About the

Stuart has had a 25-year career as a manager in various cultural venues, including London's Transport Museum, the Roman Baths in Bath and the Millennium Dome. In 2001, he returned to his home town of Norwich and eventually became Director of Norwich Arts Centre.

While working, he has also pursued a passion in studying the history of science and has had articles published about 19th-century science, particularly as regards the birth of evolutionary theory. Through doing this, he arrived at the fascinating figure of Harriet Martineau. Stuart became convinced that she was a much-neglected historical figure and, in 2012, began an intensive period of research and writing. This book is a result of that research.

ENCOUNTERS WITH HARRIET MARTINEAU

Sue,

Thanks for coming

Frank

x

ENCOUNTERS WITH HARRIET MARTINEAU

A VICTORIAN LIVING AHEAD OF HER TIME

STUART HOBDAY

This edition first published in 2017

Unbound

6th Floor Mutual House, 70 Conduit Street, London W1S 2GF

www.unbound.com

ISBN (eBook):978-191158-622-7

ISBN (Paperback):978-191158-621-0

Design by Mecob

Cover image:

© Shutterstock.com/mis-Tery

Printed and bound in Great Britain by Clays Ltd, St Ives plc

To my parents, John and Margaret Hobday

Dear Reader,

The book you are holding came about in a rather different way to most others. It was funded directly by readers through a new website: Unbound.

Unbound is the creation of three writers. We started the company because we believed there had to be a better deal for both writers and readers. On the Unbound website, authors share the ideas for the books they want to write directly with readers. If there are enough who will support the book by pledging for it in advance, we will produce a beautifully bound special subscribers' edition and distribute a regular edition and e-book wherever books are sold, in shops and online.

This new way of publishing is actually a very old idea (Samuel Johnson funded his dictionary this way). We're just using the internet to build a network of patrons for each writer. Here, at the back of this book, you'll find the names of all the people who made it happen.

Publishing in this way means readers are no longer mere passive consumers of the books they buy, and authors are free to write the books they really want. They get a much fairer return too – half the profits their books generate, rather than a tiny percentage of the cover price.

If you're not yet a subscriber, we hope that you'll want to join our publishing revolution and have your name listed in one of our books in the future. To get you started, here is a £5 discount on your first pledge. Just visit unbound.com, make your pledge and type HARRIET17 in the promo code box when you check out.

Thank you for your support,

Dan, Justin and John
Founders, Unbound

Super Patrons

Geoff & Anne-Marie Hunter
Grace Jackson
Stephen Jarvis
Natalie Jode
Dan Kieran
Neil Mackie
Tom Mahon
Sarah Marsh
James Martineau
Jeremy Martineau
Alison McFarlane
Laura McGillivray
Ben Miller
John Mitchinson
Chris Moore
Lucy Murphy
Michael Talbot & Fiona Oates
Justin Pollard
Simon Reese
Nick Roche
Anasua S. Roy
Alexandra Runswick
Valerie Sanders
Emma Shipton-Smith
Anna Sims
Kathryn Skoyles
Megan Bradbury & Ben Smart
Craig Smitherman
Beth Torgerson
Anne Vallins-Hooper
John Vint
Iris Voegeli
Jane Vogler
Ed & Eleanor Wall
Clotilde Wang
Lucy Ward
Ruth Watts
Gaby Weiner
Ian Wildboar
Maiko Yamamoto

Contents

Introduction: The Life, Career and Reputation of Harriet Martineau

Harriet Martineau lived an eventful life through tumultuous times. Born in Norwich in 1802, she died in the Lake District 74 years later, having been a participant in, an observer of and an inspiration for some of the greatest historic movements and events humankind has ever seen. Within the history of ideas, which Martineau herself claimed was the most important history, she is a much underestimated figure. Intangible and hard to measure, ideas, ideologies and philosophies can transform institutions and encourage people to make change. The restless pen of Harriet Martineau was a crucial influence during a critical time in the development of ideas that today still inform ideological movements, leaders and governments across the world.

Martineau was a rare creature. As a shy, introverted teenager she took to reading and began to develop her own philosophy based on the writings of, amongst others, Francis Bacon, Joseph Priestley, Jane Marcet, Thomas Paine and Adam Smith. She believed that humankind was on an upward curve towards freedom, better living conditions, self-awareness through education and progress through science. She had great faith in the capabilities of people if they could be encouraged, liberated and supported in free, but fair, markets. In later life, she was overtly scornful of religion, spoke out for women's rights and was ahead of her time in championing racial equality. She anticipated modern evolutionary philosophy, directly influenced the development of social science, and, to top it all, became the precursor of a modern campaigning journalist in the last 25 years of her life. While doing all this, she also defended sustainable living, better health and hospitals, self-determination of people around the world and human rights, espousing these ideas long before they became widely discussed and disseminated.

These principles have become the drivers of the modern world. Greater freedom, democracy and rights for all people have become powerful ideas, regardless of localised politics. Progress through science is a background noise to the world's activities in both natural and social sciences and in technological progress. Racial equality and the rights of women are still controversial in some countries but widely accepted by many as the way forward. Religion is still powerful but increasingly challenged by secular thinking, in the West at least. The message of education and better health and hospitals is one that continues to spread throughout the world. Martineau's understanding of sustainable living and her connection with nature in the Lake District were such that, at the start of the 21st century, we can still learn from her in the light of the human impact on the planet's natural resources and the limits of modern consumerism.

If you believe that these things would have happened anyway, then you would be agreeing with Harriet Martineau that humankind is on an inevitable path towards progress, freedom, knowledge and self-realisation. If, like me, you think that these notions need advocates and originators, then Martineau sits squarely in the frame. Although she was the first to say she merely popularised the ideas of others, I would argue that she cultivated her own, had the determination to promote them and the moral courage to speak out in the face of ridicule, and thus became a direct influence on other 19th-century individuals who would go on to help forge these developments.

The 20th century did not go exactly the way Martineau anticipated. The Marxist and fascist regimes of Stalin and Hitler were major roadblocks on the path to freedom, and she abhorred violence and despotism. But throughout the century, the importance of science and education was growing. The social science she helped to found has been instrumental in shaping institutions that encourage democracy and human rights, such as the European Union and the United Nations, backed up by the formation of thousands of non-governmental organisations, charities and pressure groups demanding respect and rights for every individual. Free markets have won the battle with socialist systems, although Martineau would have baulked at the inequality and ostentatious wealth that they have wrought. It is striking to see, however, how much of her philosophy chimes with the modern world, and it is this that has led to a resurgence of interest in her life and work.

That resurgence has been driven from the United States, and in particular American academics, who recognise Martineau as a 'first-wave' feminist. This is not entirely surprising for she developed a great connection with America during her lifetime, realising that it provided hope for a new world. She set off on an intrepid grand tour of the States in 1834, was fêted as a famed author wherever she went, met many of America's notable people, including President Andrew Jackson, and made lasting friends and contacts who helped inform her writing. Her books and articles were widely read there throughout her lifetime.

The only statue erected anywhere in tribute to Harriet Martineau was commissioned by the American abolitionist Maria Weston Chapman and sculpted by Anne Whitney, to be duly placed in front of the all-female Wellesley College in Massachusetts. Unveiled in 1883, the statue was unfortunately damaged beyond repair in a devastating fire in 1914, though a bust of Martineau remains in the museum. The love affair between Martineau and the United

States has continued with the two most prominent of her biographers being American historian Robert K. Webb and Deborah Logan, the holder of a post devoted to the study of Martineau at the University of Kentucky. Webb's book *Harriet Martineau: A Radical Victorian*, published in 1960, did much to boost the resurgence of interest and is a riveting read that vividly captures her motivation and eventful life. At several points, Webb felt the need to put Martineau in her place as a 'second-rate mind' and I've been told by those that knew him that he later regretted this. Deborah Logan's biography *The Hour and the Woman* emphasises Martineau's campaigns and her human side and Logan has also overseen much publication from America of Martineau's original writing.

This American advocacy has attracted analytical sociological studies, evident in a conference held at University College, London in 2007 attended mainly by American academics, summarised in the book *Harriet Martineau: Authorship, Society and Empire* and similarly in *Harriet Martineau: Sociological and Methodological Approaches* by Michael Hill and Susan Hoecker-Drysdale. It is not surprising that Martineau's life and work attracts this type of analysis. Being a woman writer of non-fiction in the patriarchal Victorian era was not easy. Overt, and powerful, dismissals of her were often personal and palpably based on opposition to the existence of an intellectual woman.

Of the eight existing biographies, six have been written by Americans. Martineau has had determined British advocates – particularly feminist thinker Gaby Weiner, who edited a new Virago edition of her autobiography in 1983, and Valerie Sanders, who has written extensively of Martineau's place in 19th-century literature. It is, however, a different story when we look at the prominent British historians of the Victorian era.

It is unfortunate for Martineau that A. N. Wilson's widely read *The Victorians* is dismissive of her, although he does pay her some backhanded compliments. He introduces her by saying: 'Sometimes we can learn more of a past generation by reading the authors who were popular at the time and have now sunk without trace, rather than reperusing the immortals.' He describes her initial works as 'woodenly written' but concedes they 'made a very palpable hit'. He goes on: 'Wordy, authoritative, cliché ridden, Miss Martineau had the know-all tone which so often wins journalism wide readership and short-term respect. Like many of her modern equivalents, she had all the right views – that is the views espoused in the metropolitan intelligentsia.'[1]

Wilson describes her as a 'lifetime professional invalid' and a hypochondriac; he ridicules her later championing of the fad of mesmerism and then, get-

---

1. A.N. Wilson, *The Victorians* (Arrow Books, 2003), p. 152.

5

ting his timeline confused (she toured America in 1835 and became ill well after her return, in 1840), claims that: 'Mobile once more, she could tour America and send back precisely the dispatches the comfortable middle classes wanted to read.' He gives her credit for supporting the abolition of slavery in America in the 1850s, while out of self-interest 'we find many English people turning a blind eye to America at this time, or almost wilfully missing the point', but claims Martineau was doing so in order to defend capitalist industrialism. He also gives her grudging credit for being prominent in the advent of a growth in secular thought. In this deliberately negative assessment we can ascertain that Martineau wrote about economics in a popular way, produced secular writing that was radical, wrote journalism connected to the progressive middle classes and continued the fight against slavery in the face of widespread apathy in Britain. Not a bad list of achievements for anyone, let alone a woman writing in an unprecedented way within a powerfully patriarchal society. Wilson betrays his prejudice in complaining of 'her modern equivalents' in that he seems to have a general problem with progressive, campaigning journalists.

One of the British doyennes of 19th-century literary biography, Kathryn Hughes, is certainly no fan of Martineau and in her biography of George Eliot paints a picture of Harriet as a bitter spinster gossip, who harboured grudges evident in her posthumous autobiography. It is certainly possible that Martineau made mischievous gossip when George Eliot started her affair with George Lewes (she would have been far from alone in this) but Hughes makes much of one private letter to Thomas Carlyle, which we only know of through secondary references.

The 'grudge' Hughes refers to is with Martineau's younger, and equally famous brother, James, who wrote what she concedes was a 'spiteful review'; others have seen Harriet's disconnection from her brother as a reasonable response to a sibling betrayal. As regards Martineau's autobiography, the innate beauty is in the honest portrayal of others with their qualities and foibles exposed in equal measure. In short, I believe Hughes overplays isolated private incidences and ignores the groundbreaking writing and ideas that Martineau presented to the public and inspired in others.

Anthony Wood's widely used textbook *Nineteenth Century Britain* mentions Martineau and how her writing had a 'devastating' effect but fails to explain what that effect was.[2] Simon Heffer's 2013 *High Minds: The Victorians and the Birth of Modern Britain* barely discusses Martineau and is a very male-centric history. Heffer charts the rise of a new middle-class intelligentsia in the

2. Anthony Wood, *Nineteenth Century Britain, 1815–1914* (Longman 1960), p.96.

1840s and the development of the 'Rational Mind' and secular thought in the 1860s. Martineau had been at the head of both of these movements, having forged an unprecedented career in London from 1832 and having shocked Victorian society with her atheism in 1851. For some reason, Heffer omits these facts and Harriet only appears when he comes to address the beginnings of rights for women.

In carrying out research on Martineau it is hard to find people on the ground, in libraries and archives, who have heard of her – even in places where she should be remembered, such as her home town of Norwich or in the Lake District where she settled later in life. The difference between the American and British academic views is striking, and this lack of interest in Britain has affected her reputation.

Paradoxically, it makes the study of Martineau even more intriguing. She seems to have been deliberately written out of history, which calls into question the nature of how history is remembered and recorded, the power of myth-making and why some things are deemed relevant and others not. Martineau had two important qualifications that led to her dismissal by the later 19th-century male establishment: she was an intellectual woman and also became widely regarded as an atheist.

For my History Masters I studied Darwin and the context in which his ideas were born. I broadly argued that myths have arisen around evolution because of the Victorian context. Social Darwinism, a dog-eat-dog, 'survival-of-the-fittest' view remains powerful because of the context in which natural selection was born. There was, though, always a conundrum with Darwin. How did this shy, diligent naturalist, from a conservative background, arrive at the single most radical idea in changing how humans understand themselves?

During my research a strange French name, Harriet Martineau, kept popping up. In the late 1830s, the crucial period in Darwin's fermentation of his ideas, she was right there in the room: the famous author at the centre of a free-thinking circle. I soon discovered that I shared my home town, Norwich, with her. Like Martineau, I have been greatly interested in the history of ideas, how they shape our futures and influence minds and actions, yet have a strangely intangible existence. In writing this book I have resolved to show the human side of Harriet, how she interacted with many of those in the 19th century who have been better remembered, and how she truly *lived* an eventful life. There are people, famous in their day, who fall between the cracks of history, but as I've grown more involved with Harriet Martineau over the years it has become obvious that her philosophical creed is still relevant and that, in the historical battleground of ideas, she should be much better remembered.

In this portrait of her life, I present her encounters with other 19th-century luminaries as a way of highlighting her dramatic relationships and the development of her own ideas. A radical presence in the small literary circle of early Victorian Britain, she encouraged others to pursue their own goals time and again. She can be seen as an important bridge between the 18th and 19th centuries, as she moved into both the social circle and intellectual space left by the famed 'Lunar Men' of the British Enlightenment such as Joseph Priestley and Erasmus Darwin. I hope this approach also portrays the way in which all the figures shown in the book helped to shape the times that followed. Most of the 'encounters' I've chosen to highlight are with people she knew and met. There are a few in which the interaction consisted mainly of correspondence and a couple towards the end exploring her posthumous legacy.

Harriet's life can be divided into distinct phases. Her childhood was marred by illness and shyness: in her early years she lost the senses of taste and smell, which were never to return; as a teenager she began to go deaf, so that as an adult she became reliant on, and well known for, a large ear trumpet that she would thrust towards her conversational partner.

She began to write in her twenties and she soon realised her calling. Having retreated into reading as a teenager, her informed opinions now found their voice. The 1830s were key to Martineau's life. She moved to London and her bestselling economic parables, issued monthly, became essential reading. Before long, she became a fêted figure in London society and a centre point in a radical freethinking circle. Politicians lined up to persuade her to write something in favour of their preferred economic policies.

In 1834, she set off on an American trip which was to last nearly two years. She came back to London in 1836 and produced a radical outspoken analysis of the United States, which was widely read and reviewed. Often called the 'radical Thirties', it is hard for us to relate to a time when literacy and education were not common, voting was restricted to a small male elite, modern industrial technology was just starting and there was a profound disconnection between the ruled and the ruling classes. Martineau was one of the first to consciously write about economics with the general public in mind as her readership.

The next phase of her life began in 1840, when she was taken ill while in Venice and returned to be near her doctor brother-in-law in Tynemouth, close to Newcastle. She spent much of the next five years in her 'sickroom' although she continued to write, producing a biography of the Haitian slave rebellion leader Toussaint L'Ouverture, *The Hour and the Man,* as well as several children's stories and reflections on her illness in *Life in the Sick-Room.*

She was adamant that her recovery was due to a course of 'mesmerism' (the use of electrical magnetism on the body and a precursor to modern homeopathic approaches to medicine), which, partly through her practice and publicising of it, became something of a sensation in the mid-1840s. Once better, she visited the Lake District and enjoyed it so much that she resolved to move there. She bought a plot of land in Ambleside, on which she designed and built her own house, The Knoll, which she was to call home for the rest of her life.

Martineau revelled in the beautiful surroundings of Ambleside and found there a new set of stimulating friends, including the Wordsworths and the Arnolds. She did not, however, relent in her causes, and there was no relaxation of her pen. Quite the opposite, in fact. In the 1850s, she wrote much that was overtly anti-religious and moved into some subtle and radical scientific philosophical areas, producing the three-volume *Eastern Life* after eight months of travelling in Egypt, Syria and Palestine.

By now Martineau was in regular communication with the philosophically minded Henry Atkinson and she arranged for their correspondence to be published in 1851, under the title *Letters on the Laws of Man's Nature and Development*. This volume contained writing that ridiculed religious ideas of man's origin and firmly placed the human mind as well within 'nature'. The book's publication led many friends and family to distance themselves from her. This was eight years before Darwin's *Origin of Species* caused theological tumult, and many critics, including Harriet's brother James, wrote dismissive reviews.

Harriet was undaunted, however, and followed up the book with a popular translation of *The Positive Philosophy of Auguste Comte*. His secular, progressive, scientific philosophy chimed with her own writings, and she even put her own spin on the translation. This phase of her life culminated in another illness and, convinced she was about to die of an enlarged heart, in 1855 she penned her autobiography and her own obituary.

I would contend that one of the tragedies of Martineau's life was that the autobiography did not appear until after her death, 21 years later. Had it been published in 1855, it would have caused a sensation. She still had a visible public profile and the book contained much to antagonise the religious-minded establishment, several years in advance of the Darwinian controversies. It is written in an open, honest, modern prose that would have shocked the 1850s' public. It is a stream of consciousness that brings alive the Victorian era and has a realistic tone that would become the norm in the 20th century. As it was, her fame waned in the last 15 years of her life, she was less active and visible, and what could have been a famous publication was lost in the diminished presence of her twilight years.

Despite penning her own obituary and fearing the worst, she recovered from the 1855 illness and went on to write regular leader articles for a national newspaper, the *Daily News*, a liberal alternative to the establishment *Times*. She was to write over 1,600 leaders for the *Daily News* and other pieces for journals, on topics ranging from international affairs and the effects of industrialisation to home politics. She provided the authentic voice of abolitionist America, being in direct regular correspondence with her abolitionist friends and contacts, in the lead-up to the American Civil War, which she proclaimed as America's 'manifest destiny'. This stance was all the braver when we realise that slavery was at its peak in America in the 1850s, with powerful supporters in Britain, underpinning as it did, the cotton factories of Northern England. Much of the trade and wealth was shared with America – an ongoing relationship that is conveniently forgotten in the British slavery narrative.

In the late 1860s, Martineau formed formidable partnerships with Florence Nightingale and Josephine Butler as the journalistic newspaper voice for their causes – in Nightingale's case, the need for better hospitals, hygiene and trained nurses, and in Butler's, reforming the Contagious Diseases Act to make it less harsh towards women in prostitution and less prejudiced against women in general.

Martineau finally passed away in June 1876 at The Knoll. She was found to have had a large ovarian cyst which would explain many of her health problems in the second half of her life (her 1855 health crisis has largely been put down to the menopause).

An advocate of science to the end, she offered to leave her brain to Atkinson and her ears to a hearing specialist. Both declined and she was buried in Key Hill Cemetery, Birmingham, in a family grave.

I would by no means claim that Harriet Martineau was perfect, or solely responsible for the progressive ideas she persistently wrote of and their subsequent impact. She had a bad habit of burning her bridges and several times wrote scathing reviews of the work of friends, which led to fallings out. She also made eccentric demands of friends and could be vain. Robert Webb suggests that after the publication of the Atkinson letters she 'achieved the martyrdom she so craved', and there was certainly an element of martyrdom to her causes.

For much of her life she would have been a notable presence at gatherings, with her ear trumpet no restriction to constant conversation. In 1830s' London, she was a social catalyst for a new generation of freethinkers, whilst in later life she hosted many visitors to The Knoll, such as the American writer Nathanial Hawthorne, who presents a vivid picture of her and portrays the radicalism of her atheism affectionately:

I think I neglected to record that I saw Miss Martineau a few weeks since. She is a large, robust (one might almost say bouncing) elderly woman, very coarse of aspect, and plainly dressed; but withal, so kind, cheerful, and intelligent a face, that she is pleasanter to look at than most beauties. Her hair is of a decided gray; and she does not shrink from calling herself an old woman. She is the most continual talker I ever heard; it is really like the babbling of a brook; and very lively and sensible too; and all the while she talks, she becomes quite an organ of intelligence and sympathy between her and yourself. The ear trumpet seems like a sensitive part of her, like the feelers of some insects. If you have any little remark to make, you drop it in; and she helps you make remarks by this delicate little appeal of the trumpet, as she slightly directs it towards you; and if you have nothing to say, the appeal is not strong enough to embarrass you. All her talk was about herself and her affairs; but it did not seem like egotism, because it was so cheerful and free from morbidness. And this woman is an atheist, and thinks, I believe, that the principle of life will become extinct, when her great, fat, well-to-do body is laid in the grave. I will not think so, were it only for her sake; only a few weeds to spring out of her fat mortality, instead of her intellect and sympathies flowering and fruiting forever![3]

In later life she shocked the Ambleside locals by wearing hobnail boots and smoking cigars. She lived and wrote freely herself but could be moralistic and preaching to others. A perceived weakness in her writing has been that she found it hard to relate to passion or overwhelming love. She remained single throughout her life and is assumed to have never been sexually active. She had a clinical, logical approach to life which could come across as moral superiority. Webb suggests that Martineau was probably gay, and certainly she had close connections and profound relationships with several women. This will, however, remain speculation, as it was almost certainly never physically acted upon if true.

I believe that there are some hidden virtues in Martineau's oeuvre which are relevant to the history of ideas. She wrote before modern academic divides became manifest and so had no qualms switching from economics to politics to science to fiction to biography to history. There is a freedom in her whole body of work being so diverse. Moreover, everything she wrote had a reason behind it; her writing was driven by causes, the goal being the betterment for

3. Nathaniel Hawthorne, *English Notebooks* (Randall Stewart, 1941), p. 77.

11

some other person or persons. Dickens, sarcastically but accurately, said of her that she was 'grimly bent upon the enlightenment of mankind'. She would have been nonplussed by the modern academic scene, with its niche study and endless pointless production of 'papers'. Martineau would have been much more in tune with modern campaigning journalists and popular authors who have something to say, and write in a way that will make a difference because people will actually read their writing.

The diversity and freedom in her work haven't, however, aided her legacy. She doesn't fit easily into any category, which is not helpful to libraries, bookshops or academia. She crops up in books about sociology, literature, travel, history, journalism, evolution and many biographies, but she herself has slipped through the cracks. She ought to have become famous for her autobiography alone, such is the power of its modern direct free prose and the vehemence of its secularism. However, the delay in publication and the subsequent moralistic reviews showed it was both too late and too early for such a work. Similarly, she could have become famous for her journalism in the *Daily News* but she wrote anonymously and the moment was lost.

Not only was there purpose to her writing, but she lived the ideas. Her life *was* advocacy. She experienced directly the collapse of her father's textile business in Norwich and the devastating effect this had on his workers and family; she walked the streets of London to observe poverty in the 1830s; she went to Newgate Prison to work with Elizabeth Fry; she went to America to see slavery in action for herself and felt the wrath of the mob when she spoke out against it. She was vilified in her writings simply for being a woman. The members of the radical salons she hosted in London knew they were challenging the establishment status quo.

In the Lake District, she set up a sustainable home with her own food production. She founded a building society to provide dwellings for locals. She gave lectures to the rural poor. When the American Civil War started, she sought to arrange retraining for Manchester cotton workers, whose trade was disrupted by the turmoil. She welcomed all visitors to The Knoll, including escaped slaves from America. She travelled to Ireland to see the effects of the potato famine and did a tour of the Holy Land to learn more about other religions, which she passed on to the public. She was as far away from the aloof theoretical academic world of ideas that exists today as it is possible to be. Yet she was a catalyst for positive change in her writing and through the way she lived.

Her most modern value was that she regarded every single individual to be of intrinsic value – as having some worth for their family, workplace or community. She also had great compassion for those who had fallen by the wayside, were in prison or destitute. Her answer to these problems was not socialism but freedom, support, stability in the household, a positive, productive life, in which people fulfilled their potential and there was enough income for everyone through fair, free markets and the division of labour.

Her approach was shared by other Victorian thinkers and writers such as Thomas Carlyle, Herbert Spencer and T. H. Huxley and the new evolutionary science of the 1860s and '70s. The latter made a fatal move towards what became known as 'Social Darwinism': a philosophy of superiority that was picked up by imperialists in the Scramble for Africa and was used to justify the subjugation of many peoples in the name of Empire. It culminated in the eugenics and racial ideology that would blight the 20th century.

Harriet Martineau would have abhorred this view of nature. To her, evolutionary science wasn't about superiority; it was about realising the potential of every person in the world and valuing different cultures. She had much more faith in humanity than the Social Darwinists, and one of her key insights was that people build their own societies from the bottom up, through training and education and contribution. That is why social matters, education and opportunity were as important to her as politics from on high. Ultimately, Harriet Martineau was a progressive influence on an era of new ideas, restless change and great advancement. She was a fascinating, prescient, indomitable writer and a wide-ranging, original thinker, who led an unprecedented life that should be both remembered and celebrated.

Part I: The 1820s

In the 1820s, British life was still very much rooted in its pre-industrial past. Horse-drawn transport was the norm, and horses were a common sight on the streets of every town. Most people worked in agriculture or cottage industries or on ships reliant on wind and sails. Large factories were a thing of the future, politics were the reserve of a male upper-class landowning elite and the monarch, George IV, still had an influential court. A Tory government, led by Lord Liverpool, dominated the decade. Britain was recovering from a lengthy period of war with Napoleonic France, which had ended in 1815. It was a decade of relative international peace, during which much of the basis for industrial and manufacturing development was laid. Education was limited, as was literacy, although printing presses were growing with newspapers and pamphlets more commonly read than they had been in the 18th century. The ferment of the French Revolution meant that the idea of greater democracy was in the air. Enlightened ideas of science and democracy, espoused in the previous century, were being increasingly shared with the public. This was a time of peace and industrial development, but it was also a harsh era of unrest and mob behaviour, underlined by economic poverty.

Chapter 1: Lant Carpenter

Harriet Martineau was a shy, introverted child. Prone to ill health, she did not find it easy being surrounded by the hustle and bustle of a busy household in a thriving provincial city. The sixth of eight children, she lived in Magdalen Street, Norwich, in a house just big enough to accommodate the family, fronting the main thoroughfare into the centre of town. The whole family regularly trooped around the corner to the Unitarian Octagon Chapel, designed and built by William Ivory in 1745 and renowned by the end of the 18th century for its freethinking, dissenting circle. The Martineaus came from French Huguenot stock, so it was natural for them to gravitate away from the Church of England and they became part of a non-conforming tradition in Norwich.

Harriet's parents, particularly her mother, encouraged her reading. Her naturally inquisitive mind was drawn to Milton, Austen and Wordsworth at a young age. As well as the literary greats she read the Bible, other religious texts and philosophy.

Her father's business specialised in the production and selling of bombazine, the material used for mourning dress. The textiles manufactory and warehouse were nearby and add to the intensity of Harriet's childhood. Several attempts were made to alleviate her ill health by taking her out of Norwich, for instance to Newcastle to stay with her mother's relatives and to the coast at Cromer. Born with neither sense of taste nor smell, she suffered the gradual onset of deafness in her teenage years. She reflects on this period in her autobiography:

> My health was bad and my mind ill at ease. It was a depressed and wrangling life; and I have no doubt I was as disagreeable as possible. The great calamity of my deafness was now opening upon me; and that would have been enough for youthful fortitude, without the constant indigestion, languor and muscular weakness which made life a burden to me. My religion was a partial comfort to me; and books and music were a great resource; but they left a large margin over for wretchedness.

She goes on to reflect that coping with her deafness was made more difficult due to a lack of diagnosis and that, for a long time, her family and others assumed she was merely badly behaved and difficult. It seems, however, that her hearing problems helped her develop a spirit of defiance:

> It [deafness] showed me that I must take my case into my own hands, and with me this was redemption from probable destruction. Instead of drifting helplessly as hitherto, I gathered myself up for a gallant breasting of my destiny... Here I am now, confident that this same deafness is about the best thing that ever happened to me: my grandest impulse to self-mastery and my most peculiar opportunity of helping others.

Aged 16 in 1818, in another attempt to bring her out of herself and address her struggling health, she was sent to Bristol to study at a school established by her aunt. It was linked to the Mead Chapel, and she soon came under the influence of charismatic Unitarian minister and preacher Dr Lant Carpenter. Carpenter was instrumental in developing a Unitarian creed that rejected the dogma and doctrine of Christianity and replaced it with a need to do social good. He urged moral responsibility and charity over self-interest. Hailing from Exeter, he publicly espoused views that chimed with social progressives of the industrially developing city of Bristol and he soon became a well-known figure with a loyal congregation.

Martineau responded well to Dr Carpenter's message and this was to be the most religiously active period of her life, spurring her towards her own free-thinking and moral causes. Her time in Bristol must have also brought Harriet face to face with the slave trade. Although by now abolished in Britain, slave trading continued elsewhere across the globe, and Bristol harbour would have been full of slavery-related activity and ships, with the town still profiting from this industry.

Martineau and Carpenter established a connection that was to have personal ramifications for them both. On her return to Norwich after 15 months she wrote to him:

> I may again assure you that I am not insensible to the great kindness which you showed to me, during my stay at Bristol. I trust I felt the value of your instructions, while I enjoyed the advantage of them, and now that I am deprived of them, I feel their value still more. I have not however discontinued the pursuits in which you guided me, and it gives me great pleasure, while I go through again the books which I learned under you.

Carpenter had recommended to the inquisitive Harriet the latest progressive dissenting reading that related to his causes, and soon she would have her own causes. Harriet had, herself, recommended that her younger brother James visit Bristol to learn under the doctor and preacher, and he made the trip soon after Harriet's return. Her letter to Carpenter continues:

> I hope James will make the most of the advantages which he will enjoy. It will be a severe trial to me to part with him, having just met after so long a separation, but I must console myself with looking forward to the time when he will return improved, I hope, in every respect, and when he will be a valuable companion to me.

Indeed, Carpenter's teaching was to have an even greater effect on James Martineau, who, after an initial period of learning, returned to Bristol and worked as the preacher's assistant for several years – an experience that clearly laid the path for his own career as a freethinking and controversial cleric. In later life, James's path would diverge from his increasingly sceptical older sister's, and this parting of ways would have great ramifications on their relationship.

As for Lant Carpenter, in the 1830s he began to experience regular mental and physical breakdowns until in 1839 he was sent on a voyage around Europe on a steamer, from which he would not return. One night, travelling between Italy and France, he fell into the sea and was not missed until the following day. His body washed ashore near Anzio, in Italy, two months later. Conjecture continues to this day as to whether he fell overboard or jumped. In her autobiography, Harriet portrays her penchant for black humour when she learns of Dr Carpenter's death: 'My old instructor, who had for years of my youth been my idol, Dr Carpenter, perished in a singularly impressive manner – by being thrown overboard by a lurch of the steamer in which he was traversing the Mediterranean. A strange and forlorn mode of death for a Minister.'

The influence of this new breed of Unitarian moral progressiveness – as taught, preached and exemplified by Lant Carpenter – cannot be underestimated. Lant's daughter, Mary Carpenter, established the famed 'Ragged Schools' in Bristol, setting a precedent for the education of what we would now call 'excluded' children from poor backgrounds. Mary was to become a friend and ally of Harriet's in her advocacy of education and women's rights, and was instrumental later in life in the establishment of education for girls in India, founding schools in several major Indian cities.

The famous Lunar Society (an informal meeting of progressives, so called because they met monthly under the light of the full moon) had existed around

Birmingham, and several of its members, such as Erasmus Darwin, Josiah Wedgwood, Matthew Boulton and Joseph Priestley, were influential thinkers and also active in the new dissenting progressive moral cause. From their work this Unitarian gospel became particularly powerful in America, leading, for example, to the founding of Harvard University.

Later, James Martineau became known for building on Unitarian thinking, developing his own creed that citizens had a duty to play a role in their communities. This influenced the development of local government as an idea particularly through the work of his follower George Dawson in Birmingham. These are just some examples of the hidden influence of Unitarianism.

For Harriet, Lant Carpenter had opened her mind and set her on a course to pursue her own writing. She was later dismissive of Carpenter and embarrassed by her religiosity during this phase of her life, but he had introduced her to books and writing that would shape her work – particularly those of Joseph Priestley.

Chapter 2: Joseph Priestley

Reading Joseph Priestley was a turning point in Harriet Martineau's life. Starting with his record of *Hartley's Theory of the Human Mind: On the Principle of the Association of Ideas*, she also assimilated the 'associationist' philosophy of David Hartley, in particular his founding texts on psychology, which presented a materialist view of the human mind. Now back in Norwich and spurred on in her reading, she delved further into the Priestley canon, enjoying his particular brand of scientific enquiry and political theory. His idea that life was driven by *necessity*, combined with a religious and moral optimism, struck a chord with her. Indeed, Priestley's wide-ranging interests and career (such as it was) were, to some extent, the precepts followed by Martineau in her own life.

Joseph Priestley died in 1804, two years after Harriet was born. He had led an eventful life as a cleric, scientist and agitator. He is now best remembered for his pioneering chemistry experiments, his role in discovering oxygen and in the development of electricity. In the 1770s, he had been privately supported by William Petty, the Earl of Shelbourne managed to develop his own scientific instruments and laboratory; and was one of the first people to show that air had different components.

To Priestley, this particle, chemical view of life was a natural extension of his scepticism towards established religion. He had become known for his dissenting preaching as a cleric in Suffolk but, deemed too radical for the congregation there, he moved first to Warrington and then to Leeds. Priestley was developing the Unitarian attitude to Christianity, which would follow a rejection of the Holy Trinity, less reliance on miracles, a presentation of materialist nature alongside the retention of belief in a first cause, an initial creator but not an interventionist God. He produced three volumes of *Institutes of Natural and Revealed Religion* between 1772 and 1774.

In the 1780s, Priestley's public following was developing as the minister of the New Meeting House in Birmingham. He set up a laboratory next to his house and began to feed his growing knowledge of gases into the developing industrial processes of Birmingham. He connected with the renowned Lunar Society. The meetings were also attended by the American Founding Father and scientist Benjamin Franklin when he was in Britain. The group shared a belief in freedom, education and progress, and its guiding principles were an increasing dismissal of God, the Bible, country and king.

Priestley became an important member of this group as he was the least commercially, industrially minded of them all. He infused the others with his mixture of Unitarianism and materialism, which included faith in the capabilities of the individual, and the duty of those in public life to work towards progress. Jenny Uglow describes Priestley's influence in her book *The Lunar Men*:

> Whereas Darwin (Erasmus) was intrigued by Hartley's physiological ideas of the nervous system, Priestley responded passionately to his missionary view of learning. If people were moulded by circumstances then they could change, become 'perfected' – finally reaching the happiness intended by 'providence'... In Priestley's mind this goal merged with wider political battles for liberty and reform... 'The morning is upon us', he wrote, 'and we cannot doubt that the light will increase, and extend itself more and more into the perfect day.'[1]

Joseph Priestley's chemistry stemmed from his materialist philosophy. If the world was all matter, then all things had building blocks which could be broken down. These were the mid-18th-century beginnings of modern science. He was involved in the development of observational instruments, restlessly designing microscopes and telescopes. The key to life was in the detail. But matter was also force and energy, and his material views were not in conflict with his religion, as Uglow summarises: 'Religion and politics and science swept together. Around all his experiments and ideas hovered a shimmering aura of transformation.'

Priestley, however, ran into trouble in Birmingham. The French Revolution of 1789 caused great unrest in England, with patriots of all classes steeling themselves against sympathetic progressives who admired the principles of the revolution. On the two-year anniversary of Bastille Day, Priestley attended a meeting of French supporters in the city, but a restless mob formed and turned on the properties of those at this meeting. Priestley was a well-known and obvious target. He and his family escaped to safety, but his house, chapel and laboratory were ransacked, burnt and destroyed by the rioting mob.

This violent turn of events was a shock to the Lunar Men. Erasmus Darwin (Charles's grandfather) wrote to his friend Josiah Wedgwood that: 'The Birmingham riots are a disgrace to mankind'. In Jenny Uglow's narrative it is a turning point for these 18th-century luminaries, turning away from the free-

---

1. Jenny Uglow, *The Lunar Men* (Faber & Faber 2002) p.74.

thinking philosophising led by Priestley and towards the more practical considerations of protecting their families:

> The Lunar Society had been fatally wounded by these riots – less by the damage to property, or even the departure of Priestley, but by the slur attached to all the things they believed in: 'reason', 'science', 'freedom', 'experiment'. This was a riot against intellectualism, and its abiding image is of book burning... One slogan chalked on Birmingham walls was 'No philosophers – Church and King For Ever'.

Martineau idolised Priestley and would become well aware of the sacrifices he made; it is interesting to note that she took up these causes alongside the Darwin and Wedgwood descendants 40 years later.

Priestley relocated to London, but this episode left him badly shaken and he soon resolved to move to America where, in 1794, he established himself as a Unitarian preacher in Northumberland, Pennsylvania. Becoming well known in America, he became the friend and supporter of Thomas Jefferson in his run for the Presidency. This turn of events mirrors the path taken by another of Harriet Martineau's heroes, Thomas Paine. Also hailing from Norfolk, Paine had been hounded out of Britain prior to the French Revolution after penning his seditious *Rights of Man*, which championed the basic rights of all people and the need to challenge aristocratic rule. Paine had originally found fame as an influence on the American Revolution, with his call to overthrow British colonial rule of America in *Common Sense*.

Priestley and Paine led similar lives, both having been lampooned mercilessly in the press and hounded out of England by a patriotic mob mentality. These two, free, wandering, inquisitive, progressive minds, guided by science and the need for greater freedom, would be Harriet Martineau's role models throughout her life. Indeed, the similarities between Priestley, Paine and Martineau are striking. They all believed in greater freedom from religious strictures; they all had profound connections with France and America; they were all driven to write so as to influence the public and events; none was motivated by money or fame; and all three were only semi-interested in personal relations, family and love. All three received opprobrium as well as support for their writings. And all three, despite influencing modern progressive scientific ideas, are poorly remembered in 21st-century Britain.

Martineau had a portrait of Priestley on her bookshelf and gradually she became a convinced follower of the Priestleyan philosophy of Necessarianism. This was the belief that all life was guided by nature's laws and all individuals were shaped by necessity. At the same time, Necessarianism retained the belief in a God-given first cause, an original Creation, but as this was unfathomable to the human mind, it maintained that the key to life was to track down nature's law. This doctrine presaged 20th-century debates around scientific determinism and free will. Opponents would reject Necessarianism as contrary to freedom. Priestley, and subsequently Martineau, protested that freedom and free will did exist: they were part of nature.

In his biography of Martineau, written in 1960, R. K. Webb made the link between Necessarian ideas and modern science: 'This view, stripped of its insistence on Divine Prescience (demanded by Priestley's religious commitments) is of course little different from the positivistic doctrines which ruled nineteenth century science, and much of twentieth century science still obeys them.'

He also points out that there was a clash with advocates of free will from the start:

> Materialism was hateful to most early nineteenth century thinkers, they could not easily give up the freedom which Priestley seemed to deny them. No matter how many times Priestley reiterated that he did no such thing, it was difficult to make the point stick. Everything that is granted under the use of the term freedom, he said, the necessarian allows. [2]

This built on Hartleyan Associationism, which held that all life was connected materially, unified under nature, and that one cause led to another. Charles Darwin would use this as groundwork for his study of evolution, 50 years later.

So, by her mid-twenties Harriet Martineau had a philosophy she could believe in, was imbued with moral progressiveness, retained her religious optimism, and was living in tumultuous times when the great industrial and economic fluctuations would begin to hold powerful sway over peoples everywhere. The stage was opening up for this young woman to start her own writings.

2. R. K. Webb, *Harriet Martineau: A Radical Victorian* (Heinemann, 1960), p. 80.

Part II: The 1830s

The 1830s were a time of great transition and reform. The agitation of the previous decade culminated in a progressive Whig government that passed the 1832 Reform Act. This marked a turning point in British democracy, expanding the voting franchise and introducing elected representatives from the whole country (until now the growing cities had been barely represented, with the landed gentry holding sway). The Act marked a swing in power towards the growing industrialised cities, which would drive economic growth and innovation in the coming years. It still meant that only one in five men had the vote, and the Chartist movement, which demanded universal male franchise, would emerge during this decade.

The Whig government under Lord Grey also passed the Slavery Abolition Act in 1833. This measure still had powerful opponents, such as large trading companies that benefited economically from slavery, and even King William IV, who had previously called abolitionists 'either fanatics or hypocrites' (a king, it should also be said, who was happy to parade his nine illegitimate children around his court).[1] The young Queen Victoria's ascent to the throne in 1837 represented a new era, not least in the change of tone in royal leadership.

The 1830s became known as the 'Radical Thirties', and by the middle of the decade Harriet Martineau was a pivotal figure in a literary and scientific scene, centred on London, which encouraged radicalism and freethinking. The growth in printing presses and literacy meant there was a public eager to engage with progressive ideas and good stories. The growth of the intellectual scene was mirrored by technological innovations and this was the decade when large factories employing industrial techniques began to dominate the working landscape. The first motorised buses appeared in growing urban centres, as well as the first railways connecting cities to one another. This was the time that brought witness to the advent of industrial technology, the assertion of greater democracy and the wide acceptance of progressive ideas. However, modern communication had yet to develop, ships still had sails, and the horse-drawn carriage was the common mode of transport. The new world of technology, democracy and human rights was just beginning.

---

1. King William IV in 1807 House of Lords debate, while still the Duke of Clarence and St Andrews.

Chapter 3: William Johnson Fox

In her early twenties Harriet Martineau started to write. Initially, she penned her own religious and philosophical musings, which she sent for publication in the Unitarian *Monthly Repository*. In her autobiography, she presents a picture of this period as one in which she emerged from her introverted younger years, easing into relations with those around her, partly due to her realisation that it was acceptable, in some quarters, to have doubts about the efficacy of religious doctrine and a reliance on miracles:

> It is clear that a Christianity which never was received as a scheme of salvation, which might be treated at the will and pleasure of each believer, which is declared to be independent of its external evidence, because those evidences are found to be untenable, must cease to be a faith, and becomes a matter of speculation, of spiritual convenience, till it declines to the rank of a mere fact in the history of mankind. These are the gradations through which I passed. It took many years to travel through them. But at length I recognised the monstrous superstition in its true character of a great fact in the history of the race, and found myself, with the last link of my chain snapped, – a free rover on the broad, bright breezy common of the universe.

Her first published work appeared anonymously and was entitled 'Female Writers on Practical Divinity'. It was an inherently radical article, both in highlighting neglected women writers and bringing the unknown divine into a practical realm. Her family remarked on the article at home without realising Harriet had penned it. The discovery served to make them encourage the budding writer. She followed this work with 'Devotional Exercises' which, she was gratified to learn, Lant Carpenter used in one of his sermons back in Bristol.

However, events at home were to force her to take writing more seriously. In 1825, during a national economic crisis, her father's textile business began to fail. Her older brother Thomas, affected by the strain, became ill and was sent abroad to recover. Unfortunately, he died on board a ship in transit from Madeira to Bordeaux – a death described in a letter from Harriet to James as a 'painless sinking away from exhausted strength'.

Soon afterwards, John Worthington, a college friend of James's, came to stay in Norwich. Harriet was pushed into an engagement with him by his romantic enthusiasm and her own family. However, with Harriet a reluctant fiancée, the engagement did not run smoothly and Worthington became paranoid. He seems to have convinced himself that Harriet was flirting with other suitors, which drove him mad with jealousy. Certainly, he became very depressed. Soon Harriet was demanding the return of her letters from his family in Manchester, something which would disconcert her correspondents at many points in the future. It seems as if, unsettled by his depression, Harriet broke off the engagement, perhaps glad to have an excuse. In May 1827 Worthington took his own life.

By this time the Martineau family business had collapsed. Harriet's father found the financial difficulties hard to cope with. He developed gout and liver disease and despite an attempt at a water cure in Cheltenham, he died soon afterwards. This trio of deaths between 1825 and 1827 was to be instrumental in shaping Martineau's life. She was left to fend for herself and make her own way. The economic effect of the collapsed business on her family drove much of the next phase of her writing and she would never again venture into a romantic engagement.

In her autobiography she takes a very matter of fact approach to this series of tragedies, in a passage that says much about her character:

> ... when the last of our series of family misfortunes occurred. I call it a misfortune because in common parlance it would be so treated; but I believe that my mother and all her other daughters would have joined heartily, if asked, in my conviction that it was one of the best things that ever happened to us. My mother and her daughters lost, at a stroke, nearly all they had in the world by the failure of the house and the old manufactory in which their money was placed. We never recovered more than the merest pittance; and at the time I for one, was left destitute; The effect on me of this new 'calamity' as people called it, was like that of a blister on a dull, weary pain, or series of pains. I rather enjoyed it, even at the time; for there was scope for action; whereas in the long, dreary series of preceding trials, there was nothing possible but endurance... I began to feel the blessing of a wholly new freedom. I, who had been obliged to write before breakfast, or in some private way, had henceforth liberty to do my own work in my own way... By being thrown on our own resources we have worked hard and usefully, won friends, reputation and independence, seen the world abundantly, abroad and at home, and in short have truly lived instead of vegetated.

32

William Johnson Fox entered Harriet's life at precisely the right moment. Another of the small but influential band of progressive Unitarians, he had arrived in London from Norwich in 1806. He knew of Harriet's family and the Octagon Chapel well. In 1827 Fox purchased the *Monthly Repository* and sought to grow its circulation and improve its content. He advertised for contributors and Harriet applied, offering to help with a range of reviews and articles and soon naively suggesting to Fox that some income would be useful.

Fox immediately recognised her intelligence and talent for progressive writing. The letters between them in this initial phase are those of mentor to pupil. Indeed, Valerie Sanders suggests Harriet has a 'schoolgirlish flirtation' in their early dealings.[1] Fox became a crucial supporter of Harriet's writings just as she was ready to express herself, but, more importantly, just when she needed some income. Soon she was on a retainer of £15 a year which supplemented her earnings from skilled needlework.

In 1830, she took part in a *Monthly Repository* writing competition that had three sections: how to convince Muslims, Jews and Catholics of the superiority of Unitarianism. Harriet entered all three parts anonymously, using different handwriting for each essay. She won all three prizes. The judges tried to change their decision when they realised she was the sole prize recipient but Fox insisted they stick with their original choice. She had won fair and square.

Soon Harriet moved to London, where she stayed with relatives but worked out of Fox's study in north London. She was writing reviews, sketches and even poems. She made new friends and enjoyed her first taste of London life. Harriet Taylor, who would later inspire philosopher John Stuart Mill to write a feminist tract, was in Fox's congregation. The beautiful and talented Eliza Flower was another Fox collaborator, and took Harriet under her wing. Radical doctor Thomas Southwood Smith, friend of Jeremy Bentham, was also in the circle. James Martineau was concerned that his sister had been kidnapped by a 'free-thinking and free-living' clique and declared on her return to Norwich that she was 'full of Saint-Simonism'.[2] (Saint Simon was the radical French philosopher who proclaimed science over religion and someone who would come back into Harriet's life 20 years later through the Positivism of Auguste Comte.)

Harriet suggested that she should write a novel but Fox encouraged her to illustrate social change and economics through short tales. By now she was

1. Valerie Sanders (ed.), 'Introduction', in *Harriet Martineau: Selected Letters* (Oxford University Press, 1990), p. X.

2. James Martineau, quoted in transcription of letter dated 20th June 1824, *Harriet Martineau: Further Letters*, ed. Deborah Logan (Lehigh University Press, 2012), p. 447.

becoming a known writer and other publishers were interested, although none made her a firm offer.

It was William Fox and his brother Charles who would oversee the initial publication of Harriet's *Illustrations of Political Economy*, issued monthly at a shilling a piece. The Fox brothers were circumspect in their publication of the first *Illustrations*, demanding that she get 500 subscriptions in advance and also stipulating that they would stop after two editions if sales were less than 1,000. In fact, the first, *Life in the Wilds*, was an immediate hit. The first tale sold thousands of copies and was much talked about; the Fox brothers need not have worried and soon they shared a royalty of £600 with their author.

Sometimes presented as a bolt from the blue, Harriet had in fact already built up a good following for her writing, and had growing connections in Norwich, Bristol, London and Birmingham, all of whom she urged to purchase the first monthly edition, while her mother had the bright idea of sending one to every Member of Parliament.

The success of these initial economic tales was partly due to good timing. In the early 1830s interest had developed in economic theory, backed up by increased middle-class literacy. With the Great Reform Act about to signal greater democracy, the plan by Martineau and Fox to interpret the theories of the classical 18th-century economists came at just the right time and brought the talented writer fame within months of first being published nationally.

Life in the Wilds is an intriguing idea, even now. Martineau had been imbibing the economic theories of Adam Smith, and in this tale she aims to illustrate his free market ideas, but also to question 'what is wealth?' and to show the importance of the 'division of labour', as Smith had done. In her tale, a group of British travellers are robbed of everything they own and left on a remote beach so that they have to live in a cave and learn how to survive. It takes economics back to basics: what do we need to survive and how do communities develop? It shows that wealth is not only measured in money but is also found in what can be grown, or used as food or clothes, and considers what conditions are needed for survival. Martineau implies that from these basic needs, trade will follow. Economic historian John Vint has commended Martineau's accurate depiction of Smith's ideas in this tale and acclaims it as a good, very human, portrayal of basic community needs. At one point in the story, the perceived leader of the group says to the others:

> I wish... that people in England who think that wealth consists of
> gold, silver and bank notes, would come here and see how much
> their money is worth in our settlement. A thousand sovereigns

would not here buy a hat, nor a roll of bank notes a loaf of bread. Here at least money is not wealth… Wealth is made up of many things – of land, of houses, of clothes, food and of the means (whether gold or silver or anything else) by which these things may be obtained. Whatever lives, or grows, or can be produced, that is necessary, or useful, or agreeable to mankind, is wealth.

To Martineau, this was not far from the Necessarianism of Hartley and Priestley. It was the survival instinct within people that drove human life, as left to us by nature. *Life in the Wilds* contains a good depiction of the importance of productive labour. The settlement grows, connects with other settlements and trade increases. Martineau provides an illustration of Adam Smith's 'division of labour' for which she gives the humorous example of a plum pudding:

Think of the toil of preparing the vineyards where raisins grow; of the smith and the carpenter who made the press where the grapes are prepared, and of the miner, the smelter, the founder, the furnace builder, the bricklayer, and others who helped make their tools, and rope makers, the sail makers, the ship builders, the sailors who must do their part towards bringing the fruit to our shores.

As John Vint writes: 'It is not a surprise that 'Life in the Wilds' was such a success. There was a clear popular appeal in the little settlement fighting back and winning through after suffering a massive setback. As a picture of illustration of some key ideas of Adam Smith it is very well done.'[3]

In February 1832, after the initial good sales of *Life in the Wilds* Harriet wrote an excited letter to Fox detailing her plans for further tales and explaining how her mind was preoccupied with what she should present to her new-found audience: 'What a blessing it is to have an empty picture gallery all to myself & to have hundreds perhaps thousands urging me to fill one panel after another… it is well for me that this is a work of the imagination, else I should dwell more than is at all good for me.'

She concluded: 'How I have rattled on! Good night and remember whatever becomes of me and my scheme, that all the success will have been owing to you. If there be failure, it must be mine.'

In another letter to Fox soon afterwards, we can see that she was receiving much encouraging correspondence, and it also suggests, perhaps, that she was enjoying society more: 'If I had not been pretty much used to drams of late, I

3. John Vint, *Harriet Martineau: 'The Wealth of Nations' and 'Life in the Wilds'* (Martineau Society Conference Paper 2014), p. 8.

should have been tipsy with some of the letters we have had this week. Nothing but prophecies of the most complete success.'

Martineau knew now that she had to be in London, and after writing the first few *Illustrations* in Norwich, in the autumn of 1832 she took lodgings in Conduit Street, just off Regent Street. She arrived in London, where she was regarded as the hottest writing talent around and not only fêted and sought out by society types, but also by politicians who attempted to influence her popular tales.

William Johnson Fox continued to be an important link in London society but Harriet was moving on to pastures new. Late in 1833 she was commissioned to write some specific *Illustrations of Taxation,* which would not be published by the Fox brothers. They tried to claim that their agreement extended to include all of her output, while she perhaps remembered their initial reticence. The dispute is outlined in a letter later summarised by James Martineau:

> She has been deeply hurt by a claim on the part of Mr Fox and his brother to one half of the proceeds of her projected 'Illustrations of Taxation'. The lawyers pronounced that the Foxes 'had not a leg to stand on' and they had to yield but the trait of character could not be forgotten.

Within a year of being in London, not only had the young author gained enough confidence to stand up to her publisher but she also had lawyers on her side, which she could now afford. In addition, she had the backing of the Lord Chancellor, Henry Brougham, who had become a vocal supporter, and who was pushing for the taxation tales.

The split with Fox was accentuated when he left his wife and moved in with Eliza Flower, a move that attracted scandal, social opprobrium and brought about his official expulsion as a Unitarian minister.

In a letter to Fox in 1838, Harriet was upfront about her disapproval. She suggests that their relationship changed when her success occurred: 'I could not but be aware of a change in your feelings towards me from the moment my success became great. You were too ready to be certain that I should be spoiled, – that I was spoiled.'

This is the age-old tale of the protégé's fame and popularity leaving the mentor behind in its wake, although Martineau goes on: 'I still regard you as my chief benefactor, because you first helped me out of the trammels of fears and prejudices from which I suffered grievously. And do not suppose that this is a mere private acknowledgement. Everyone who knows me knows my sense of obligation to you.'

Despite the effect the scandal had on his life in the 1830s, Fox proved himself a survivor. His affair with Eliza Flower ended with her premature death in 1846, at which point he moved to Lancashire and became MP for Oldham. Whilst it was said his preaching style was not suited to the House of Commons, he supported important moves towards national education and increased suffrage. He and Martineau occasionally corresponded, though this ended in the 1850s when he refused to destroy the letters she had sent him. He became reconciled with his first wife later in life, and died in London in 1864.

Harriet Martineau had been fortunate in her partnership with William Johnson Fox in the early 1830s. Firstly, she had a publisher in tune with her Unitarian progressive dissenting background, who was supportive of her and could introduce her to influential like-minded people in the capital. Secondly, he supported her financially at a crucial moment, which meant she could devote time to her reading and writing. Finally, she chose, with his encouragement, to write about economics at a time when the public was ready and eager to engage with the subject matter and willing to pay for the privilege. William Johnson Fox opened the door and Martineau, clutching her restless pen, burst through it.

Chapter 4: Elizabeth Fry

In 1833 the *Illustrations* regularly sold 10,000 monthly copies with a readership that Fox estimated to be close to 150,000 – enormous for the day. The books were a worldwide hit, with readers in Europe and America. With help from her brother Robert, Harriet moved into a house in Fludyer Street (a street that was later demolished to make way for the Foreign Office), just behind Downing Street and close to Parliament.

Harriet hosted visitors most afternoons, after spending the mornings writing. It was easier to manage if people came to her, particularly as she was now regularly using a large ear trumpet, which she would disconcertingly place in the face of any interlocutors. Within a year of being in London she had reinvented herself from the shy, deaf girl she'd been in Norwich into a 'literary lion', a confident, famous woman. She juxtaposes the two situations in her autobiography:

> The change from my life in Norwich to my life in London, was certainly prodigious, and such as I did not dream of when I exchanged the one for the other. Before we lost our money, and when I was a young lady 'just introduced' my mother insisted on taking me to balls and parties, though that sort of visiting was the misery of my life. My deafness was terribly in the way, both because it made me shy, and because card players and dancers of a provincial town, are awkward in such a case. Very few people spoke to me and I dare say I looked as if I did not wish to be spoken to. From the time when I went to London all that changed. People began with me as a deaf person; and there was little more awkwardness about hearing, when they had once reconciled themselves to my trumpet. They came to me in good will, or they would not have come at all.

Elizabeth Fry (née Gurney) was born in the same house as Martineau – Gurney Court off Magdalen Street in Norwich – in 1780, 22 years before Harriet's own birth. (The house was leased to the Martineaus by the Gurneys for a few years at the start of the 19th century.) The Gurneys were a Quaker and banking family, based in the large Earlham Hall, just outside Norwich. Elizabeth had been inspired as an 18-year-old by an American Quaker preacher William Savery and resolved to dedicate herself to working for the poor and destitute, and for prison reform. She married Joseph Fry in 1800, moved to London and had eleven children over the next 20 years.

During her procreating years Elizabeth Fry had not forgotten the most deprived in society, and she came away from a visit to Newgate Prison horrified at the treatment of incarcerated women and children. In 1816 she founded a school for the children at Newgate and, a year later, helped to found the 'Association for the Improvement of the Female Prisons'.

In addition to their shared birthplace, Martineau and Fry had something else in common: they both felt the impact of the financial crisis of 1825–8, which in Fry's case bankrupted her husband. This freed Elizabeth to form a formidable partnership with her brother Joseph John Gurney. Together they campaigned to improve conditions in prisons across the country, which included the initiation of new legislation.

During 1833 Harriet received a letter from Elizabeth Fry – a request to meet up at Newgate Prison. Harriet would have been keen to meet her Norwich role model as well as see the conditions in the prison. The main record of the meeting comes from Martineau's autobiography in which she reports that Fry and Gurney had recently read Martineau's tale *Cousin Marshall*, which influenced their campaign for the reform of the existing Poor Law in Parliament. Both women now had an acute awareness of how to make change happen; they had both become effective parliamentary lobbyists at a time when women could not vote and the presence of any women (other than cooks or cleaners) in the Houses of Parliament was a great rarity.

In *Cousin Marshall*, Martineau made the case that charity and dole money for the unemployed and poor created a situation of dependency that should not be encouraged. The system of parish relief and workhouses gave no incentive for people to climb out of their situation through education or endeavour. This, of course, is a debate that is still raging in the modern world, with the perceived 'underclass' living a life of dependency on state benefits, a seemingly insoluble problem that most acknowledge but are unsure as to how to approach it: with the carrot of jobs or the stick of withdrawing support payments. Martineau provides an accurate prediction of what has come to pass nearly two centuries later and, rereading her *Illustrations* now, it is striking how many of the economic factors and the people's stories she presents are still relevant to modern life.

Cousin Marshall can be interpreted as coming directly from Martineau's own experience of the death of her father, the collapse of his business, and what might have happened had she and her mother not had anything to fall back on. It shows how the parish workhouse was not a healthy, motivating environment for anyone and would probably lead to its inhabitants ending up on the wrong side of the law. It is one of several presentations in the *Illustrations* of a working woman being able to shoulder wider responsibilities. *The Spectator* reviewed the story positively, beginning: 'The first day of each month is marked by no publication of more importance than Miss Martineau's "Illustrations of Political Economy". Each succeeding number increases our admiration for the writer's abilities.'

The review gives an outline of the story's protagonist's situation:

> Cousin Marshall is the wife of a steady and respectable working man who brings up a large family decently and virtuously by the frugal employment of scanty wages. However a fire destroys the business, the man, John Marshall dies and the family end up in the workhouse which is laid open before us, and all its disgusting scenes... the painful process of degradation, shamelessness and ultimate vice worked in those who come look upon the parish as a rightful labour fund.

Cousin Marshall, however, shows fortitude:

> ... such is the force of her admirable qualities of industry, frugality, and energy possessed by her... the impression conveyed through the whole book, is that of a poor but high minded creature, worthier of respect than duchesses in their robes or countesses in coronets and carriages. Miss Martineau is the real painter of the poor: she has all the truth of Crabbe, with more hope and more reason.

Her approach was idealistic: she believed that societies were built from the bottom up, by individuals finding their vocation, being educated and trained, then contributing to the economy and creating fair pay for good labour. The Welfare State didn't exist in the 1830s, but the Poor Law reform that Martineau and Fry both wanted included the introduction of incentives for work to get people out of their dependent situation. Martineau remembered:

> She [Fry] told me that her brother, J. J. Gurney, and other members of her family had become convinced by reading 'Cousin Marshall' and others of my tales that they had been for a long course of years unsuspectingly doing mischief where they meant to do good: that they were now convinced that the true way of benefiting the poor

1. Spectator review of 'Cousin Marshall' (8th September 1832) as reprinted in *Illustrations of Political Economy: Selected Tales*, ed. Deborah Logan (Broadview Editions 2004), p. 418.

was to reform the poor law system. Understanding that I was in the confidence of the government as to this measure, they desired to know whether I could give them an insight into the principles on which it was to be founded. They desired that their section of the House of Commons should have time and opportunity to consider the subject… I had no scruple in communicating the principles… Mrs Fry noted them down, with cheerful thanks, and assurances that they would not be thrown away. They were not thrown away. That section of members came well prepared for the hearing of the measure, and one and all unflinchingly supported it.

In her 1937 biography of Fry, Janet Whitney puts a positive spin on this meeting:

A conversation between two such women has an intrinsic interest of its own, but it is still more interesting in the direct evidence it affords of Elizabeth Fry's conscious influence in Parliamentary affairs.

It was she who requested the interview. They met at Newgate in the Matron's room. Miss Martineau, knowing the conversation was to have to do with politics, astutely brought a witness. The careless, easy Mrs Fry never thought of such a thing. But the clergyman friend was a quiet fellow; and the mutual admiration of the two ladies made the conversation easy. Mrs Fry had heard that Miss Martineau was informed on some of the measures, especially those touching Poor Law reform, that were shortly to come before the House of Commons. And she wondered if it would be honourably possible for Miss Martineau to pass on some of that information, in order, said Mrs Fry candidly, that 'our section of members might come prepared.' Miss Martineau was able to give useful information on the principles of the proposed measures without betrayal of confidence, and willingly did so. Mrs Fry took notes, gave her cheerful thanks, complimented Miss Martineau on her books, and the ladies parted, with expressions of mutual esteem. The results were excellent. 'Our section' of members came well prepared, and one and all 'unflinchingly support' the reform measures.

At the time of this naively wire-pulling conference Miss Martineau was thirty-one and Mrs Fry fifty-three. No doubt Miss Fry, always conscious of intellect when she met it, regarded Miss Martineau half-enviously as 'really clever'. But Miss Martineau regarded Mrs Fry as nothing less than 'sublime'.[2]

In fact, I suspect that the meeting was businesslike rather than friendly and that Elizabeth Fry may have found the younger woman a tad impertinent in her confidence. It is very unlikely that Fry and Gurney suddenly turned their backs on a lifetime of charitable inclination as a result of reading *Cousin Marshall*. Fry didn't report the meeting in her own journal and made no record of it.

Fry and Gurney were Quakers and were about to recruit that other notable Norwich woman, Amelia Opie, into their Quaker ways. Their moral puritanism, abstinence and charity were strong components of their philosophy, whereas the Unitarian clan of Norwich had been a more practical circle, less puritanical, urging scientific progress and change rather than charity. Martineau was the model of an opinionated, clever woman, a precursor of the modern feminist. She imbibed economic theory but lacked compassion for the poorest in society, suggesting that work and wages were the only answer to alleviating poverty, which was, and is, good in theory. Fry was dealing with the reality of those unable to find work, buried in the cycle of crime and poverty. As the mother of eleven children, Fry took a maternalistic approach to fallen people, despite coming from a family of bankers. It was no contest as to who would eventually appear on a £5 note.

Amelia Opie had spoken out against slavery in the 1790s. In the famous portrait of the 1840 anti-slavery convention by Benjamin Robert Haydon, which hangs in the National Portrait Gallery, a small handful of women are seen present, and Opie is prominent in the picture, although she was not allowed to speak at the meeting. This was the convention that the Boston Female Anti-Slavery Society came over from America to attend, only to be turned away at the door because they were women. Harriet Martineau was invited to be their honorary delegate but she was too ill to take up the invitation.

Elizabeth Fry, Amelia Opie and Harriet Martineau all came from large Norwich families. All three had unprecedented careers which influenced social change. They shared a dissenting religion, a regional city background away from the London establishment, the encouragement of those around them, the huge challenges thrown up by the new industrial era, stepping into arenas shamefully vacated by the prominent men of the day. These three Norwich women set determined, steadfast, pioneering examples of real reform over appearance or fashion and showed individual courage over conformity.

2. Janet Whitney, *Elizabeth Fry: Quaker Heroine* (George Harrap & Co, 1937), pp. 269–271.

Chapter 5: Thomas Malthus

In her fifth and sixth *Illustrations* Martineau addressed the work of Thomas Malthus, who had written *An Essay on the Principle of Population* in 1798, broadly arguing that if population growth continued unchecked, it would outgrow the production and distribution of adequate food for a growing population. This would have significant economic consequences: the price of food would escalate with the potential for starvation amongst poorer people. Much of his essay uses similar arguments to those portrayed by Martineau in *Cousin Marshall* – essentially, that the Poor Law accentuated poverty rather than relieving it by creating unsustainable dependency.

Martineau's two tales, *Ella of Garveloch* and *Weal and Woe in Garveloch*, are set in a Scottish fishing village and present the problem of population as a reproductive concern for women. Deborah Logan sets the scene for Ella:

> Ella of Garveloch is notable for its strong and memorable characterisation of a Scots fisherwoman. Life in this Scottish fishing village is difficult and strenuous, and Ella faces more challenges than most: she is young and inexperienced, poor and without resources, and resented by a jealous overseer. As the head of her family of orphaned brothers, Ella proves herself equal to the task; by negotiating directly with the 'Laird', an absentee landlord who is scandalised by her rough, unladylike appearance, but impressed by her character and determination… the men in this patriarchal fishing village resent Ella's forthright honesty and seemingly limitless capacity for hard work, but she is undeterred in her aim to provide for her family. Ella is a compelling feminist prototype and the narrative was reputed to be one of Princess Victoria's favourites.[1]

The follow-up tale *Weal and Woe in Garveloch* caused some scandal, with its portrayal of a discussion between Ella and her friend Katie about sexual abstinence and how they could control their own reproduction – a discussion that was becoming more relevant under the new pressures of growing industrial cities. These tales were engaging, relevant to people's lives and popular. The Victorian establishment was shocked by their candour but the new wider-reading public lapped it up. Logan concludes:

---

1. Deborah Logan (ed.), 'Introduction', in *Illustrations of Political Economy: Selected Tales* (Broadview Editions, 2004), p. 55–6.

She suggests that sexual abstinence could easily improve the economic status of the poor, she was as praised by some for addressing this difficult topic as she was condemned by others for what was regarded as a direct affront to the period's revered material ideology. Written at a time when any woman who was not producing babies regularly was a social anomaly – like Harriet Martineau, for instance – the promotion of 'preventive checks' as a primary tenet for social reform was daring indeed.

Presenting reproduction as a choice for women was far ahead of its time, and would not enter public discourse in the West until the push for birth control in the 1960s.

Malthus's work, and Martineau's advocacy of it, were controversial because they seemed to promote one rule for the poor and another for the rich: the poor should not procreate, but the rich should be allowed to do so. Taken to its full course, it could be seen as an argument for population control at the bottom end of society, almost as if it was acceptable to let poor people starve. This stigma became attached to Malthus in the 20th century when 'Malthusian' was regarded as akin to eugenics, the argument being that if food and resources were not available, then it was simply nature's way that people should die.

In fact, Malthus was not 'Malthusian' (or at least not what became mythologised as 'Malthusian') and neither was Martineau. Both were sounding a warning about what we would now describe as sustainability. Population growth needed to be controlled in line with natural resources, but each individual also needed to have a life of work and fair pay in order to feed their family. Martineau added to this the suggestion that women, as exemplified by her character of Ella, could take the lead in influencing the future of the family and its sustainable survival.

A letter from Harriet to her brother James in June 1832 suggests that she had not found writing this easy, and that she knew she was on controversial ground. In James's transcription:

> Harriet then describes the struggles she has had to go through in facing and honestly treating the population problem in her Political Economy tales. She had taken courage to deal with it as Malthus himself did, like a moral and social question of fundamental importance and not to be shirked.

Malthus liked Martineau's exposition of his ideas and she received word in London that he would like to meet his populariser. They met, initially, at a gathering organised by a Mrs Austin in November 1832. As later recalled in her autobiography, Harriet was apprehensive, partly because she knew that Malthus had a speech impediment caused by a cleft palate and that she would be using her ear trumpet:

> I could not decline such an invitation as this: but when I considered my own deafness, and his inability to pronounce half the consonants in the alphabet, and his hare lip which must prevent my offering him my tube, I feared we should make a terrible business of it. I was delightfully wrong. His first sentence, slow and gentle, set me at ease completely.

Harriet describes how Malthus and his wife then invited her to Haileybury College in Hertfordshire, where he resided and taught, and where all facilities would be made available to her if she so wished. She took up this offer in August 1833:

> It was a delightful visit. The well planted county of Herts a welcome change from the pavement of London in August... My room was a large and airy one with a bay window and a charming view, fitted up with desk, books and everything I could possibly want... My friends had somehow discovered from my tales that I was fond of riding and horse habit and whip were prepared for me. Almost daily we went forth when work was done, a pleasant riding party of five or six, and explored all the green lanes and enjoyed all the fine views.

This happy summer scene also linked them to the Darwin and Wedgwood circle. By now, Martineau had connected with this group in London through her near-neighbour Erasmus Alvey Darwin with whom she shared Unitarian links. Malthus was a long-time friend of the Mackintosh family who were about to be joined to the Wedgwoods through the marriage of Fanny Mackintosh and Hensleigh Wedgwood. Indeed, Malthus's daughter was a bridesmaid at the wedding. Meanwhile Charles Darwin, far away on board the *Beagle*, was opening his mind, ready to connect with this circle when he came back to England three years later.

These connections were to have great ramifications for the future of science and Martineau anticipates their significance in a letter to William Johnson Fox in June 1833:

> We were together at the Wedgwoods on Sunday, when Darwin

[Erasmus Alvey] brought out the Examiner and we all, including the Malthuses, read it together. I could scarcely help laughing that day to think what the 'Age' should have said if it would have seen us sitting after dinner; I, dancing Mrs Wedgwood's baby and Malthus patting its cheeks.

Just a few years later, reading Malthus's essay on population gave Charles Darwin his 'Eureka' moment with regard to natural selection: if scarcity of resources led to death, then those that survived would retain traits that would aid them. He extrapolated this to all life on Earth.

In recent years, Martineau has received credit for being a link between Malthus and Darwin, in the comprehensive biographies of Darwin by Adrian Desmond and James Moore, and in the biography of Malthus by Robert Mayhew:

> On his return from the Beagle voyage in the mid 1830s Darwin had become enmeshed via his brother in the London Circle around Harriet Martineau, whose Malthusian popularizing we have encountered. This was the moment when Malthus's influence was at its peak and Darwin was close to the eye of the storm in his acquaintance with, and entrancement by, the Martineau circle. And thus his auto-biographical comments about stumbling upon Malthus 'by chance' are somewhat misleading; he was bound to encounter Malthus's ideas by the company he kept.[2]

The link between Malthus, Martineau and Darwin can be stretched even further back. Malthus had written about, and had been portraying, laws of nature, while Martineau picked up on the work of Malthus because it chimed with the Necessarianism of Priestley and Hartley. Indeed, Malthus, in becoming a cleric, had been educated at the dissenting academy in Warrington developed by Priestley. Malthus always leant towards the freethinking side of Unitarianism which is part of his connection to the Darwin–Wedgwood circle. There is a line of dissenting thought, pursuing natural laws before God's, that runs directly through Priestley, Malthus, Martineau and Charles Darwin.

Martineau's addressing of Malthus did much to stimulate a popular debate about population and resources, as well as to make ordinary people aware of their own place within the economic system by suggesting that their own actions would be of consequence in building a more equal society. Later in

---

2. Robert Mayhew, *Malthus: The Life and Legacies of an Untimely Prophet* (Belknap Press, 2014), p. 145.

the 19th century this didn't cast Martineau in a positive light with the growing number of socialists who, alongside religious people, particularly those from
Catholic backgrounds, shared the thinking that if ordinary working people
wanted a large family, that was their choice.

In his biography of Malthus, Mayhew presents a convincing case that the
problem has never gone away and still provides the framework for modern concerns over population growth in an environmental context. The academic battle between Paul Ehrlich and Julian Simon in the 1970s and '80s was, in fact,
debating Malthus's predictions. Ehrlich wrote *The Population Bomb* in 1968 as
a wake-up call to the impending doom he envisaged should world population
growth continue unabated. He believed that food production was going to be a
huge future issue. Julian Simon countered Ehrlich with economic and technological analysis, claiming that human ingenuity would mean that food could be
produced to keep pace with population growth. In his 1981 book *The Ultimate
Resource* he went back to Malthus:

> We must recognise what Malthus came to recognise. After he pub-
> lished the short simplistic theory in the first edition of his 'Essay on
> Population' and after he had the time and inclination to consider the
> facts as well as the theory, he concluded that human beings are very
> different from flies or rats. When faced with the limits of a bottle-like
> situation, people can alter their behaviour so as to accommodate to
> that limit... And people can alter that limit – expand the 'bottle' – by
> consciously increasing the resources available.[3]

Simon is making the case for human technology: that it will always stay ahead
of natural pressures. This is still a live debate in modern environmental science.
Technology is working to stay ahead but there is a limit to the number of people that the Earth's resources can sustain. This is the debate that Malthus, Martineau and Darwin started. Interestingly, all three of them underestimated the
potential of technology. They were writing at the start of the industrial age
and could not foresee that the science they were advocating would advance so
quickly in the biotechnology of the 21st century. In 1830 the world's population was around 750 million people; it is now over 7 billion. Food technology
has managed to keep up with food demand so far, in that there is enough food
produced to go around (although it doesn't always get to where it is needed);
and the problems of rising population may now be more to do with the demand

3. Julian Simon, *The Ultimate Resource*, quoted in Robert Mayhew, *Malthus: The Life and Legacies of an Untimely Prophet* (Belknap Press, 2014), p. 206.

for material goods and transport, and the effect of consumerist production on the Earth's atmosphere, particularly in rising levels of carbon dioxide and global warming. It is an issue which isn't going away.

Martineau's writing on the effects of population and runaway reproduction are worthy of consideration and recognition. She was humanising the theory in her stories, taking it back to how economic and natural fluctuations affected people's lives. The danger of the globalised, hyper-tech world we live in is that we forget the basics of human existence. The system should be created for people to lead healthy lives and to be able to provide for their families. It should recognise that people's actions will influence wider outcomes and that women are important in taking decisions which will affect economic futures. Indeed, in modern environmental thinking and in worldwide policy making there is an accepted correlation between women's education, their decision making, and population growth. Increasing women's education about reproduction in many parts of the world is now a UN policy priority. Martineau's economic writings in 1832 were about issues that are still alive, her pioneering outlining of them was important and her views are still relevant.

Chapter 6: World Leaders

One of several amazing aspects of Harriet Martineau's life and career is how she spent her twenties as an introverted, shy, deaf young lady in Norwich and then, in her thirties, seen not just in the company of the Great and the Good, but celebrated by the world's most prominent statesmen. All this in the 1830s, a time when women were to be seen and not heard and to bear children. Harriet Martineau was nothing if not a novelty.

Barely three years after moving from the family home in Norwich to London, she was staying with James Madison in his legendary palatial home in Montpelier, Virginia in America. Madison had been the fourth President of the United States between 1809 and 1817 but he was more famous as the 'Father of the Constitution', having played a key role in drafting the American Constitution and the Bill of Rights. Harriet must have had to pinch herself, although in the year before her trip to America she had got used to meeting the top politicians at home.

Living with her mother and aunt in Fludyer Street in 1834, Martineau received a steady stream of random visitors as later recalled in her autobiography:

> When my morning work was done, there was usually a curious variety of visitors, such as it bewilders me more to think of now than it did to receive at the time. More than once, my study door was thrown open, and a Frenchman, Italian or German stood on the threshold with one hand on his heart and the other almost touching the top of the door, clearing his throat to recite an ode, of which he wanted my opinion. Sometimes, it was a lady from the country, who desired to pour her sorrows into my bosom, and swear eternal friendship.

She was also regularly called upon by politicians from around the corner in Parliament and Downing Street. The Lord Chancellor, Henry Brougham, was a regular visitor and supporter, and she developed a rapport with another Cabinet member, Lord Durham. In her autobiography she describes how she became something of an intermediary between these two leading figures of the government. Brougham had been supportive of her, but she lambasts him for being 'false' around women as well as drunk and boorish on occasions. Lord Durham was more statesmanlike. Both tried to give Brougham the benefit of the doubt but she reports on one occasion: 'His swearing became so incessant, and the indecency of his talk so insufferable, that I have seen even coquettes and adorers turn pale.'

After one particular afternoon when she was not sure if Brougham was 'drunk or insane', she reflected: 'My impression remains that no man who conducted himself as he did that summer day in 1834 could be sane and sober.'

Lord Durham had summoned her to discuss the Society for the Diffusion of Knowledge and she brazenly told him of the widespread distrust of Brougham and 'his teaching and preaching clique' to which Durham reportedly replied: 'Brougham has done foolish things enough but it would cut me to the heart to think that Brougham was false.'

She adds:

> ... the words and the tone were impressed on my mind by the contrast which they formed with the way in which Brougham and his toadies were in the habit of speaking of Lord Durham. Brougham's envy and jealousy of the popular confidence enjoyed by Lord Durham at that time were notorious. If Lord Durham were unaware of it, he was the only person who was.

The divide between the two statesmen was to have serious repercussions when they eventually clashed in the House of Lords. Martineau recalls the dramatic intervention of the King, William IV:

> The terror of the feeble king, who dissolved parliament to preclude the encounter, deprived Brougham of his Seals and sent Lord Durham on a foreign mission... My heart swelled many a time when I recalled the moment of Lord Durham's first reception of a doubt of Brougham's honesty... In seven years from that time he was in his grave – sent there by Brougham's falseness.

It seems bitter infighting within governments, even amongst appointed peers in the House of Lords, is nothing new.

Martineau's economic parables continued to be lapped up by an eager public. The pressure of the writing and the high-profile visits were punctuated by regular weekend escapes to, for instance, the Wedgwoods or Malthuses, or to Birmingham to see her brother Robert and his family. She received word that her works were being translated and read across Europe, particularly in the royal courts of Russia, Austria and France, in the restored monarchy of King

Louis Phillippe. She held no great regard for aristocracy, however, and managed quickly to ruin this new-found continental fame: her twelfth tale, *French Wines and Politics*, was one of her most popular but espoused the importance of 'égalité' in France, leading Louis Phillippe to withdraw his support.

A regular visitor to Fludyer Street was the writer on economics, the now elderly Jane Marcet. She had retained her French contacts and was surprised that Martineau would deliberately upset the French king, recalled by Harriet in her autobiography as: 'I thought I had told you that the King of the French read all your stories, and made all his family read them; and now you have been writing about *égalité*, they will never read you again.'

Martineau's defiant response was:

> My good friend could not see how I could hope to be presented at the Tuileries after this and I could only say that it had never entered my head to wish it. I tried to impress on my anxious friend the hopelessness of all attempts to induce me to alter my stories from such considerations as she urged. I wrote with a view to the people, and especially the most suffering of them; and the crowned heads must, for once, take their chance with their feelings.

Tsar Nicholas I had ordered copies of all previous issues of the *Illustrations* for his court and all the schools of Russia. Harriet's 13th tale was *The Charmed Sea;* ignoring her popularity with the Tsar and disconcerting her publisher, the story criticised Russia for its treatment of Poland in general and its unsympathetic attitude towards Polish immigrants in particular. Tsar Nicholas promptly had all Martineau's volumes rounded up from Russia's schools and burnt. For good measure he also banned the author from Russia – not that she had any plans to visit.

In the pre-Victorian era, monarchies still had great power and prestige in a Europe where elected leaders were rare and an aristocratic system of inherited status still dominated governments. Martineau arrived as a popular writer at a time when democratic ideas were making inroads alongside great economic and industrial change. Her Tom Paine-like lack of deference to royalty was significant. Martineau was one of a new breed.

Her fourth tale had been *Demerara,* an argument against the economic institution of slavery in America and an explicit statement of the immorality of buying and selling human beings. Published in 1833, the same year as the abolition of slavery in the British Empire was passed in Parliament, this may not seem such a controversial stance. However, Martineau's approach to political economy told her that the slave system of labour was still central to American trade and to its whole way of life. She also knew that this was an issue which continued to arouse sensitivities. In the preface she wrote:

> If I had believed as many do that strong feeling impairs the soundness of reasoning, I should have avoided the subject of the following tale since slavery is a subject which cannot be approached without emotion. But convinced as I am on the contrary, that reason and sensibilities are made for cooperation, and perceiving as I do, that the most stirring eloquence issues from the calmest logic, I have not hesitated to bring calculations and reasonings to bear on the subject, which awakens the drowsiest, and fires the coldest.

Her decision to visit America in 1834 seems sudden and intrepid. It also interrupted a period of great fame, increased income and of her being honoured by London politicians, writers and artists. She was, though, young and restless and realised that America was in an interesting phase of development, having only released itself from the mother country 50 years earlier. There were still important links between the two countries and, moreover, she wanted to see the system of slavery for herself.

Another reason for the trip, which was revealed in her autobiography many years later, was that relations with her mother had become strained. Elizabeth Martineau was a strict, matriarchal woman and one can only guess at what she made of her daughter's life in London where they now lived together.

In the published letters between Harriet and her brother James we can see that she had been planning the America trip for about a year and had pleaded with him to come with her. However, he repeatedly turned her down, increasingly tied as he was to his own family and preaching commitments. Harriet eventually found a travelling companion in the independent-minded Louisa Jeffrey, and in August 1834 the two set off for Liverpool to board a sailing vessel, the *United States,* for a 42-day journey across the Atlantic. Martineau revelled in her first sea journey. She presented a rose to every passenger on board but then requested that she be left alone to her reading and writing, often sitting 'alone in the stern' to witness 'the boundless sea'.

The ship was hit by a bad storm and to the crew's probable incredulity, Martineau asked to be strapped to a mast so as to get the full experience, perhaps compensating for her deafness. Her subsequent description in *Retrospect of Western Travel* is memorable:

The sea was no more like water than it was like land or sky. When I had heard of the ocean running mountains high, I thought it mere hyperbolical expression. But here the scene was of huge wandering mountains with leaden vales between. The sky seemed narrowed to a mere slip overhead... the heavens seemed rocking their masses of torn clouds, keeping time with the billows to the solemn music of the winds; the most swelling and mournful music I ever listened to. The delight of this hour I shall never forget.

The voyage had an effect on Harriet's developing philosophical mind:

The first few days after a voyage go far towards making one believe that some things have a quality of stability, however one may be metaphysically convinced that the sea affords a far truer hint of the incessant flux and change which are the law of the universe. If I had rejoiced in the emblem at sea, I now enjoyed the deception on land.

Martineau and Jeffrey reached America at a time of ferment, with historical forces colliding. On their arrival in New York, the harbour master sought reassurance about Miss Martineau's views as regards slavery. The city was in the grip of mob violence against abolitionists and potential incendiaries would not be allowed to enter. He received a guarantee that she had come only to learn, and they were allowed to embark. Initially greeted and housed by Unitarians, soon after the well-known author had many wanting to meet her, particularly once the New York newspapers announced her arrival. Even the Vice President himself, Martin Van Buren, turned up one evening at their hotel in Albany, but only managed to reinforce his image of being an uninspiring and compromised figure.

Martineau was keen to get out and about, experiencing the wilderness by staying in a log cabin and then returning to the city to visit the recently established New York State Prison. Later she set off with a small group to visit Niagara Falls, after which she recorded that the emotion of being there would be 'never renewed or equalled'. She also paid a moving visit to Joseph Priestley's house in Northumberland, Pennsylvania, and placed flowers at his grave, lamenting the neglect shown to both.

In January, three months into the trip, she found herself in Washington. She was invited to a Congressional dinner at the White House, where she sat opposite President Andrew Jackson who quizzed her about the governments of England and France. A few days later she witnessed an assassination attempt on the President, observing the 'insane culprit' enveloped by a crowd and President Jackson being: 'the old soldier thrown into a tremendous passion'.

Her intriguing encounter with James Madison occurred in February 1835 when the travelling ladies were invited to Montpelier in Vermont to spend a few days at the large house of the former president. Martineau's private quest while travelling across America was to see how the country was measuring up to the original principles established in its idealistic constitution. She would have been well aware that Madison had been present as America gained independence from Britain and, indeed, had been the author of the all-important First Amendment of the American Constitution, outlining the right to freedom of speech and other individual freedoms. By the time of Martineau's visit, Madison was 83 but well cared for by his wife and he was not lost to the pleasures of conversation. As described in her *Retrospect*, Martineau had almost met her match:

> He appeared perfectly well during my visit, and was a wonderful man... He complained of one ear being deaf, and that his sight which had never been perfect, prevented his reading much but he could hear Mrs. Madison read, and I did not perceive that he lost any part of the conversation... His voice was clear and strong, and his manner of speaking particularly lively, often playful. It was an uncommonly pleasant countenance.

Unlikely though it may have seemed, these two were kindred spirits and Harriet was impressed by the still lively mind of this former Founding Father:

> His relish for conversation could never have been keener. I was in perpetual fear of his being exhausted but when I left my seat he was sure to follow and sit down... I was glad enough to make the most of my means of intercourse with one whose political philosophy I deeply venerated.

They were both religiously sceptical and progressive, would very likely have swapped views on Tom Paine, and shared sympathy on the recently announced death of Malthus. She must, however, have been surprised at his views on slavery. He declared himself a 'coloniser' – affiliated to a movement in America that saw the only resolution to slavery as being the establishment of a new colony abroad in which to place all the ex-slaves. Implicit in this was an assumption that black and white people could not possibly live together.

Martineau enjoyed her tête-à-tête with Madison and resolved to travel to the Southern States to witness slavery in action. The picture of an entrenched system she had already gained from the North must have surprised her. Abolitionists were a controversial fringe group of idealists. The whole country was economically dependent on slavery and was not going to change easily. She bade a fond farewell to Madison and voiced her desire to visit again on her way back but, alas, James Madison died a few months later.

Harriet's encounters with elite politicians and royalty between 1833 and 1836 firmed up her belief in the need for greater democracy and human rights. She had come face to face with governing male elites and, while respectful of their views,f she was not impressed by their government of the people. Martineau was at the vanguard of a new breed of commentators who lacked deference to upper-class rulers – a less deferential attitude that would continue to spread. These first-hand encounters also hardened her resolve to challenge the great inequalities she observed. She summarised her own journey, and her own shifting views, in a letter to the Manchester Association for Cooperatives who had written to her with their appreciation of her work:

> Within a short time, and happily before the energy of youth is past, I have been awakened from a state of aristocratic prejudice, to a clear conviction of the Equality of Human Rights, and of the paramount duty of society, to provide for the support, comfort and enlightenment of every member born into it. All that I write is now with a view to the illustration of these great truths; with the hope of pressing upon the rich a conviction of their obligations, and of inducing the poor to urge their claims with moderation and forbearance, and to bear about with them the credentials and of intelligence and good deserts.

Chapter 7: William Lloyd Garrison

Harriet Martineau spent all of 1835 touring America. During that time two things dominated her trip, both of which would have great ramifications for the rest of her life. Firstly, she came face to face with the reality of the slave system as a way of life; secondly, following on from this, she came to appreciate the steadfast determination of those campaigning in America for the abolition of slavery. She realised that this group, widely regarded as radical extremists at the time, needed to be lauded and supported. The unofficial leader of this extreme group in 1835 was William Lloyd Garrison. Meeting and observing Garrison was to have a profound effect on Martineau, and vice versa: receiving the public support of the famous English author boosted Garrison and would fortify others in the abolitionist movement, particularly encouraging women to get involved in the struggle.

As Martineau and Louisa Jeffrey navigated the Southern States they were made welcome and enjoyed much of the scenery and cities, particularly a steam-boat trip along the Mississippi and a few days in Cincinnati. Martineau's record of a social meeting with slave-holders in *Retrospect of Western Travel* suggests she wasn't actively confronting the issue but the publication of *Demerara* preceded her and those working the system were keen to make their case:

> It was likewise a rule with me never to conceal or soften my own opinions, and never to allow myself to be irritated by what I heard. The first time I met an eminent Southern gentleman, a defender of slavery, he said to me (within the half hour) 'I wish you would not be in such a hurry away. I wish you would stay a year in this city. I wish you would stay ten years, and then you would change your opinions.'
> 'What opinions?'
> 'Your opinions on slavery.'
> 'What do you know of my opinions on slavery?'
> 'Oh, we know them all well enough; we have all read Demerara.'

Martineau's *Illustrations* had sold well and been widely read throughout America. Published three years before this meeting, the anti-slavery *Demerara* created a level of notoriety, particularly significant as she toured the Southern states. Her recollection of her spirited debate with these slave-holders continues:

> ... We had engaged to dine with this gentleman the next week... in order to hear his exposition of slavery. He was well prepared; and his statement of facts and reason was clear, ready, and entertaining. The fault was in the narrowness of his premises; for his whole argument was grounded on the supposition that human rights consist in sufficient subsistence in return for labour. Before he began I told him that I fully understood his wish not to argue the question, and that I came to hear his statement, not to controvert it; but that I must warn him not to take my silence for assent. Upon this understanding we proceeded; with some little irritability on his part when I asked questions, but with no danger of any quarrel. I never found the slightest difficulty in establishing a similar clear understanding with every slaveholder I met.

Martineau, travelling in the South, was not publicly opposing the slave system but when challenged in private on what were known to be her views, she would not back down:

> In the drawing room of the boarding house at Richmond, Virginia, three gentlemen, two of whom were entire strangers attacked me in the presence of a pretty large company, one afternoon. This was a direct challenge, which I did not think fit to decline and we had it all out. They were irritable at first, but softened as they went on; and when, at the end of three hours we had exhausted the subject, we were better friends than when we began.

In fact, it was the wider impact of the slave system that shocked Martineau and most affected her views. She reported the case of two brothers taken to the woods to face a 'lynch court' because they had been teaching their slaves to read, and described slaves accused of misdemeanours facing mob justice and being burnt alive. She also observed the number of mixed-race children, the direct result of the sexual abuse of young female slaves by their white masters, a practice that was financially beneficial to them as the mixed-race children could be sold as slaves. All of this could only be learnt on the ground and was a long way from the high-minded, theoretical moral arguments of Wilberforce and the Wedgwoods.

Martineau returned to Boston in the autumn of 1835 and connected with

Garrisonian abolitionists, though she felt some guilt about the friendly welcome she had received in the South. William Lloyd Garrison had set up his abolitionist newspaper *The Liberator* four years earlier as an idealistic 25-year-old demanding immediate and total freedom of slaves as a moral imperative. He had a small band of vocal supporters including Maria Weston Chapman, who made a profound connection with Martineau that would last for the rest of their lives.

In mid-November, Garrison's newspaper headquarters were ransacked by a mob and he was dragged through the streets. He was lucky to survive, thanks to the intervention of a stranger who managed to get him to the local prison where he was locked up for his own protection. It was probably Chapman who asked Martineau to attend the next meeting of the Boston Female Anti-Slavery Society which convened on 18 November with a mob abusing attendees as they arrived. Martineau was passed a note by a gentleman friend requesting that she speak on the cause's behalf. She realised straight away that if she spoke at the meeting it would have a big impact on her future: 'I foresaw that almost every house in Boston, except those of the abolitionists, would be shut against me; that my relation to the country would be completely changed, as I should suddenly be transformed from being a guest and an observer to being considered a spy.'

Martineau was introduced, stood up and addressed the audience, most likely in her own quiet reserved way which must have made her words all the more effective, so obviously did they come from an English author rather than an American preacher:

> I will say what I have said through the whole South; that I consider slavery as inconsistent with the law of God, and as incompatible with the course of his providence. I should certainly say no less at the North concerning this utter abomination and I now declare that in your principles I fully agree.

The abolitionists were ecstatic. Harriet's words were quickly printed by Garrison in *The Liberator* and would be widely reprinted. Gradually, word spread that the prominent author was supporting this widely despised, radical group and she soon received death threats and was warned not to return to the South. As she later wrote: 'The hubbub was so great, and the modes of insult were so various, as to justify distant observers in concluding that the whole nation had risen against me.'

Martineau changed her travel plans and Louisa Jeffrey returned to England for her own safety. Several times in the last few months of her American visit

Harriet was verbally and physically threatened. Intriguingly, she took refuge for several weeks in the house of the great American writer and transcendentalist philosopher Ralph Waldo Emerson who rose above the fray, seemingly regarding the slavery issue as beneath him. His own metaphysical philosophy interested Martineau but differed from her materialism. They did however remain friends, and Emerson would visit Martineau in England later in life.

Meanwhile, Harriet became closer to Garrison and Chapman. She interviewed Garrison twice and he also wrote of a friendly social evening they spent together. They would stay in touch in a way that was mutually beneficial, Garrison feeding her later journalism about America, and Harriet writing articles for *The Liberator*.

In the short term Martineau made her way back to England and, with publishers waiting, penned two books: the shrill blast of *Society in America* and the more journal-like *Retrospect of Western Travel*. *Society in America* was an analytical text measuring America's young society, not very positively, against its founding principles. Martineau exacted her revenge for the pro-slavery threats by explicitly exposing slavery as a corrupt, morally bankrupt system. She wrote of the violence and sexual exploitation of slave-holders and the corruption of politicians. It was a book read and admired by, amongst others, Charles Dickens, Charles Darwin and Florence Nightingale, and one that did much to influence the developing social sciences. Indeed, it is one of the first books aimed at providing an evidence-led analysis of a 'society'. It was also a major fillip to the abolitionists in America, and although the book attracted negative reviews and abuse, it must have done much to prick the conscience of the pro-slavery American middle classes.

The travelogue *Retrospect of Western Travel* is one of Martineau's most enjoyable and readable books. It is much more positive about her own experiences in America, though it is still punctuated by the violence and degradation of slavery as well as describing some close scrapes with outbreaks of cholera. It is also funny in places, with memorable displays of her dark humour. While on the *Mississippi* boat she remembers:

> I was privately told by a companion that the man who had forced his way on board had died of cholera in the night and been laid under a tree at the wooding place a few minutes before. Never was there a lovelier morning for a worn wretch to lie down to his long sleep.

On attending a concert in a society house she provides the following memorable review: 'There was a young girl, in a plain white frock, with a splendid voice, a good ear, and a love of warbling which carried her through very well indeed, though her own taste had obviously been her only teacher.'

Not so funny was the follow-up article, 'The Martyr Age of America', published in the widely read *Westminster Review*. She clearly stated her own view of the abolitionists and Garrison in particular:

> William Lloyd Garrison is one of God's nobility – the head of the moral aristocracy whose prerogatives we are contemplating. At present he is a marked man wherever he turns. The faces of his friends brighten when his step is heard: the people of colour almost kneel to him; and the rest of society jeer, pelt and execrate him. Amidst all this, his gladsome life rails on… this serene countenance, saint-like in its earnestness and purity.

This article was reprinted and widely read in America, as well as having considerable impact on British middle-class intelligentsia. It was also prescient. Garrison and his abolitionists would be campaigning for another 30 years before Lincoln became President and the brutal American Civil War resolved the slavery issue. Indeed, the emancipation of slaves in 1865 saw Garrison and Chapman largely lay down their abolitionist pens, tired and exhausted from 30 years of collaborative haranguing. Martineau paid fulsome tribute, particularly to Garrison, in the *Daily News*:

> *We may not hear much of him henceforth. He said he would be heard; he was heard effectually; and now he proposes to be silent. It is to be hoped that we shall not for such a reason forget him. History certainly will not… for there was one great man – the second printer's journeyman who did a great work for his country – William Lloyd Garrison.*

The history of slavery has not always been kind to the white abolitionists. It has been argued since that they may have served to accentuate opposition (the same was later said of British Suffragettes), and slavery historians have preferred to show the efforts of slaves themselves in achieving their own freedom. They state that it was in the interest of the white establishment in Britain and America to make it seem as if they had supported the emancipation of slaves all along when, in fact, the slave system had powerful supporters right up to, and during, the American Civil War.

In reality there is no reason to neglect the heroic efforts of Garrison, his followers and his British allies who were outspoken, courageous and determined to see the end of the slave system of labour in America. Their campaign did have an important impact in gradually turning public opinion around both in America and abroad. Garrison himself knew the importance of Martineau's intervention in America and on her death in 1876 he wrote:

> Never shall I cease to remember with gratitude and admiration the sublime exemplification of her great character when she was in this country in 1835, the most perilous period of the anti-slavery struggle, when any sympathy evinced for it was sure to be followed by social ostracism and public contempt... She met the issue modestly, bravely, uncompromisingly. The service she rendered to the anti-slavery course was inestimable... I am under the deepest obligations to her for the steadfast countenance she gave to me in that dark hour and the unfaltering friendship with which she honoured me to the close of her remarkable life.[1]

1. William Garrison, letter quoted in Harriet Martineau, *Autobiography*, Vol. 2 'Memorials' (Elibron Classics, 2005), p. 577.

Chapter 8: Charles Darwin

Harriet Martineau returned to Britain from America in September 1836. Soon she was back in Fludyer Street and preparing to write up her findings while they were fresh in her mind. Three publishers competed to issue them. Meanwhile, she caught up with her London friends who were eager to hear about her adventures.

Erasmus Alvey Darwin was Charles's older brother, five years his senior. The two boys had had a close relationship throughout their lives, Charles following Erasmus to Shrewsbury School, Edinburgh University Medical School and Christ's College Cambridge, none of which did either of them much good in helping their careers. Charles rejected his Edinburgh medical training and his Cambridge theological course to pursue the path of a naturalist. Eventually, abetted by the backing of his Uncle Josiah, Charles persuaded his father to endorse him, and he set off on his voyage on *The Beagle* in 1831.

Erasmus similarly rejected both the medical and priestly paths and, by now, seemed to have been pensioned off by his father in light of his vulnerable constitution. He was set up with a house in Great Marlborough Street, just off Regent Street, and became known as a 'man with a cab' as he owned an elegant horse-drawn carriage, with a distinctive grey horse, with which he consciously sought to accompany independent-minded women. It was not easy for women at the time to walk around unaccompanied so a chaperone with transport was useful, and this is perhaps how Martineau was first integrated into the Darwin–Wedgwood circle: Erasmus was to provide this service to the Wedgwood and Darwin sisters, and to Jane Carlyle, as well as to Harriet, her initial lodgings on Conduit Street being just the other side of Regent Street from his own house on Great Marlborough Street.

In recent years, thanks to the comprehensive biographies of Charles Darwin written by Janet Browne and jointly by James Moore and Adrian Desmond, both Erasmus Darwin and Harriet Martineau have emerged from the shadows and been given credit for their encouragement of Charles in the crucial period of the second half of the 1830s. The letters written by them and their circle portray the three of them as close at this time and part of a freethinking, progressive London scene.

Erasmus was a genial freethinker with scientific interests and was the perfect companion to Harriet in also being a good listener. In 1834, while sailing on *The Beagle*, Charles had received a package of Martineau's political economy tales from his sister with the accompanying note: 'Erasmus knows her and is a very great admirer and everybody reads her little books.'[1] Soon after arriving back from his five-year voyage, and shortly after Harriet's return from America, the twenty-seven-year-old Charles stayed with Erasmus in Great Marlborough Street. He wrote to his sisters to say that Erasmus was like a slave to 'Miss Martineau', driving her out morning, noon and night, and that 'Ras' had advised him that 'it would be better to view her as a man rather than a woman', a statement that says much about how different Martineau was and how even the progressive Darwin and Wedgwood circle had an entrenched attitude towards gender roles. The impression of the closeness of Erasmus and Harriet in this period is reinforced by letters from the Darwin sisters to their father, Robert Darwin, in Shrewsbury, which speculated that they may have become engaged. In fact, having a companion such as Erasmus may have been a useful guard *against* any romantic entanglements.

Martineau's American writings were soon published as the radical *Society in America*, an outspoken, critical book outlining to Americans how far they were straying from their original constitutional principles of freedom and democracy. It portrayed corrupt politicians and a compromised press, and lambasted the economic system based on slavery. It contained a chapter on 'The Political Non Existence of Women' and directly accused slave owners of the sexual exploitation of young female slaves in a passage that, in the mid-1830s, must have leapt off the page:

> There is no occasion to explain the management of the female slaves on estates where the object is to rear as many as possible, like stock, for the southern market: nor to point out the boundless licentiousness caused by the practise: a practise which rung from the wife of the planter, in the bitterness of her heart, the declaration that a planter's wife was only 'the chief slave of the hareem'... and that it was understood that the female slaves were to become mothers at fifteen.

Martineau goes on to explain how a law had been passed to stop mixed-race slaves being sold so that the planters could no longer 'sell their own offspring to fill their purses'. She overtly accuses white Southern American slave-holders of deliberately impregnating slave women for their own profitable purpose, and concludes, 'I met with no candid southerner who was not full of shame at the monstrous hypocrisy'.

The book was widely read and reviewed, including in America. The argu-

---

1. Adrian Desmond and James Moore, *Darwin* (Michael Joseph, 1991), p. 206.

ments had a patronising, high-minded tone, as if Martineau were scolding Americans. Understandably, they didn't respond well to this, and American reviews were bitter and personal. In the *Charleston Reporter*, the reviewer invited her back so that they could cut out her tongue. Another reviewer described her as an 'ugly, deaf, sour old crab-apple'. Some reviews stated her deafness as the root cause of her failings. Martineau's notoriety increased greatly in 1837 as a result of this outspoken book, one of the first to analyse a society and its social mores closely, critically and with a scientific eye, well before social science was an established field.

The young, impressionable Charles Darwin moved in next door to his brother in Great Marlborough Street in the spring of 1837. He lodged alone, perusing his naturalist notes, visiting the nearby Regent's Park Zoo, connecting with scientists and other naturalists, and using his brother's house for evening meals and joining in with the Erasmus/Harriet soirées. Adrian Desmond and James Moore, in their 1991 biography *Darwin*, made much of the febrile, free-thinking atmosphere which Darwin fell into at this time, and the fact that he read the works of the famous author in his midst:

> Charles was in and out of his brother's house this spring. He never strayed far from Eras… Eras's was a hive of intellectual activity. After five lonely years at sea Charles embraced his brother's ready-made circle of friends, revelling in the intimate dinners with Eras and Harriet Martineau. Here the buzz was radical and dissenting and 'heterodoxy was the norm.' He gained reassurance from this home circle.

The period between 1836 and 1840 has been underestimated as regards Darwin's intellectual breakthrough.[2] Martineau was the famous author in his small immediate circle. Moore and Desmond quote two letters in which Darwin describes having one-to-one talks with Martineau and enquiring about her writing routine:

> I called on Miss Martineau and sat there nearly an hour. She was very agreeable and managed to talk on a most wonderful number of subjects. She is overwhelmed with her own projects, her own thought and own abilities. Erasmus palliated all this by maintaining one ought not to look at her as a woman…

Later in 1838, Darwin wrote a small portrait of Martineau as a writer, in

---

2. He came up with the idea of Natural Selection in 1838 while at Great Marlborough Street.

which he reports an empathy with her around his own writing struggles and is gratified to find that she too finds the process exhausting:

> I had a very interesting conversation with Miss Martineau,—most perfectly authorial,—comparing our methods of writing.—it seems wonderful the rapidity with which she writes correctly.—I felt, however, no small gratification, to find, that she is not a complete Amazonian, & knows the feeling of exhaustion from thinking too much. I thought she was quite invincible; but she confesses, a few hours consecutively exhausts every grain of strength she possesses.

Now in her mid-thirties, Martineau was seven years older than Darwin, but she was experienced and confident as a radical challenging writer. It has always been a conundrum how Darwin went from being a gentleman naturalist, with a traditional upper-class public school and Cambridge upbringing, to becoming obsessed with the question that he knew would undermine the religious foundations beneath much of the tradition he was surrounded by.

Certainly, in their one-to-one talks, Martineau would have openly ridiculed religion. She already saw it as an absurd man-made construct, and several passages in *Society in America* shocked the religious reading public. Moore and Desmond give Harriet much credit for radicalising the young 'fermenting' Darwin: 'Radical Unitarians saw reform and evolution as going hand in hand. A self-developing nature held no terrors for them. Eras's group, with Martineau at its centre, gave Charles the licence to work out his own deterministic theories.'

To mark the 150th anniversary of the publication of *On the Origin of Species*, Desmond and Moore produced a follow-up to their original biography, entitled *Darwin's Sacred Cause*. In this later book they made the link with the Unitarian background shared by Darwin's family and social circle – the 'Sacred Cause' being the abolition of slavery – and they went further in placing Martineau at the centre of this development:

> He now not only had the only detailed castigatory travelogues of Southern slavery – Martineau's three volumes of Society in America, and three more of retrospective Western travel, all published within two years of Darwin's return – but their author mooching around the dinner table. He would read them all. But there was no rush while she was a fixture at Erasmus's brilliant parties next door and stood ready to compare 'our methods of writing'.

Martineau's two years of fact finding was intended to measure

American society against the nation's founding beliefs, but she was never a neutral observer. Even before returning home, she had come out for immediate and complete emancipation without compensation for slave owners. Any Darwin or Wedgwood woman visiting America might have had the same experience. They all shared the same radical Unitarian–Humanitarian heritage to which Harriet added the moral obligation to speak out.[3]

Darwin was being galvanised by a spirit of moral and scientific progress, and gaining the confidence to examine what he had seen on his travels and how his principles of nature applied to all of humankind. Martineau's conversation and writing were very much in his mind at this time, particularly her determination as regards the rights of black American slaves, as Moore and Desmond continue:

> For abusing Southern hospitality the slave-holders hated her. News-papers invited her back so they could cut out her tongue. In Charleston they called her a secret 'incendiary'. The prospect galvanized her: she wrote Society in America in the white-hot hope of mobilising a moral army to free the blacks. This was Darwin's frequent dining companion as he penned his own incendiary racial-evolution notes.

Darwin's eureka moment came on re-reading Malthus's original essay on population, and this was no accident. Malthus had been part of the Darwin–Wedgwood circle; Martineau had known him and had written of his theories. Darwin now saw the correlation between a population too big for the amount of food available, the death of those excess numbers unable to obtain food, and the survival of those with ready access to nourishment. This was not an active war in nature, not a battle. It was an intrinsic drop-off from the limit in available food.

Darwin extrapolated that those animals which continued to live would be able to reproduce, and their traits would be passed on. They would gradually become married to their environment and a system of life would settle through the twin arbiters of survival and reproduction. In 1838 he intensively noted all this down while also working on his first major text, *The Voyage of the Beagle*, which was to come out the following year.

It would, however, be another 20 years before natural selection was announced to the world. Much has been made of 'Darwin's delay' and Moore/Desmond both tie Martineau into this. Certainly, Darwin read and assiduously

---

3. Adrian Desmond and James Moore, *Darwin's Sacred Cause* (Allen Lane, 2009), p. 127.

recorded in a log book every work of Martineau's he read; she appears six times over the years – more than any other author and, indeed, the only woman author included.

In 1851 Harriet produced *Letters on the Law of Man's Nature* with Henry Atkinson. The book was ridiculed in the press for its overt atheism. Darwin's aunt, Fanny Allen, wrote to Fanny Wedgwood that these were 'two criminals' and many in Martineau's former circle were upset and distanced themselves from her. Darwin read this book and would have been well aware of the reaction in literary London to its perceived atheism. This would not have encouraged him, still stalling, to publish his own challenge to religion.

In 1840, Charles Darwin married his cousin Emma Wedgwood and moved to Gower Street. Martineau mentions in a letter that she and Erasmus had been out house-hunting for the newlyweds. Darwin has a note in his diary, in 1840, that he was visited at Gower Street by Martineau, and in a letter to Emma around this time, he writes 'he will get advice from Martineau on finding a suitable and reliable housekeeper'.

Erasmus remained a loyal friend to Harriet for the rest of their lives. When she was taken ill during a European tour and retreated to Tynemouth, in 1840, it was Erasmus who rallied round her friends to give her some income. A letter from Emma Darwin, written in Gower Street in May 1841 to her Aunt Sismondi, gives a good portrait of the relationship:

> I must tell you a nice thing of Erasmus as you used not to like him, but it is a profound secret so you must not tell anybody. The other day he wrote to Miss Martineau, thinking that owing to her long illness she might be in want of money, to ask if he could help her. He carried about his letter in his pocket for some days without having courage to send it; but he did at last and poor Miss M. was very much gratified by it, though she would not let him help her. She refused very nicely by openly entering on her affairs with him and telling him exactly what she had, to show him that she was not in want. She has nothing but what she has earned. I am afraid she has little chance of recovery, which I am very sorry for. Life was of great value to her, though she seems resigned to quit it. She told him she would let him know if she was in any distress.[4]

In July 1840, Martineau wrote to Jane Carlyle from Tynemouth: 'So Erasmus is

4. Emma Darwin, letter to Aunt Sismondi, May 1841, *Darwin Correspondence Project* <https://www.darwinproject.ac.uk/> [accessed 01/05/15]

really coming: and you probably and Mrs Wedgwood possibly. Hurrah! What a season is before me then!' At first she refused the money Erasmus offered, but by 1842 she needed extra space and he insisted on helping financially. Martineau then showed some of her eccentricity by insisting that the financial gift be partly paid 'in plate': a silver dining set rather than money. This seems to have irritated her London friends and Deborah Logan suggests: 'The coolness of some of her friends may relate to the silver plate episode, which some thought a bizarre extravagance for one in Martineau's precarious position (both in her health and in her capacity to earn a living)'.[5]

Although Erasmus had been romantically linked with Martineau, with speculation fanned by his own sisters, he was actually holding a flame for Harriet's close friend Fanny Wedgwood – something that had long been an open but unspoken secret in their circle. However, while he and Fanny retained a lifelong close relationship, she had spurned his advances by marrying the more reliable and industrious Hensleigh Wedgwood. Their friendship took an uncomfortable turn when Fanny and Hensleigh moved in with Erasmus for practical reasons, and Harriet wrote to Jane Carlyle in sympathy with Erasmus:

> I would point out how very uneasy he has been about Fanny Wedgwood since the beginning of January and how unwilling to go anywhere but to Gower Street. I wholly agree with you as to the prudence, or other morality, of making no enquiry and no effort, in such a case. When people who love each other and have to live together, – then I think every movement should be known, every little difficulty dispersed as the days pass but in the case of our dear friends who seem to cool gradually, I think the only way is to have a loving and trusting patience. But his growing cool when once warm is inconceivable to me.

Neither Darwin brother was impressed by the mesmerism that became a Martineau-inspired fad in the mid-1840s. Charles Darwin wrote to the publisher Charles Fox on the subject in December 1844:

> Shd your zeal still continue, I wd write to Miss Martineau & propose your visiting her (my Brother wishes to avoid all communication with her on this subject) — When in London, I saw a letter from her (not to my Brother), in which she says crowds of people are coming to her from all parts of England...

5. Deborah Logan, note to letter dated 25th August 1844, in *The Collected Letters of Harriet Martineau*, Vol. 2, ed. Deborah Logan (Pickering and Chatto, 2007), p. 264.

The Darwins' scepticism was probably representative of the scientific community; Martineau's advocacy of mesmeric cures seems to have affected her reputation in scientific circles.

Over the next twenty years, Eramus and Martineau remained in touch: he visiting her in Tynemouth and Ambleside; she attending the 1850 Great Exhibition at Crystal Palace, with him and a party of Wedgwoods. In 1858 Martineau wrote to *Edinburgh Review's* editor Henry Reeve from her Ambleside house: 'Mrs Wedgwood and Eras Darwin are benevolently coming next week; & that will be a great treat & every way a benefit, – they know so much & so wisely!'

This was perhaps also recognition that Fanny and Erasmus had remained close companions if not partners. Some have speculated that by this time Fanny was a closer companion to Erasmus than to her austere husband Hensleigh, and a trip to the Lake District to visit their old friend Harriet may have been the perfect excuse for them to be together.

In 1859 Erasmus sent Harriet a copy of *On the Origin of Species*. She was immediately rapturous:

> What I write is to thank you again for sending me your brother's book. As for thanking him for the book itself one might say 'thank you' all one's life without giving any idea of one's sense of obligation. I believed and have often described the quality and conduct of your brother's mind; but it is an unspeakable satisfaction to see here the full manifestation of its earnestness and simplicity, its sagacity, its industry, and the patient power by which it has collected such a mass of facts, to transmute them by such sagacious treatment into such portentous knowledge.

And she wrote to fellow secularist George Holyoake effusively:

> What a book it is! – overthrowing revealed religion on the one hand & Natural (as far as final causes and design are concerned) on the other. The range and mass of knowledge take away one's breath.

She had one complaint, however – that Darwin had left in the word 'created': 'the theory does not require the notion of a creator & my conviction is that Charles D does not hold it'.

In 1868 she wrote to Erasmus in sympathy with his brother having to deal with his critics:

I have always hoped and felt confident that the hostility of the ignorant and prejudiced did not trouble him... Really, what nonsense it
is to stop, scream and struggle, and have a faction – fight at every
mile on the road to knowledge!

In 1871 Charles published his follow up to the *Origin* by which time Harriet
was rarely writing and unable to get around. This did not, however, dim her
enthusiasm for reading his latest work. In March of that year, she wrote to her
niece Mary: 'And we get absorbed in Chas Darwin's new 'Descent of Man', in
the reading of which there is no stopping. 5000 sold in 3 weeks or so!'

Martineau had very different relationships with the Darwin brothers. With
Erasmus she shared great friendship and freethinking philosophical discussion.
They looked back fondly on their London days in the 1830s, riding out in his
cab and hosting dinners and parties with the like-minded. Though romantically
linked in this period, it is likely they valued each other as a buffer to romantic
speculation, a smoke screen of companionship, and they shared the knowledge
of his yearning for Fanny Wedgwood. He regularly sent Harriet champagne
and oysters once illness and age precluded their meeting up.

They both acted as mentor to Charles Darwin in his crucial, restless young
years between 1836 and 1840. They encouraged his radicalism and, in Martineau, Charles had an example of what could be achieved through the written word. It is also worth reflecting that Darwin's experience of, and attitude
towards, women changed in this period. He had gone from the laddish Cambridge atmosphere onto an all-male ship for five years, but now discovered
women who were independent and intellectual.

Certainly when Darwin wrote down his ideas in 1838 he knew their implication and many of his scientific and naturalist male friends, including his mentor Charles Lyell, baulked at the confrontation with religion. But Martineau
had no such qualms – if it was true it should be said. Her understanding of the
implications of natural selection 20 years later indicated that they were not far
apart in their radicalism. Martineau would never have claimed credit for helping to produce the revolutionary idea, partly because Darwin formulated it in
the privacy of his lodgings, but the encouragement he received in being radical,
and in pursuing his ideas, was crucial, and it is right that Martineau should be
recognised for her outspokenness in favour of science, against religion and for
the unity of all peoples, in that central London 1830s freethinking ferment.

Chapter 9: Thomas Carlyle

Being part of the Darwin-Wedgwood circle or, at least on the edge of it, Thomas Carlyle was, in the late 1830s, beginning to establish himself as a historical theorist, polemical writer and social commentator. As for Martineau, the late 1830s were something of a golden period: living in London and now in her mid-thirties, she had more confidence, knew more people and had the renown from her American trip as well as the relief she must have felt on returning.

On the surface, Carlyle and Martineau had a friendship that was tetchy and not always bound by respect, a picture partly gained from Carlyle's letters and journals. At times he dismisses her writing, calling her a bore and 'tediously talkative'.[1] In the 1840s it seemed to both Carlyle and his wife Jane that Martineau had gone a bit mad. But in truth, Carlyle could be very cutting in private about most of his friends and acquaintances – his was a mind often beset by melancholy – and these negative remarks overlook other passages that show friendship and respect. Moreover, Martineau regularly visited Carlyle's house in Chelsea between 1837 and 1839, and the lively conversation that ensued spurred them both on. Indeed, they shared several key characteristics in their personality and work.

Carlyle and his wife moved to London in similar circumstances and at a similar time to Martineau. They had previously flirted with the capital, but Carlyle was still loyal to his native west coast of Scotland. However, they eventually settled into a house on Cheyne Walk, Chelsea. Like Martineau, Carlyle was an outsider with little tolerance for flighty airs or graces or aristocratic superiority. They both valued hard work, steadfastness and, above all, honesty – a quality which they would pursue relentlessly in their writing. Carlyle came from a stricter religious background, one he would never fully shake off, but, like Harriet, he valued the liberal attitudes and freethinking found in London.

Carlyle was, from a modern perspective, a depressive – something that Martineau somehow understood and embraced. He had a difficult relationship with his wife and it seemed to observers that the marriage became loveless, sexless and difficult for both of them. Several times, particularly once he was famous, it looked as though he was on the verge of leaving her. He never did, however. He needed Jane: she understood his difficult personality, and when she died he was inconsolable and lived unhappily ever after.

But, like the Darwin-Wedgwoods, Carlyle and his wife would look back

---

1. Thomas Carlyle, quoted in Fred Kaplan, *Thomas Carlyle: A Biography* (Cambridge, 1983), p. 269.

on the late 1830s in London as a happy time. Carlyle wrote to his mother in November 1836 that Martineau was 'very intelligent looking, full of talk tho unhappily deaf almost as a post, so that you have to speak to her through an ear-trumpet'.[2]

A few months later he wrote to Ralph Waldo Emerson after reading *Society in America*:

> I have read it for the good authoress's sake, whom I love much. A genuine little Poetess, buckramed, swathed like a mummy into Socinian and Political-Economy formulas; and yet verily alive in the midst of that!... I admire this lady's integrity, sincerity; her quick, sharp discernment to the depth it goes; her love also is great; nay, in fact, it is too great; the host of illustrious obscure mortals whom she produces on you, of Preachers, Pamphleteers, Antislavers, Able Editors, and other Atlases bearing (unknown to us) the world on their shoulder, is absolutely more than enough.

In her autobiography Martineau reminisced about this period:

> No kind of evening was more delightful to me than those spent with the Carlyles. About once a fortnight a mutual friend of theirs and mine [very likely Erasmus Alvey Darwin] drove me over to Chelsea, to the early tea table at number five, Cheyne Walk, the house which Carlyle was perpetually complaining of and threatening to leave, but where he is still to be found.

She describes an evening there with Giuseppe Mazzini, the man who would go on to lead Italian independence, 'before he entered openly on the career of insurrection by which he has since become the most notorious man in Europe', as well as one spent with Leigh Hunt, the poet and critic, who had become a neighbour of the Carlyles on Cheyne Walk and who had been a friend to Keats and Shelley. She describes Carlyle at this time as having 'a rugged face, steeped in genius', but he sometimes looked 'as if he was on a rack' and was 'as variable as possible in mood', all of which she seemed to embrace.

A letter from Carlyle to his sister in Scotland in March 1838 gives us great insight into Martineau's life during that year:

> On the way home, I went to a soirée of Miss Martineau's. There

---

2. Thomas Carlyle Carlyle, letter to his mother dated 20th November 1836, quoted in *Carlyle and his Contemporaries*, ed. John Clubbe (Duke University Press, 1976). p. 78.

were fat people and fair people, lords and others, fidgeting, elbow-
ing, all very braw and hot. 'What's ta use on't?' I said to myself, and
came off early, while they were still arriving at eleven at night. I go
as rarely as I can to such things for they always do me ill. A book at
home is suitabler with a quiet pipe in the evening, innocent spoonful
of porridge at ten, and bed at eleven.[3]

Martineau's soirées from this time are sometimes presented as sedate, intellectual
affairs, but the picture above suggests that they were lively occasions attended
by a diverse crowd, 'braw and hot' in Carlyle's Scottish brogue and carrying on
well into the night.

Carlyle was a step apart, ready to brood at home, but Martineau would seek
him out. Indeed, she was encouraging and helpful with his first seminal book
Sartor Resartus, a portrayal of a man struggling to keep his spirituality in the
modern scientific world. Martineau recommended it to her American friends
and even sold copies of it for him so as to show up his publisher. Simon Heffer
describes Martineau's forwardness in his biography of Carlyle:

> Miss Martineau embarrassed Carlyle by bringing him the profits
> from these sales and pressing the money into his hand. He overcame
> his embarrassment by buying both Harriet and Jane signet rings with
> the proceeds, his wife's marked 'Point de faiblesse', his friend's 'Frisch
> zu!'. When Harriet realised more money from her imports, she gave
> Carlyle bottles of his favourite French brandy rather than the cash.[4]

Quite what Carlyle meant by the ring for Martineau marked '*Frisch Zu!*' is open
to interpretation. The German '*frisch*' means 'fresh' in English and so a generous interpretation is that Martineau had brought fresh life and thinking into his
world. A more cynical interpretation might be that he was suggesting that she
was going too far in bringing him cash for his books.

Martineau and Carlyle shared an intellectual progressiveness and impa-
tience, as well as an interest in spiritual matters. The genial freethinker Erasmus
Darwin was a mutual friend and a good listener to both. This resulted in a
three-way trick played on the Carlyles' cleaner as reported by Thea Holme in
The Carlyles at Home:

> Helen Mitchell, the Carlyles' maid, was a constant source of comedy

3. Thomas Carlyle, letter to his mother dated March 1838, quoted in J.A. Froude, *Thomas Carlyle: A History of His Life in London*
(Longmans, 1885), p. 132.
4. Simon Heffer, *Moral Desperado: A Life of Thomas Carlyle* (Weidenfeld and Nicolson, 1995), p. 174–5.

in the household. Witty. The Carlyles adopted many of her phrasings for their own amusement. She was a great reader 'when she could snatch a bit of time'; and evidently borrowed from her employer's library. Her pithy comments on Harriet Martineau's Maid of All Work were repeated by Jane [Carlyle] for the entertainment of Erasmus Darwin, who passed on the criticism to the authoress. Miss Martineau must have referred to it the next time Helen opened the door to her: Helen was overcome with confusion. 'It was a rail insipid trick in Darwin to tell Miss Martno,' she declared.[5]

However, the onset of Martineau's illness and her removal to Tynemouth, was to put some pressure on the friendship with the Carlyles. The extent of how friendly they had become is suggested by a letter from Harriet to Jane Carlyle, requesting, jokingly, that they could move in with her at Tynemouth: 'We can knock through the wall – we can nod out of the window – you can run in the back door without your bonnet and I shall invite myself to tea with you. My neighbours hear us laugh now sometimes... thou much more when you come!'

This betrays the fact that they had some fun evenings in Cheyne Walk as well as some serious conversation. The Carlyles visited the invalid in Tynemouth at least twice in her first year in the 'sickroom'. Thomas wrote to their mutual friend, the poet Monckton Milnes:

> As for poor Harriet... I found her confined to a sofa, dangerously ill I believe though brisk, alert, invincible as ever. There is a kind of prepared completeness in Harriet, which does honour to nature and the Socinian formula. In my travels I have met with few more valiant women.

At this time the friendship started to drift. The Carlyles were part of the group rounded up by Erasmus to provide Martineau with a fund, which she eccentrically insisted should come as a set of silver dining plate. They were surprised she rejected a state pension and nonplussed to receive a request to destroy their correspondence. Carlyle was no fan of Mesmerism and also ridiculed her writing about being ill. Martineau's actions in this period left her old London circle thinking she was losing her marbles, and the Carlyles distanced themselves from her.

There was also an interesting divergence in their work in the 1840s. Carlyle was progressive but conservative and began to use his history writings to

---

5. Thea Holme, *The Carlyles at Home* (Persephone Books, 2002), p. 27.

suggest that some people were superior to others. He didn't see any need for greater democracy and was dismissive of women's rights. In his book *Chartism* he was sympathetic to the demands of workers but essentially believed the English nobility had a right to lead and the rest should be grateful for good governance; not that they should be given greater opportunity to govern or have a say in national affairs.

Martineau, meanwhile, continued to write from her sickroom. She produced a fictionalised biography of the slave rebellion leader Toussaint L'Ouverture, showing the potential of ex-slaves if they were given their freedom. This respect for other races ran counter to the racial superiority Carlyle was now peddling. Indeed, the widespread acceptance of Carlyle's racism shows that Martineau's writing, in choosing to champion L'Ouverture, had not lost its radical edge.

After recovering her health, Martineau visited London in the early 1850s and managed a visit to Cheyne Walk to see the Carlyles, but she would have found a much frostier atmosphere between the couple and a further divergence from her own intellectual output, with Carlyle dispensing a Christian 'great man' view of history and Martineau entering her phase of championing science and rejecting religion. Carlyle was not a great advocate of science and liked to sound warnings about technology going too far.

In her autobiography Martineau produces one of her most astute assessments of Carlyle's character. Several of his biographers have claimed that she captured the conflicted, moody nature of the historian well:

I have seen Carlyle's face under all aspects, from the deepest gloom to the most reckless or most genial mirth; and it seemed to me that each mood would make a totally different portrait. The sympathetic is by far the finest, in my eyes. His express of sympathy has been, I believe, the master-pain of his life. He does not know what to do with it, and with its bitterness, seeing that human life is full of pain to those who look out for it: and the savageness which has come to be a main characteristic of this singular man is, in my opinion, a mere expression of his intolerable sympathy with the suffering. He cannot express his love and pity in natural acts, like other people; and it shows itself too often in unnatural speech. But to those who understand his eyes, his shy manner, his changing colour, his sigh, and the constitutional pudeur which renders him silent about everything that he feels the most deeply, his wild speech and abrupt manner are perfectly intelligible.

Part III: The 1840s

In the 1840s the world was moving on apace, driven by industry, technology and commerce. It was something of a tragedy for Harriet Martineau that she spent the first half of this relentless, industrial decade as an invalid in Tynemouth, recovering from a serious illness.

This was the decade of 'railway mania' in Britain and America: in 1846 alone 272 acts of the British Parliament were passed allowing new lines to be built. In America the Monroe Doctrine was enacted which allowed expansion into the West. Freed slaves such as Frederick Douglass were given a voice but the slave system remained for the time being. The transcendentalism of Emerson became popular in this decade, another direct personal connection that Martineau could have made had she not been ill, having stayed in his New England house for several months in 1836.

In the middle years of this decade Martineau was associated with the phenomenon which became known as 'mesmerism'. Named after the German Anton Mesmer, this theory postulated that everything was magnetically connected and that controlling the magnetic field around and within people would have health benefits. The effect of the practice was similar to hypnotism and it became something of a sensation. Martineau was introduced to it, learnt its techniques and became a convert as her health improved. She published an article on the subject in the *Athenaeum* and people travelled to Tynemouth to observe her mesmeric methods. She fell out with her brother-in-law, doctor Thomas Greenhow, who had been caring for her, and he wrote an account saying that she had recovered, as he had predicted, from his conventional approach.

Mesmerism had an effect on Martineau's reputation in scientific circles and previous friends distanced themselves. Martineau would send scientific articles to people showing evidence of magnetism, but linking mesmerism to rapid cures tainted it as a fad. The whole mesmerism period anticipates modern-day debates around 'alternative' homeopathic medicine and methods such as acupuncture.

After her recovery Martineau moved to Ambleside in the Lake District where she designed and had built her own house, The Knoll. In 1848 she spent eight months touring the Middle East and was moving into a more radical and outspoken phase. Yet it is difficult to avoid the sense that the world moved on without Martineau in the 1840s, as she got sidetracked by illness. However, her recovery would culminate in a trip to the Great Exhibition held in the Crystal

Palace in Hyde Park, showcasing to the world the extent of Britain's industrial and technological progress.

Chapter 10: Toussaint L'Ouverture

Martineau's first few months in Tynemouth were a period of illness and exhaustion during which her pen was unusually dimmed. She was attended by Thomas Greenhow, the doctor husband of her older sister Elizabeth, based in Newcastle, who she lauded for his calming presence and reassurance. The room she was ensconced in can be seen today as part of the 'Harriet Martineau Bed & Breakfast' in Tynemouth, and from there she had a great view of the coast and the sky, which led to her arranging with her friend Elisabeth Reid to acquire a telescope to keep a closer eye on the natural, and no doubt human, scenes.

Having recovered the motivation and energy to start writing again, though not well enough to leave her sickroom, she embarked on an historical novel about Toussaint L'Ouverture. Entitled *The Hour and the Man*, this work can seem a bit random – another change of direction from the eccentric, wayward author, particularly as it is often grouped with the other books she produced in Tynemouth. She followed *The Hour and the Man* with four children's books, which became known as *The Playfellow* series, then *Life in the Sick-Room*, a book about her time spent holed up battling her illness. Together with her later well-known enthusiasm for mesmeric cures, written up and published in journals, this Tynemouth period has often been characterised as eccentric and inconsistent, partly as a result of the response of the London literary circle.

In fact, her biography of L'Ouverture makes perfect sense when we delve into the context. François-Dominique Toussaint L'Ouverture was the 'Black Spartacus', the leader of a successful slave rebellion in Haiti in 1791–4. Admired for his leadership and progressive principles, he tried to create a democratic, inclusive society of freed slaves in Haiti, until Napoleon had him imprisoned in 1802. He died soon afterwards, but France was not able to retake Haiti, and the society L'Ouverture created continued into the 19th century. For Martineau he was a prime candidate for heroism, not only in her crusade against slavery in America but also in her espousal of economic fairness, freedom and citizen participation.

She would have known of the poetic tribute 'To Toussaint L'Ouverture' by her childhood hero William Wordsworth, written in 1802 (the year of Martineau's birth) in the months between L'Ouverture's imprisonment and death, in his elegy:

Though fallen thyself, never to rise again,
Live, and take comfort. Thou hast left behind
Powers that will work for thee; air, earth, and skies;
There's not a breathing of the common wind
That will forget thee; thou hast great allies;
Thy friends are exultations, agonies,
And love, and man's unconquerable mind.[1]

Martineau would have been reminded of the legend of Toussaint while in America, where she observed first-hand the ongoing slave system of the Southern states. She herself had written in her 1832 tale *Demerara* of a state of freed slaves that succeeds in Liberia, and of her moral repugnance at the institution of slavery.

In 1838, while enduring vociferous criticism of *Society in America*, she wrote a short biographical piece on L'Ouverture for the *Penny Magazine*. This was during her healthy and productive phase and, from correspondence at the time, it is clear who her target was. She wrote to Fanny Wedgwood:

Do you care about Toussaint L'Ouverture? I have been doing a life of him for the Penny Magazine. My chief object is to get at the Southern States, where they reprint the P.M. fearlessly, and will never dream of meeting me. I hope a few hundred people there will learn what a negro has been, and what other negroes therefore may be... he (L'Ouverture) has given me three happy days, if he does no further good.

During 1837–8, Martineau kept a diary, excerpts of which were published alongside her autobiography in the *Testimonials* of 1877. She mentions this article in her diary entry for 11 April 1838: 'Finished Toussaint with a great relish. How I have enjoyed doing this, and how infinitely do these emotions transcend all pleasures of sense and all gratifications of vanity!'

Her life in London at this time is revealed by her diary entries between February and April 1838, which accentuate the picture of her as at the hub of a dissenting, fermenting circle:

February 6th – Note from Carlyle, most hearty, about my book...
Mr Wedgwood called... Met C. Darwin, Mr F. Edgeworth and Mr

1. William Wordsworth, 'To Toussaint L'Ouverture', in *The Collected Poems of William Wordsworth*, ed. Antonia Till (Wordsworth Editions, 1994), p. 363.

Hamilton, brother in law of the Duke of Wellington, who had been reading my book.

April 11th – Erasmus Darwin and Browning called... Dressed for the Bullers and walked there through the park. Roebuck was there, long talk with him; the Gaskells, Carlyle, and Lady Baring came to see me... I told Buller I could sympathise with Voltaire, Fenelon & co seeing that the truth is that all of us are right and all are wrong. Does it follow that there is no truth? Surely not.

The change from this life, after she was taken ill in Venice and retreated to her Tynemouth sickroom, was drastic. Some have suggested that it was the pressure on her caused by writing and socialising that made her ill. Certainly her writing was incessant in the years 1836–9, and this Toussaint article is an example of work which is often overshadowed by the American writings and the radical blast of *The Martyr Age of the United States* and later the popularity of the novel *Deerbrook*.

She embarked on *The Hour and the Man* in the middle months of 1840 and described it as 'An Historical Romance', constrained by her sickroom from doing any further research. Instead she built a novel around the basic story of the rebellion leader, partly remembering how much she had enjoyed the previous experience of writing about him. She wrote to Fanny Wedgwood saying: 'I have it fully in my head and heart; and I fancy I may do it gently and easily in my seaside lodging.'

The result is a long novel and one of Martineau's less readable works. It is most memorable for her radical idea of championing a black slave rebellion leader as a great man and example, and of hailing the potential society that could be created by slaves when freed. Her portrayal of L'Ouverture was idealistic and the racial elements of the book were overt:

Toussaint was requested to name a day when he would take the oaths publicly, and receive the homage of the grateful colony; and in his reply he took occasion to declare with earnestness that his present course of action originated altogether in the decree of the Convention in favour of the negroes; and that the resources of his power and influence should all be directed towards raising his race to that intellectual and moral equality with the whites, without which they could neither enjoy nor retain the political equality which the Convention had decreed.

Her description of it as 'An Historical Romance' implies that she knew it was an embroidered version of his life story. Even admirers of the book suggested that it seemed improbable, as Lord Jeffrey wrote at the time:

> I have read Harriet's first volume, and give my adhesion to her black prince with all my heart and soul. The book is really not only beautiful and touching, but noble; and I do not recollect when I have been more charmed, whether by very sweet and eloquent writing and glowing description, or by elevated as well as tender sentiments... Toussaint himself, I suppose, really was an extraordinary person; though I cannot believe that he actually was such a combination of Scipio and Cato and Fenelon and Washington as she seems to have made him out... the book however, is calculated to make its readers better, and does great honour to the heart as well as the talent of the author. I would go a long way to kiss the hem of her garment or the hand that delineated this glowing and lofty representation of purity and noble virtue.[2]

Maria Weston Chapman summarised the impact of the book in America:

> The title of the book was chosen as the one best calculated to conceal the hero's colour, as this complexional prejudice was running high in the United States, and she hoped the work might tell in favour of her cause there. It was republished there immediately and has since been republished at different intervals and in different forms; and our most admired and impressive orator, Wendell Phillips, seizing the subject for lecturing tours on behalf of the cause, bore it the whole land, deep into the prejudiced hearts of the people.

It had other admirers at the time, including Florence Nightingale and Crabb Robinson. R. K. Webb, in his Martineau biography, says that criticism of it on the grounds of probability or style is beside the point: 'Artistic success to Martineau was secondary to moral considerations, and the moral considerations of this book had considerable impact at the time.'

For her part, in her autobiography, Martineau would distance herself from the book artistically, and although she fondly remembered engaging with Toussaint, the writing of the book itself was a struggle while battling her illness:

---

2. Lord Jeffrey, quoted in Harriet Martineau, *Autobiography* (Elibron Classics, 2005), p. 353.

Jane Carlyle died in 1870 and Thomas Carlyle was never quite the same. He outlived his old sparring partner, Martineau, by six years, dying in 1881 and on her death he wrote:

> She had a sharp eye, an imperturbable self-possession, and in all things a swiftness of positive decision, which, joined to her evident loyalty of intention, and her frank, guileless, easy ways, we both liked. Her very considerable talent would have made her a quite shining Matron of some big Female Establishment.

He had, though, become very suspicious of her religious scepticism and this had been a growing divide in the second half of their lives so that he finished this tribute with a diminishing remark: '[her talent] was totally inadequate to grapple with deep spiritual and social questions'.

Thomas Carlyle had a great influence on the Victorian narrative with his ideas of racial superiority and the importance of 'Great Men' through history – ideas that were lapped up by empire builders and Social Darwinists in the 1880s and '90s. Today these ideas are discredited, but he remains a much better remembered figure than Martineau and his house in Chelsea is a National Trust museum. Martineau's advocacy of racial equality, human rights, democracy and free-market economics have all come to fruition to some extent in many parts of the world and yet, in comparison to Carlyle, she barely gets a mention. On a personal level, he disparaged her and distanced himself from her, while she showed him respect and infinite patience, drawing a veil over some of his more unpalatable views. I know who I believe should be better remembered.

My affections sprang back to the character and fortunes of Toussaint L'Ouverture. I speedily made up my mind to present that genuine hero with his actual sayings and doings to the world. When I had been some time at Tynemouth, finding my strength and spirits declining, I gave up the practise of keeping a diary... I find in the sickly handwriting in that spring of 1840, notices of how my subject opened before me and of how, as I lay gazing upon the moonlit sea, in the evenings of April and May, new traits in the man, new links between the personages, and a clearer perception of the guiding principle of the work disclosed themselves to me... my notice is that I was sadly tired with the effort, but more struck than ever with the springing up of ideas in the act of writing... This work was a resource, and some anxiety to me, all summer.

This is followed by a passage in the autobiography that says much about the character of Harriet Martineau. She describes her emotions on receiving the news that *The Hour and the Man* was neither received nor selling as well as it could have been, and quotes a journal entry from the time:

> ... as I sat at work, my spirits rose, the more I thought it over. It always is the way with me, and has been since I grew up, that personal mortifications put me in a happy state of mind... It is always so with hostile reviewers;- the more brutal, the more animating, in a very little while'... The lighting upon this entry reminds me of some marked days in my literary life made happy by this tendency in me.

It is significant that Thomas Carlyle read and had a strong reaction to *The Hour and the Man*. He wrote to Lydia Emerson that it seemed to have been written with a 'child's heart' and from 'so shrewd a head as that!'[3] He ridiculed the presentation of L'Ouverture as a mixture of 'Washington, Christ and Macready', and it would be in the following years that Carlyle would write his notorious exposition of white racial superiority, partly in a direct slap down of what he regarded as Martineau's naivety.

Carlyle was part of the circle that, by the end of 1842, thought that Martineau was somewhat losing her sanity, and this book may have added to that feeling. She had rejected a government pension, requested that her friends destroy their letters and begun her dalliance with mesmerism. In fact, all of these

---

3. Thomas Carlyle, letter to Lydia Emerson 21st February 1841, in *The Carlyle Letters Online* (http://carlyleletters.dukeu-press.edu/) [accessed 14/02/17]

things are consistent with Martineau's guiding principles, although they perhaps took on an eccentric edge given her isolation in the North-East. She didn't want to rely on taxpayers' money; she wanted her own financial footing. As a public author she was sensitive about letters because she wanted to be honest in them and so was wary of their publication – she was not alone in this. Her writing in this period continued to be honest, radical, inquisitive, analytical and without fear.

Her follow-up book *Life in the Sick-Room* was a reflection on illness and the human condition and the need to survive psychologically, and was seen by some as self-indulgent and part of her hypochondria. However, she was genuinely ill, as was discovered on her death when a large cyst was identified. Bed-bound periods of recovery were not uncommon in Victorian Britain, and Martineau's recuperation of several years was mirrored by Elizabeth Barrett Browning's in London.

Both *The Hour and the Man* and *Life in the Sick-Room* have been a boon to sociologists: the former for its white middle-class idealisation of black races and universalism within an assumption of British imperial superiority; the latter as an early analytical account of illness and the socio-cultural implications of human frailty and how it is presented and perceived. Both books stand out as being different in the early 1840s, if nothing else.

A modern sociological analysis of *The Hour and the Man* by Lauren Goodlad appears in *Harriet Martineau: Authorship, Society and Empire.* It is a good example of how social science has developed since pioneers such as Martineau began to provide structural criticism of society with a clear moral background. Modern analysis has moved from trying to influence real causes to creating retrospective censure, enveloped in convoluted language:

> Evoking a Toussaint who both is, and is more than, a Europeanized subject, Martineau's narrative of Haitian rebellion engages the conundrums of a temporalized post-Enlightenment liberalism. As the black Spartacus, Toussaint figures self-discipline as the successor to liberatory insurrection, creating an imaginative space for the white middle class feminist to negotiate her desire for the collective politics she has renounced. Moreover as tropicopolitan, Toussaint is the persistent placeholder in Martineau's thought for a cultural otherness she struggled to recognise through the competing liberal terms of abolitionist universalism and cultural pluralism... in both ways, 'The Hour and the Man' provides a glimpse outside the trajectory

that saw British feminism serving imperialisms increasingly racial-ized geopolitical ends.[4]

She concludes with a critical tone:

> As the exponent of this imperial romance of improvement, Mar-tineau ceases in any fashion either to heed her own ethnographic principles, or admire the self determination of tropical subjects. If she steers mainly clear of the racism that pervaded later feminisms, there is no more hint of a South Asian Spartacus to inspire her than of respect for cultural difference in her anti-Russian diatribes. Her pre-scient clash with the 'Clash of Civilisations' is an object lesson for today.

Goodlad is critical of Martineau for favouring black American slaves over Indian colonial subjects or slavery elsewhere in Asia in the 19th century. This retro-spective criticism seems very harsh to me given that Martineau was going out on a radical limb to make a distinct point to the cultural and literary society in which she existed at the time. That society was about to enter a long and intense period of ideological racial superiority writ large in imperial ambitions. Mar-tineau's is a lone voice of non-racial superiority, advocating the potential of all peoples, like a stubborn reed in a sandstorm. And this was still 20 years before Darwin's ideas of evolution would suggest that humankind was a single species, closely tied with all animals, key aspects of which would then be misused to provide a basis for Social Darwinism, with devastating effects on the world.

The Hour and the Man had genuine results, and for Martineau was part of a real campaign, not 'an imaginary space', to get the system of slavery over-thrown. It was read widely in America, by, among others, the abolitionist John Brown who adopted the tactics he'd read about in the book and whose mar-tyrdom did much to trigger the American Civil War. Years later Brown's fate would be reported by Martineau in the *Daily News*.

In its blatant confrontation with racial prejudice, *The Hour and the Man* preceded, by 120 years, Harper Lee's *To Kill a Mockingbird*, often celebrated as one of the first novels to tackle systemised racism with its idealised (white) hero Atticus Finch. Martineau's portrait of the potential of black slaves, and the black man as an effective leader, was truly groundbreaking.

---

4. Lauren M. E. Goodland, 'Imperial Woman: Harriet Martineau, Geopolitics and the Romance of Improvement', in *Harriet Martineau: Authorship, Society and Empire*, ed. Ella Dzelzainis and Cora Kaplan (Manchester University Press, 2010), p. 203.

Chapter 11: Elizabeth Barrett Browning

Harriet Martineau and Elizabeth Barrett Browning were well aware of each other before they entered into a three-year period of intense correspondence. Barrett Browning was five years younger and had read and admired Martineau in her twenties, particularly *Deerbrook* and *Society in America*. She came from a family whose fortune was built on slavery and had close ties to farm holdings in Jamaica. Rejecting her family background in the 1830s, she started to write, and developed a growing reputation as a poet. The ending of the slave trade badly affected her father's business, and this – mirroring Martineau's own experience – served to provide encouragement for her writing and for making her own way.

The Barrett family were forced to sell their country house and move to Wimpole Street, London in 1838. Harriet knew of Elizabeth's poetry by the late 1830s, and when she moved to London they had many mutual acquaintances in the literary scene. But they never met, partly because Barrett rarely went out. By now her life had taken on a tragic dimension: she had a physical affliction affecting her spine which made her increasingly immobile. She was also dealing with the tragic death of her favourite younger brother on a sailing trip to visit her on the south coast, where she was recuperating – a visit of which her father had disapproved. The incident had worsened the situation at home, where she lived with her domineering father, her mother having died ten years previously. In Wimpole Street, Elizabeth Barrett retreated to her room, to her poems and to her correspondence.

By 1843 Martineau had been in her own 'sickroom' for two and a half years, and she wrote to the poet in admiration and to share their experience of solitude and being an invalid. Barrett, who had expressed her admiration of Martineau to others, was delighted. Martineau wrote in praise of the poem 'Pan Departed':

> The stanzas of that poem have run in my head and raised my thought, ever since the first reading... These few words may perhaps not come amiss from one who has for friends some who are yours – who has, like you, lost health and become inured to the want of it.

Barrett was gratified and was soon sending new poems for Martineau to comment on. She had a picture of Harriet in her room alongside those of Wordsworth and Tennyson, 'because she was a woman and she was admirable'.[1]

A few months after the correspondence started, Martineau wrote to the poet and politician Edward Bulwer Lytton:

> What a wonderful woman she is! – her genial and glowing morale so self sustained, regulated and cheerily sympathetic under the inspiration of her genius and learning and the very hard pressure of her suffering life. She is better, however, and there seems some distant hope of her rising to a condition of something like ease and strength.

Barrett continued to describe Martineau in glowing terms. She valued her writing advice, and in September 1844 wrote to her teacher Hugh Stuart Boyd:

> ... And oh, such a letter I have had from Harriet Martineau! She had bound herself by a promise to tell me the full truth about the books, – let it be pleasant or unpleasant truth – and because her letter was long in coming, I began to fear that it would be unpleasant. But there was never a more delightful generous letter, or one fuller of fervent sympathy. She tells me that every day she has had the volumes open before her, and that their power over her is of the deepest. What particularly pleases me, is, that her predominant impression, she says, is of their entire 'originality'. Also she observes upon what she calls the 'immense advance' on the former work... I was very much delighted by this letter from such a person, who unites to high logic, a deep sensibility to poetry – certainly the most manlike woman (in the best sense of man) in the three Kingdoms.

A month later she wrote again to Boyd:

> ... With regards to Miss Martineau, as Arabel has been telling me what you say, I must say something again. As far as she is a political economist, I can judge no more of her ability than I can judge Mrs Somerville's in mathematics. But as an eloquent writer and lucid thinker, – as possessing singular powers of description and pathos, – and as the possessor of an original and originating mind endowed with high logic and imaginative sensibility, I consider her very superior to Mrs Somerville.

1. Gardner B. Taplin, *The Life of Elizabeth Barrett Browning* (Yale University Press, 1957), p. 88.

Martineau was a little embarrassed to be giving advice on poetry to a full-time poet of great promise, though that didn't stop her, and she advised Elizabeth to be 'simple, direct and modern' and avoid over-elaboration. On receiving the updated edition of *Poems* from Barrett, Martineau was full of praise: 'I was swept through it... I find ideas which are grand, moving and beautiful beyond my power of acknowledgement.'

When Martineau's record of being an invalid, *Life in the Sick-Room*, was published anonymously towards the end of 1844, it was erroneously attributed – to her amusement – as a work by Elizabeth Barrett. Both women took the mistake as a compliment. By this time Martineau had also recommended Barrett to Maria Weston Chapman in the United States and some of her poems appeared in *The Liberty Bell*, helping to raise funds for the abolitionist cause, but also helping Barrett's profile as a poet in the New World.

In 1845 both invalids started to find more energy. Martineau was convinced that her course of mesmerism had cured her and she shared this with Barrett: 'My affectionate maid has mesmerised me twice a day. My sickness and distress left me: appetite returned – then sleep – then nerve and spirit. I kept silence lest any possible relapse might tell against the Mesmerism. It is so. There is a change.'

Barrett, however, was not so sure and, while interested in the mesmerism fad, wrote in her journal: 'There is something horrible and cold to me in the whole matter and mystery, like the undressing of the soul from its familiar conventions and the plunging of it, shiveringly, into a new element.'[2]

In April 1845, Martineau wrote to Barrett about her writing plans now that she was on the mend: 'This year, my longings are all for fresh air, beauty and idleness, a yearning which I do not fear to indulge because I know the need to work will recur quite soon enough.'

For her part, Barrett also wrote in a fit of newly found optimism: 'There is no saying what foolish thing I might do.' Her life, by now, was moving apace. The 1844 publication of *Poems*, which Martineau so admired, had been a big hit, giving Barrett her own steady income and the confidence to move away from her father.

In the spring of 1846 Martineau, now in the Lake District and possibly showing off a new friend to Barrett, wrote: 'Surely almost everything may be hoped for you now – perhaps even that you may one day sit on my terrace with old Wordsworth stretchered by your side, playing with a flower and discoursing of things great and trivial.'

2. Dorothy Mermin, *Elizabeth Barrett Browning: The Origins of a New Poetry* (University of Chicago Press, 1989), p. 155.

But Barrett had other plans. She had fallen in love with the poet Robert Browning who had been wooing her (and with whom Martineau had had mixed experiences as acquaintances in the 1830s London literary circle) and that summer they eloped and got married in Paris, soon moving onto Florence. She also penned her most famous poems, *Sonnets from the Portuguese*, including the immortal 'Sonnet 43':

> How do I love thee? Let me count the ways.
> I love thee to the depth and breadth and height
> My soul can reach, when feeling out of sight
> For the ends of being and ideal grace.
> I love thee to the level of every day's
> Most quiet need, by sun and candle-light.
> I love thee freely, as men strive for right.
> I love thee purely, as they turn from praise.
> I love thee with the passion put to use
> In my old griefs, and with my childhood's faith.
> I love thee with a love I seemed to lose
> With my lost saints. I love thee with the breath,
> Smiles, tears, of all my life; and, if God choose,
> I shall but love thee better after death.[3]

In this poem and others the sense of freedom and relief from Barrett's 'old griefs' is palpable. And it feels inevitable that her marriage to Browning would mean an end to the Barrett–Martineau mutual-admiration society: Browning was not a Martineau fan, and Harriet and Elizabeth had now both been set free from the invalidism that they once had in common. Modern commentators Deborah Logan and Valerie Sanders have each suggested that Martineau was instrumental in giving Barrett the confidence to emerge from her father's shadow, as well as aiding a flowering of her poetry.

Sanders also suggests, however, a great divide between the two women. Her summary of Martineau's life was entitled *Reason Over Passion* and it is not difficult to see that Barrett had chosen passion, throwing herself wholeheartedly into her relationship with Browning. As would later occur with George Eliot and Charlotte Brontë, Martineau did not understand women who gave up their own independence for romantic love. For her part, Barrett Browning did not become an advocate of women's rights as others did in the 1850s, and in her

---

3. Elizabeth Barrett Browning, 'Sonnet 43', *Sonnets from the Portuguese* from *The Collected Poems of Elizabeth Barrett Browning*, ed. Sally Minogue (Wordsworth Editions, 2015), p. 300.

devotion to Robert Browning on the Continent, she became separated from the groundbreaking literary scene of Martineau, the Brontës, Gaskell and Eliot.

In her autobiography, written in 1855, Martineau is still full of admiration, referring to Barrett Browning as a 'true genius' and paying tribute to her husband: 'A real genius was Robert Browning, assuredly; and how good a man, how wise and morally strong, is proved by the successful issue of the perilous experiment of the marriage of two poets.' However, she would later be critical of Barrett Browning for not being in touch with reality and overly living in her own imagination. In her autobiography, she goes on to hint at a criticism that was bubbling underneath:

> Her poems were to me, in my sick room, marvellously beautiful; now that my life has been transferred to the free open air of real, practical existence, I still think her poetry wonderfully beautiful in its way, while wishing that she was more familiar with the external realities which are needed to balance her ideal conceptions. They are a remarkable pair, whom society may well honour and cherish.

She was less guarded in a letter to a Reverend in August 1856, by now having to defend her own highly materialist output:

> About the Brownings... I am persuaded that she has not the remotest conception of what it is to know anything and therefore to believe any thing... As for her husband, I knew him only in his hoity-toity days, twenty years ago and it would be hard to judge him by that but his insolence, quarrelsomeness and conceit were then only equaled by Robertson's.

Martineau then challenges what Barrett Browning had felt about her mesmerism, demonstrating perhaps that she harboured a grudge that this had not been accepted by Elizabeth at the time: 'Mrs Browning is irrational when she jumps to the conclusion that the phenomena are occasioned by "spirits". One can expect nothing else from a woman who does not know what science is and who has been in one long reverie about "spirits" all her life.'

Inevitably, this divide had a public manifestation. In an 1860 article for an American newspaper about European politics, Martineau was critical of Barrett Browning's recent poems concerning political events in France and Italy and, in particular, her 'vulgar worship of success' as regards Napoleon III and an 'ideal and unpractical habit of mind.' Barrett Browning described this as 'monstrously unjust and absurd'.

It was certainly not an admirable trait in Martineau that she continued to bear grudges from her past for, by now, Barrett Browning was very ill again and would die in Robert Browning's arms in Florence a few months later.

Chapter 12: The Wordsworths

Harriet Martineau became a neighbour of William Wordsworth and his wife Mary in the Lake District in 1845. Wordsworth's sister Dorothy was also resident in the famous house, Rydal Mount, on the edge of Grasmere about a mile and a half from Martineau's house, The Knoll, in Ambleside. The great poet was aged seventy-five and would only live another five years, his most creative period now long behind him, as well as his youthful radical optimism. However, the connection between Martineau and Wordsworth was much deeper than the mere fact that they were neighbours.

The evocative, lyrical poetry of William Wordsworth first became popular in Britain when Harriet was an avid teenage reader. Between 1815 and 1820 his poems were widely read and Martineau was smitten: she had a picture of the dashing poet in her bedroom and would later describe how she learnt all his poems 'by heart, by the bushel' and that it was 'the joy of her youth'. A particular favourite that she shared with her younger brother James was *The Excursion*.

Wordsworth made a great impact on the impressionable Martineaus with his engagement with nature. His vivid descriptions of the beauty and grandeur of the Lake District, and the sense of freedom he garnered from it, would always stay with them. However, *The Excursion* is much more than that; it is a book-length poem in which a poet, a wanderer, a man of solitude and a pastor debate life's big questions, and it helped to lead the Martineau siblings towards a questioning of religion which would eventually spell trouble. Wordsworth opens it with a preface, setting the scene:

> On Man, Nature, and on Human Life
> Musing in solitude, I oft perceive
> Fair trains of imagery before me rise,
> Accompanied by feelings of delight[1]

Martineau would spend much of her life 'musing in solitude' and Wordsworth's description in *The Excursion* of his walks in the Lake District stayed with her to the point where she would replicate it very closely:

> I roved o'er many a hill and many a dale,
> With my accustomed load; In heat and cold,

---

1. William Wordsworth, *The Excursion* (Wordsworth Editions 1994), p. 897.

Through many a wood, and many an open ground,
In sunshine and in shade, in wet and fair,
My best companions now the driving winds,
And now the 'trotting brooks' and whispering trees,
The music of my own sad steps

This sense of the freedom, wildness and even solitary melancholy found in nature became a yearning in Harriet that wasn't easy to fulfil. She relished the natural sights of America, such as Niagara Falls and the Mississippi River, but her initial career as a radical writer kept her in London. Later, in Tynemouth, on her sick bed for five years, she longed to fully experience a natural landscape. Deborah Logan has suggested that *Life in the Sick-Room* has 'Wordsworthian themes':

> This valuing of natural scenes, to be fully appreciated in the moment as well as stored in the imagination for later pleasure, was a practice she cultivated for the remainder of her long life, from her release from this illness to her nightly communion with the stars from her terrace at The Knoll in old age. The idea that 'the outward man must decay the inward man is renewed day by day' points, like everything else for Martineau, to the human capacity for perfection, which finds its most apt expression in communion with the natural world.[2]

From her sickroom in Tynemouth she could observe the tides coming and going, and had a telescope for the night sky. In the face of her own mortality she developed a sense of awe in nature, which led her into a deeper spiritual correspondence with Henry Atkinson, marrying her Priestleyan Necessarianism to the Wordsworthian communion with the natural world. Even her belief in mesmerism was part of her revelation that nature was everything. This realisation was a great leap forward in her own life and thought, and influenced her move to the Lake District. Increasingly she longed to feel the open air and experience a landscape under foot. It was no accident that she took control in designing her own house in the great natural context of Ambleside.

Wordsworth and Martineau also shared an anti-slavery connection. Wordsworth had publicly admired *The Martyr Age of the United States* and had himself penned a poetic tribute – 'To Toussaint L'Ouverture' – in 1802, which may well have given rise to Harriet's initial motivation to write *The Hour and the Man*.

---

2. Deborah Logan, *The Hour and the Woman* (Northern Illinois University Press, 2002), p. 121.

At the time she moved to The Knoll, Martineau was corresponding regularly with Elizabeth Barratt Browning and she summarised her excitement
about moving into Wordsworth's neighbourhood:

> Wordsworth was an educator of infinite value to me, a worthy idol
> during many of the best years of my life… in his poetry I find my
> pleasures arise more from the echoes of old raptures than from new
> disclosures but I do honour and love the poet very deeply.

The relationship between the Wordsworths and Martineau as Lake District
neighbours has at times been dismissed as unfriendly. One Wordsworth biographer says that 'they could never get on'. In fact, for William, for a period of
time, it was a shot in the arm. After initially inviting the Wordsworths round
for tea, Harriet asked her great idol to plant a tree in her garden, which he gladly
did. They would regularly play host to her when she stopped at Rydal Mount
on her hiking route. After living in the Lakes a few months, she wrote to Mary
Carpenter (Lant's daughter) in shock at how many tourists would head to Rydal
Mount and be welcomed: 'On an average 500 strangers per season thrust themselves on Mr Wordsworth, consuming his time and wearing out the old man's
strength.'

In 1849, Martineau published a monthly journal of a year in Ambleside in
which she gives good descriptions of local life and her relationships with her
neighbours. She wrote it as a fundraiser for the American abolitionists and it was
only published in the obscure *Sartain's Union Magazine* in Philadelphia in 1850
– never in Britain. Fortunately, Barbara Todd, who now lives in The Knoll,
rediscovered this manuscript and had it republished in 2002 under the title *Harriet Martineau at Ambleside*. In it, Martineau gives more detail on how and why
she moved to Ambleside, describing it as a choice between the city and the
countryside and concluding: 'If I chose the country, I might as well choose the
best, and this very valley was, beyond all controversy, the best. Here I could
write in the serenest repose, I could rove at will, I could rest.'[3] She name-drops
Wordsworth numerous times for her American audience, telling of his 'summer
tea festivals', how he could give the history of the eagle sightings in the area and
how Mrs Wordsworth is the 'beloved of us all!' It is a great picture of the Lake
District in the middle of the 19th century.

The relationship between Martineau and Wordsworth was generally cor-
dial, and he valued having another writer in the area. He warned people to
beware of Martineau's invitation 'to go for a walk', as it would mean joining

---

3. Barbara Todd, *Harriet Martineau in Ambleside* (Bookcase, 2002), p. 57.

her on her daily 10-mile hike, which was sometimes longer and often intrepid. She, meanwhile, grabbed her opportunity to get to know her teenage idol and quiz him about his poetry, even showing him some of her own that had been published early in her career. The aged poet grumbled that he hadn't made the money he should have done from his early success, and they observed each other's eccentric habits. For example, Martineau complained at his generosity in giving milk away to strangers so that there was none left to share with his guests: 'The mixture of odd economies and neighbourly generosity was one of the most striking things in the old poet.' Later, she had to time her visits to Rydal Mount so that the great lyrical poet still had his teeth in. Once he'd taken his dentures out in the evening it was too difficult to decipher what he was saying.

Harriet despaired at Wordsworth's innocent take on the local people who she was determined to improve. Wordsworth had an old countryman's attitude to Cumbrian life, whereas she saw the opportunity for progress everywhere. She wrote to Elizabeth Barratt Browning complaining about him in 1846:

> I, deaf, can hardly conceive how he, with eyes and ears, and a heart that leads him to converse with the poor in his incessant walks, can be so unaware of their moral state. I dare say you need not be told how sensual vice abounds in rural districts. Here it is flagrant beyond anything I ever could have looked for; while every justice of the peace is filled with disgust and every clergy with despair at the drunkenness, quarrelling and extreme licentiousness with women – here is good old Wordsworth forever talking of rural innocence.

Martineau became convinced that the cause of the moral degradation was a lack of good housing. She resolved to set up a building society, secured financial help from her friend Elizabeth Jesser-Reid to do so, and encouraged local people to contribute monthly savings so they would eventually have enough for the locally built houses. It was a big success and of great reward to Martineau, who later wrote to Fanny Wedgwood:

> It is no small matter to see the life and spirits aroused among the people. Instead of dandering to the pothouse, they come up to me with their eager notions about the land and the dwellings; and we have merry meetings on the ground, and there is work for the old and the feeble, as well as for the builders... it is not a small matter considering how much health, morality and domestic welfare of every sort depends upon the experiment.

This was just one way in which Martineau was a whirlwind of progressive innovation in her first years at Ambleside. In building her self-designed house she insisted the builders were paid in cash every week, and the watching locals were amazed at how quickly the house developed. In her first five years she added growing areas, vegetable patches and livestock to her two acres; she offered housing and good pay to several people to work on her self-sustaining farm, and enabled them to sell any excess fruit and vegetables in the village. She was a caring, democratic employer.

An essentially traditional, conservative couple, the Wordsworths admired Martineau's industry and energy but were suspicious of some of her opinions. They would baulk at the mesmerism. Mary Wordsworth, in particular, disapproved of Harriet's growing atheism and the way she assigned mesmeric cures to natural 'miracles', while the more freethinking influence of William's sister Dorothy had dimmed. She resided with them but was by now stricken with what we would describe as dementia.

Although some subjects were off-limits in their discourse, perhaps, in Harriet, William Wordsworth found not only a disciple but also a reminder of his younger radicalism: his days of walking through France after the Revolution and revelling in optimism, which he subsequently lost in the Napoleonic War years. Interestingly, in 1848, a few years after Martineau first met Wordsworth, the latest unrest in France, mirrored in England by the growing Chartist movement, led to the government seeking to commission an article by Martineau to show the negative effects of the original French Revolution. She declined the opportunity, replying: 'I really have much sympathy with our malcontented classes.'

By the late 1840s, however, the light social callings and intellectual discussions had been replaced in Wordsworth's life by grief. In July 1847 his beloved daughter Dora died after an illness. The great poet was inconsolable. Martineau recorded the effect on him in an obituary of his wife Mary twelve years later in the *Daily News*:

> After the lingering illness of their daughter she encountered the dreariest portion of her life. Her aged husband spent the long winter evenings in grief and tears – week after week, month after month. He could not be comforted. She, who carried as tender a maternal heart as ever beat, had to bear her own grief and his too.

In an 1849 letter she remarked that Wordsworth was obviously not long for the world, and at this time he gave clear instructions to the local cleric that he

The social vibrancy Martineau enjoyed in the late 1840s when she moved to Ambleside is easily evident, yet so is its replacement with her own infirmity and isolation by the 1860s – although this would still not silence her pen. In getting to know William Wordsworth at the end of his life, Martineau engaged with one of her idols, but this is always a mixed blessing, as rarely do our heroes live up to expectations. Her own later reservations reflect this, but there is also something amusing in seeing these radical high minds being brought down to Earth by local gossip and the mundane reality of day-to-day life, represented for both of them by Mrs Wordsworth and the Ambleside locals.

They did, however, share an important philosophical belief which has gained in importance as the frailty of the Earth's environment has come into view. Martineau was an instinctive environmentalist, building a self-sustaining home and leading a low-impact, vegetarian, lifestyle. Inspired by Wordsworth, she saw that, for any individual, embracing the planet's natural elements, enjoying long, invigorating walks, taking in the mountains amongst the Lakes and seeing the delicate balance of nature at work, is of spiritual and life-sustaining importance to all. When Wordsworth and Martineau were meeting up, they were just two of fewer than 1 billion people on the planet; 150 years later they would have been horrified at how a global population of over 7 billion people has encroached, and negatively affected, the natural context of life.

Chapter 13: The John Murrays

Five generations of Murrays, all called John, were in successive charge of the family publishing company, established in Edinburgh in 1768. The firm grew in the 19th century and moved to Albemarle Street in London, where it became known for progressive non-fiction writers such as Babbage and Malthus, and poets such as Coleridge and Byron. Harriet Martineau, however, did not have any luck with the company. John Samuel Murray contemplated publishing her novel *Deerbrook* in 1838 but pulled out. His son John Murray agreed to publish *Eastern Life* in 1848 but, then, he also got cold feet.

In her autobiography, Martineau's attitude to both setbacks was that it had been the publishers' loss, since both books became good sellers. Her interaction with the company, however, betrays a deeper reality. Both books were rejected for having modern subversive aspects: *Deerbrook* for its advocacy of science and a middle-class doctor hero, and *Eastern Life* for being disrespectful towards Christianity. Martineau brushed this off with typical stoicism but it is yet another way in which her career was unprecedented. There are very few authors who have had agreements reneged upon because they were making arguments against religion. It is indicative of the battles she faced, and suggests why she has not been well remembered. The establishment wields power by turning its back.

In fact, John Samuel Murray liked *Deerbrook* but his associate and supporter, Mr Lockhart, did not like the storyline, which is built around an apothecary who becomes a hero during a fever epidemic in a village, having previously faced local ostracism for political reasons. The not very subtly named Dr Hope finishes the novel admonishing the superstition of religion alongside the lies of the local gossips who had been against him: 'How alike is the superstition of the ignorant and of the wicked! My poor neighbours stealing to the conjurer's tent in the lane, and this wretched lady, hope alike to bribe Heaven in their extremity, – they by gifts and rites, she by remorse and reparation.'

Valerie Sanders has suggested *Deerbrook* is an important bridge between Jane Austen and Charlotte Brontë and George Eliot. It contains storylines that would recur in novels to come and, as Sanders says, includes a positive portrayal of a doctor that went beyond even Austen: 'Her portrait of Edward Hope, the conscientious country doctor corresponds with the rise of the medical practitioner as a middle class professional and consequently as a new kind of hero, to displace the landowner or superior clergyman who were his immediate literary predecessors.'[1]

She also makes the point that Martineau knew the life of doctors well from her uncle and grandfather in Norwich, who did much to establish the city hospital, and her brother-in-law Thomas Greenhow, who would soon be administering to her in Tynemouth. Sanders concludes: 'Martineau goes much further than Jane Austen in showing how a small social community works. This is largely because she is more interested in, and knowledgeable about, the lives of professional men.'

Martineau reported the response from publisher John Murray in her autobiography: 'He [Murray] was more than civil, he was kind and sincere in his regrets… Mr Lockhart's clique gave out on the eve of publication because the hero was an apothecary.'

The book was picked up by another publisher, Edward Moxon, and was a success. It had a big influence, particularly on Elizabeth Gaskell (who was socially connected to Harriet and who would start her own stories of village life a few years later), as well as on George Eliot (it has many themes that would be revisited in her masterpiece *Middlemarch*) and Charlotte Brontë. Where Martineau fell down with *Deerbrook* was to include a lengthy passage of preachy philosophising interspersed within the narrative, a fault she would happily point out herself later in life.

More controversial was the rejection, by John Murray the third, of *Eastern Life* ten years later in 1848. In 1846, Martineau was newly energised by her recovery from illness and had made the move to the Lake District. She was now offered the chance of a trip to the Eastern lands of Egypt, Sinai, Palestine and Syria – invited by a wealthy couple from Liverpool, Mr and Mrs Richard Yates. After a rough crossing over the Mediterranean, they spent three months seeing the Pyramids, the Holy Land, the Nile and all of the main Middle Eastern cities using a variety of modes of transport, including camels, which Harriet became adept at riding.

In *Eastern Life: Past and Present*, Martineau cast an analytical eye on religions past and present. R. K. Webb introduces the book by criticising precisely what I like about it: 'It is both descriptive and didactic, a book of travels and a torrent of philosophising'.

It was a dark book with much description of different ways of dying and celebrating death. In effect, it became the first in a series of works in which Martineau openly challenged the religious establishment, and as Webb also says,

---

1. Valerie Sanders, 'Introduction', in Harriet Martineau, *Deerbrook* (Penguin Classics, 2004), p. XXIV.

did a 'final demolition' to her 'old structure of faith'. It is a genuinely ground-breaking work that takes a scientific, dispassionate approach to religion, suggesting it is part of human nature, as in this section analysing the Egyptian past:

> I lament that aspiration, in its young and irrepressible activity, must make so many flights into a dim world of dreams, and come back perplexed and disheartened before it can learn to fly up to the glorious and unfailing light of nature, to replenish its life, but this regret is only what one feels every day in exploring the only true history of man – the history of ideas.

She then suggests that if we look at any religious faith it has similarities because all men share the same moral intuitions under nature:

> Amidst these natural regrets remains the comfort that the great governing ideas of mankind, – the guiding lights of the intellect – have never failed, and have scarcely suffered eclipse. The great ideas of moral obligation and strict retribution, of the desirableness of moral good and the eternal 'beauty of holiness' pass from system to system.

Martineau is proposing here that religion occurs because all humankind shares a moral mind, which manifests in different ways. As an idea this has only really come to the fore in the 21st century, with the same suggestion in work by the likes of Steven Pinker, Marc Hauser and Robert Wright. This is the basis of Martineau's whole approach in *Eastern Life.*

She is, however, empathetic and respectful. She anticipates some of the 20th-century Middle Eastern antagonisms, observing religious tensions on her travels. She is critical of Protestant missionaries who have shown no respect for Eastern traditions and history. She is sympathetic to the poor but not to the keepers of harems, whom she lambasts for their treatment of women. Martineau calls slavery and polygamy the 'two hellish practices'. She presents religion as a stepping stone towards 'the supreme presence of facts' and argues that science will provide a 'new order of knowledge and wisdom'.

Some of the text would have been quite shocking to John Murray as he read the manuscript, and he didn't take long to renege on his agreement to publish, sending the book back with a short note. Martineau was dismayed and angry, and fired off a letter in response to request an explanation. Murray replied that the book had 'infidel tendencies', and later Martineau wrote that he had also felt it was a 'conspiracy against Moses', from 'One who overthrows the veracity (!) of the bible'. She also later claimed Murray was hampered by the 'untraveled clergy' but, in an angry letter to him, she said his rejection was 'presumptuous and immature'.

Edward Moxon was again the beneficiary, for the book did sell and was widely read. Harriet wrote to him: 'I certainly do not doubt the success of the enterprise in the hands of an untrammelled man who respects freedom of opinion and promotes the spread of knowledge.'

Seven years later, in her autobiography, Harriet wrote of Murray: '... we may suppose that his clerical clients interfered to compel him to resign the publication, and I understood, on good authority, when the success of the book was secure, that he heartily regretted the mischance.'

The dispute is reported in a 1932 book written by George Paston entitled *At John Murray's*, although having been published by John Murray the book may be safely assumed to be a little biased: 'She – plain, deaf, sickly and nearing middle age – had been lionized and run after in the literary society of London... Murray knew this, but apparently he did not know that, though Miss Martineau had shed her Unitarian views, she had adopted no other form of religious faith.'[2]

Paston then reproduces a note with some of the sentences which Murray objected to:

> A paper which appears to have been intended to accompany one of
> Murray's letters gives a list of 'Objectional Passages'. For example:
> 'The object of these pages is to prove that the Bible chronology
> is altogether wrong.'
> 'Moses and Plato so compared as to imply that the former had
> no divine aid.'
> 'A much greater antiquity can be assigned to the human race
> than that which can be deduced from the Bible.'

Paston does not condemn Murray's actions although he does report Martineau's parting shot: 'I regret your mistake in beginning our negotiations as a man of business and breaking it off as a Censor.'

Meanwhile, *Eastern Life* was lapped up by Charles Darwin, who liked the dark themes and the scientific analysis of human nature, as Moore and Desmond describe in their Darwin biography:

> The travelogue was a thinly disguised critical history of religion, and
> to Darwin's taste. The dominant note is death; the text is littered with
> tombs. The 'black pall of oblivion' followed her from Egypt across

---

2. George Paston, *At John Murray's: Records of a Literary Circle 1843-92* (John Murray, 1932), p. 74.

the Sinai desert to Palestine... Darwin was intrigued by Martineau's message, that Christian beliefs about reward and punishment were based on heathen superstitions... He had done with superstition, and he enjoyed Martineau's excursus.

Darwin would, however, have been aware of Murray's refusal to publish and of the book's reviews, which found the secular writings difficult, and he would continue to prevaricate over whether to publish his own ideas. Yet it would be John Murray who would publish *On the Origin of Species* ten years later, so creating the world's first major public collision between religion and science after Martineau's skirmishes. Perhaps Murray felt he had to do something to maintain the company's progressive reputation after his faint-heartedness with Martineau.

Eastern Life had one unusual consequence which was reported back to Harriet, and which she greatly enjoyed. After reading her descriptions of how dirty his palace was, the Viceroy of Egypt had all the windows replaced, at great expense – a practical housekeeping measure, amidst the philosophical controversies, of which Martineau would have thoroughly approved.

In fact, Harriet's publication of *Eastern Life* can be seen as the halfway point in a lifetime's engagement with the Middle East. Her initial writings in the *Monthly Repository* in the early 1830s included the *Traditions of Palestine* and *Providence as Manifested through Israel*, both later produced as booklets and showing remarkably detailed knowledge of Middle Eastern religions. Martineau's Unitarian approach saw religion as a worldwide engagement with spiritual problems and kept an inquisitive open mind to the different solutions found. This work continued after *Eastern Life*, particularly in her later journalism for the *Daily News*, where her travels to the Middle East were useful in providing an accurate picture.

In September 1860 she wrote a leader for her newspaper in support of the British Consul in Jerusalem, whom she had met in 1847 and who was trying to mediate in a violent uprising of Muslims in Syria. It is a remarkable piece which could have been written today:

> Times such as the last few weeks in Syria and Palestine, try men's souls... We are safe enough at Jerusalem; we have a great duty to do there, not only to immigrants and Jews, but also to Muslims. There is no real obstacle to our living in friendship with them. They look up to us with respect and reliance; and to keep up a good understanding with Muslims in any centre of influence is to support the Turkish

Empire in the best way, and to strengthen the chances of peace in Europe; but to do our duty fully, we must support our representative more liberally.

This is a short but convincing portrait of the dilemmas that have existed in the European engagement with the Middle East both before and since, and which have become very pressing in recent years: the problem of Western involvement, the interplay with Turkey, the religious tensions and the role of diplomats. Martineau makes a plea, in a newspaper which was read around the world, that it is possible to 'live in friendship' – an appeal which has been so rarely heeded since.

In both *Eastern Life* and in her journalism, Martineau implied that religion was no reason to go to war, and that if we could recognise it as part of a localised history and culture we could be empathetic to each other. Engaging with science and accepting nature would move humans on from religion and lead to less conflict in the world. She was advocating the modern liberal humanist position 100 years before it gained momentum in the Western world. This was radical writing for which her rejection by a progressive publisher such as John Murray acts as very symbolic of the overall reaction.

should be buried near his daughter. He died in April 1850, after which Harriet seems to have worked to compensate Mrs Wordsworth with extra visits – so much so that in 1851 Mary wrote to a friend that 'she is a pest', and she is reputed to have occasionally hidden herself on seeing the restless radical marching down the lane towards her house. However, a respect and rapport did grow between the two women, who found common ground in encouraging thrift and moral responsibility amongst the locals.

In 1855 William's sister Dorothy died, having received round the clock care from Mary for many years. Mary Wordsworth was now left in Rydal Mount on her own. At the time, Martineau was penning her autobiography in which she paid fulsome tribute to Mary but was slightly less adulatory in her praise of William Wordsworth, implying that he should have pulled himself together after the death of his daughter. This is a typical Martineau trait, which reminds us of her own stoic reaction to the death of her father 30 years earlier. She says of Wordsworth: 'After his daughter's death, I seldom saw him except in his phaeton, or when I called. He gave way sadly, and inconsiderately as regards Mrs Wordsworth, to his grief and I heard that the evenings were very sad.'

Martineau recovered from illness to pick up her pen after 1855, but the old days of striding around the Grasmere fells were gone, very likely to Mary Wordsworth's relief. In 1858 she wrote to Henry Reeve encouraging him to visit, but the scene is very different from her earlier energetic days, with an implication that she would not be able to do much with him:

> Would not you like to go to Fox How? The Arnolds are here in great force right now. Maria will be happy to go with you there & to the Wordsworth garden. Mrs Wordsworth is extremely aged & blind & few see her but the pretty garden and terraces where 'The Excursion' was meditated, you can become acquainted with.

Mary Wordsworth died in 1859 and in her tribute for the *Daily News* Martineau went on to describe the situation she was left with:

> Not one is left now of the eminent persons who rendered that cluster of valleys so eminent as it has been. Dr Arnold went first, in the vigor of his years. Southey died at Keswick; Hartley Coleridge on the margin of Rydal Lake; the Quillinans under the shadow of Loughrigg; Professor Wilson disappeared from Elleray; the aged Mrs Fletcher from Lancrigg; and the three venerable Wordsworths from Rydal Mount.

Discount Book Voucher

10% off* all books purchased on your next visit to The Open Book

valid until...

signed...

The Open Book

10 King Street, Richmond, Surrey TW9 1ND
theopenbook@btconnect.com   020 8940 1802

* unless previously discounted

Part IV: The 1850s

At the beginning of the 1850s, Harriet Martineau was actively involved in a Lake District society of great literary pedigree. The Great Exhibition of 1851 marked a moment of optimism in the country, and Martineau reconnected with some of her London contacts. But in the middle of the decade things started to go awry both for her and the country.

The Crimean War of 1853–6 between Russia and a European alliance led by Britain knocked British optimism. The war was complicated and brutal, with outcomes which were not clear, encapsulated by the disastrous 'Charge of the Light Brigade'. It was quickly followed in 1857 by the Indian Mutiny, in which the Indian people undermined the rule of their country by the East India Company, only for that rule to be replaced by the British crown. There is a sense in this period that Britain was not as welcome in the world as she thought she was. The unquestioning progress of empire and industry was suddenly brought into question, and this was reinforced by events in Ireland where over 1 million people died due to famine and many more emigrated to America.

For Martineau, the early 1850s was an era when she became increasingly known as an atheistic writer. For many people this was too much to bear. This was a time of scientific enquiry and the growth of universities, but the religious controversy of evolution did not arrive until the next decade. Martineau experienced her second major illness in 1855 and, convinced she was about to die, penned her honest autobiography. But she survived, and the autobiography did not appear for another 22 years. Her physical vigour was diminished and she rarely left The Knoll after this illness. However, her writing mind and defiant attitude remained steadfast and journalistic opportunities afforded her the chance to be heard on the issues of the day.

Chapter 14: Henry G. Atkinson

Henry Atkinson played a significant part in the development of Harriet Martineau's writing, philosophy and public profile, and yet he remains a curiously mysterious character. He didn't publish anything himself. No photographs of him have been seen and later in life he retreated into obscurity – so much so that his year of death is not known, though it is thought that he had drifted to Boulogne in France and died there sometime in the 1890s.

Yet Atkinson is the man behind the 'sensation' of mesmerism in the 1840s. Later, through their meetings and letters, he drives Martineau towards greater religious scepticism and, in partnership with her, causes a scandal with the publication of some of their correspondence in 1851 under the title *Letters on the Laws of Man's Nature and Development*.

Most of what we know about Atkinson comes from either their published correspondence or from Martineau's autobiography. It seems that Martineau was introduced to Atkinson by a mutual acquaintance in recommendation of his mesmeric ideas while she was ailing in her sickroom in Tynemouth. In her memoir Martineau explains that she was not personally 'mesmerised' by Atkinson but that she took advice from him on the methods, and used a lady recommended by him. She gives a humorous description of one of their first meetings: 'I believe that, amidst the stream of talk I poured out upon him, it was impossible for him to believe how truly I really did desire to hear his views and opinions. In spite of this he did tell me much which I thought over when he was gone.'

In time she claimed that the mesmerism had cured her. Her brother-in-law, Doctor Greenhow, who had attended her in Newcastle when she had first been taken ill, was not impressed with her attributing her recovery to mesmerism, and wrote up an alternative account. Mesmerism was, however, quite the thing for a time, with many people wanting to know the techniques which could bring cures to various ailments, and Martineau was one of its principal popularisers.

Atkinson wrote to her initially about the practice, saying that it all came about through natural causes, and their letters soon became a meditation on what nature could account for. In 1847, Martineau wrote to him about her plans for travelling in the East and her ideas that religion itself needed to be analysed dispassionately. This chimed with Atkinson, and their correspondence on the make-up of the mind and the materiality of everything began in earnest on Martineau's return from the Middle East, and a friendship developed.

Atkinson visited her in Ambleside and, while as the older author and experienced traveller she mentored him, she was also in thrall to his mystical materialism and scientific freethinking. If Atkinson had lived in the 20th century he would have perhaps been hailed as a visionary like Adam Watts or a counter-cultural figure such as R. D Laing. As it was, when Martineau foisted his rather long-winded letters on the public, they were regarded, as Kathryn Hughes suggests, as a bit 'crackpot'.[1]

Martineau arranged for the publication of their letters in 1851, and it is a curiously enigmatic production. Atkinson's long meditations on nature, the mind, religion and mesmerism are followed by Martineau's ecstatic responses. The mesmerism is, to an extent, an unnecessary distraction from their main theme that the human mind – the human thought process – had no special powers and was as much a part of nature as any other body part or animal. From this they extrapolated that humankind fell within nature's laws. Religion had no special domain: it was part of human nature and that would be the great area of future study. The letters are excitable, particularly on her part, and resemble at times the correspondence between two young lovers, interrupted by a discussion of the materiality of brain and mind. They have a mercurial optimistic quality that somewhat undermines the radical philosophical ideas.

Some of the initial Martineau letters make an explicit link between humans and other animals, anticipating the evolutionary theory that would soon follow from Darwin:

> The point of most importance appears to me to be the consciousness of self, indicated by the dog and the monkey. I am constantly told that this consciousness is an attribute of the human being alone; whereas I cannot see how the jealousies, the vindictiveness, the moral fear, the love of approbation of brute animals, can be exercised without a sense of the ego. We know but little of the powers and experience of brutes… but what we do know indicates consciousness as clearly as sentience.

Atkinson replied with a long letter in which he linked findings in phrenology – at the time a growing area of interest arguing that the brain could be broken down into distinct areas– with his ideas about the human mind and stated that dreams, sleep and the effects of mesmerism were all part of material reality, the

---

1. Kathryn Hughes, *George Eliot: The Last Victorian* (Fourth Estate, 1998), p. 128.

results of brain activity. He was radical in his own right: 'The brain is the organ from whose action arises all that class of phenomenon which we term Mind: in which I include all our sensations, perceptions, emotions, judgements and intuitions; consciousness, will, and certain forces which tend to regulate, stimulate and control the other functions of the body.'[2]

He later added:

Men have smiled, and ridiculed, and blasphemed against every truth as it has been revealed. When will the world learn wisdom by the past, and hope for the future, and be ashamed and humble when it wants knowledge? Only I think, when the philosophy of Man and Mind, raised from its true basis of material fact, is developed, and admitted as a Science by the world. That men cannot imagine beyond their knowledge, is clear from every new truth being at first considered impossible and unnatural... we are as yet on the very threshold of knowledge... the true philosopher will be all patience for the present and confidence for the future.

Martineau replied to this letter ecstatically: 'I do not like to say anything after your last letter. I do not like to touch it, or the state of mind it produces in me.' And her expression of the freedom she found through these ideas was effusive:

What a feeling it is – that grows up and pervades us when we have fairly returned to our obedience to Nature! What a healthy glow animates the faculties! What a serenity settles down upon the temper! One seems to have a new set of nerves, when one has planted one's foot on the broad common of Nature, and clear daylight and bracing breezes are about one, no more raptures and agonies of selfish hope and fear – but sober certainty of reliance on the immutability of Nature's laws; and the lofty liberty that is found in obedience to them. We are still, and our kind must long continue to be, injured in power and in peace by the operation of past ignorance, which has mournfully impaired the conditions of human life; but the emancipation which may be obtained is already precious beyond all estimate. Ignorant as we yet are, hardly able yet (even the wisest of men) to snatch a glimpse of the workings of Nature, obvious as it is that our condition is merely that of an infant waking upon the world of exis-

2. Henry George Atkinson and Harriet Martineau, *Letters on the Laws of Man's Nature and Development* (John Chapman, 1851), pp. 26–29.

tence, the privilege of freedom, as far as we are able to go, is quite inestimable.

Martineau would spend the next few years denying it, but her position was overtly atheistic. A passage in the same letter explicitly challenged any possibility of life after death, and suggested that religion was a man-made construct, with God built in our own image:

> What an emancipation it is – to have escaped from the little enclosure of dogma, and to stand, free to learn! How I wonder at myself now for having held (and very confidently held forth upon it, I am ashamed to say) that at all events it was safe to believe dogma: that whether there was a future state or not, it was safe and comfortable to believe it, that if there was no God, serving as a model to man, – the original of the image – it was safe and tranquillizing to take for granted that there was.

She gives the example of a young man entering a church who blamed himself for his doubts, as a result of his 'personal sinfulness', and offers this lesson: 'I saw clearly how enervating and depraving is the practise of harbouring, through timidity or indolence, what is suspected to be untrue. The exclusion of the truth is a prodigious evil.'

In his biography of T. H. Huxley, Adrian Desmond referred to the Atkinson–Martineau letters as '… for many people their first encounter with the unimaginable'.[3] Their argument was that the Earth fell well within a natural planetary system, there had to be a 'first cause', but this was unknowable to man's restricted experiences of life on Earth, unknowable to man's mind. The world was not ready for this sophisticated position in 1851.

The reaction was vitriolic, as summarised by Webb:

> The publication of the 'Letters' brought her the martyrdom she predicted. The book made a great noise, the reviews, almost without exception, were harsh and contemptuous, and Miss Martineau's friends and acquaintances were appalled… Mrs Reid, Mrs Arnold, Julia Smith, Crabb Robinson, Macready, most of her old friends were shocked, and some never resumed the friendship. Others, who had already quarrelled with her, like Tremenheere or Mary Howitt,

---

3. Adrian Desmond, *Huxley: The Devil's Disciple* (Michael Joseph, 1994), p. 185.

found their worst suspicions confirmed: 'This is what your strong-minded women come to,' wrote Tremenheere.

Charles Knight, who had published her recent *History of the Peace,* wrote to say that he would no longer support that book or her work in general, and put out a public statement to that effect. The publication of the Atkinson letters scandalised literary London, which was not ready for such an overt challenge to the principles of Christian religion. The *Quarterly Review* was typical, and took a sarcastic tone:

> ... our friends of the New Light school profess themselves devout believers in the new philosophy. Of course we have nothing to adduce in the form of testimony in support of Christianity, that will admit of comparison with the series of lucid proofs now placed before our readers. Nothing can be more reasonable, than that we should be called upon to sympathize deeply with these ingenuous, much suffering inquirers after truth, and we should give them full credit for sincerity when they profess their painful inability to see any sufficiency or force, in what we call the Christian evidences.[4]

In *Punch* the editor Douglas Jerrold quipped: 'There is no God and Harriet Martineau is his prophet!'

The Darwin–Wedgwood circle in London, which Harriet had been closely connected to in the 1830s and '40s, was shocked. The mood of many of them can be ascertained from the content of a letter from Charles Darwin's Aunt Fanny Owen to his sister-in-law Elizabeth Wedgwood: 'Miss Martineau's publication in partnership with Mr Atkinson has shocked all her friends. I cannot understand the motive that guided these two criminals in the publishing of their miserable theory.'

The private reactions of some of Harriet's literary acquaintances also betrays the general response. George Eliot wrote to a friend that it seemed 'studiously offensive', while Charlotte Brontë reacted against the atheism in a way that would have ramifications on her friendship with Martineau. Others quietly distanced themselves.

But the bitterest pill, or, as Maria Weston Chapman later described it, 'The Life Sorrow', came with the review written by Martineau's brother James in the Unitarian *Prospective Review*, entitled 'Mesmeric Atheism'. The review described Atkinson as an 'ignorant man', ridiculed his mesmerism, and argued

4. 'The New Lights', *Quarterly Review*, XV (1852), p. 372.

that in the book they were falsifying Baconian philosophy and being reckless with 'Moral obligation'.[5] The review was spiteful and sarcastic, but it was also influential, ridiculing both the mesmerism and the atheism in the book. In her letters, Martineau says her main objection was that James had disrespected Atkinson, but she obviously also felt a personal betrayal, which she was unable to get over and the siblings had no further contact.

Harriet would always protest that the publication of the letters did not affect her reputation, suggesting that she lost no real friends through it, but deep down she knew otherwise. In her autobiography, written four years later, she recorded: 'It seemed to me probable that, after the plain speaking of the Atkinson Letters, I might never be asked, or allowed, to utter myself again... i anticipated excommunication from the world of literature, if not from society.' She was, though, still frustrated that the response both in society and in reviews had failed to engage fully with the book's main points:

> When our book came out, and was abused in almost every periodical in the kingdom, it amused me to see how very like my old self the metaphysical reviewers were; how exclusively they fastened on the collateral parts of the book, leaving its method, and all its essential part untouched... Scarcely any part of it indeed was touched at all, except the anti-theological portion, which was merely collateral.

In fact, the Martineau–Atkinson *Letters on the Laws of Man's Nature and Development* remain radical even today. It was neither a philosophical essay nor a scientific paper. Despite having a pretence of being scientific theory it lacked recourse to evidence. However, as a cogent argument for the mind being within nature, it anticipates evolution; it portrays religion as man-made and explores freedom within natural laws.

Even mesmerism is more palatable to modern eyes, if seen as an argument for atomic magnetism – it certainly anticipates the discovery of the atomic make-up of the world. Their message was that even apparently mysterious things can be measured through material reality. This was 1851, a long time before modern atomic physics and nine years before evolution was presented by Wallace and Darwin, causing such a shock to the religious world. Even then, the existence of a mind shared by all humans through nature was an idea Darwin chose not to put forward. This had to wait for 20th-century advocates.

The Atkinson letters were never republished, were rarely referred to by writers or thinkers, being too unscientific for science, too outlandish for polite

5. James Martineau, 'Mesmeric Atheism', *Prospective Review*, 26 (1851), p. 234.

society, too atheistic for the literary world. Despite her insistence to the contrary, Martineau's reputation never fully recovered, as both the general public and the establishment turned their backs on her.

Chapter 15: Charles Dickens

Charles Dickens was born ten years after Harriet Martineau, an age difference that would have significant bearing on their fascinatingly fractious relationship, which developed through the eventful times they shared.

Dickens was a fledgling writer in his twenties when Martineau became famous for her monthly-issued fictional tales illustrating politics and economics. He is often credited with having started this trend, but Martineau was a decade ahead of him and he surely must have been influenced by her example in this regard. After reading *Society in America*, Dickens called it the 'finest book' on that country. When he carried out his own American tour ten years after Martineau, he told their mutual friend, the actor William Macready, that he was determined to avoid the mistakes of previous British authors visiting America. Dickens's biographer Michael Slater suggests that Martineau was in his mind while visiting, and subsequently writing about, America in the 1840s:

> A writer of the opposite political persuasion to the Tories was the redoubtable and progressive-minded Harriet Martineau. After an investigative tour lasting two years she published her three-volume Society in America in 1837, followed by a further three volumes, A Retrospect of Western Travel in 1838... Dickens certainly knew them (both works feature in an 1844 inventory of his library), and of all his predecessors in the field of the American travel book it is Martineau with whom he seems to be most in dialogue in American Notes.[1]

While in America, Dickens wrote to Jane Carlyle suggesting that no one had a good word to say about Martineau, and showing how, after her American writings, Martineau had caused revulsion with her outspokenness. Dickens himself became interested in the slavery issue, and on his return he flirted with becoming a Unitarian, although he didn't quite take the plunge away from Anglicanism. Modern Dickens scholar Jerome Meckier has analysed Dickens's early writings on America and suggests he was clearly being competitive, not just with Martineau, but also with Frances Trollope, who had written a travelogue about the developing nation. Meckier concludes that Dickens was frustrated with the result:

---

1. Michael Slater, *Charles Dickens* (Yale University Press, 2009), p. 176–177.

In Dickens the tendency manifested itself as presumption: he had expected to come to the fore as England's finest analyst of America by discrediting Mrs Trollope's many complaints and eclipsing Harriet Martineau's many encomiums with an unrivalled paean to the new democracy; it was to be based on his sounder grasp of politics, Rousseau, and republican principles. To his chagrin, he found himself forced to undo one woman's praise and outdo the other's severity.[2]

In the late 1830s Martineau was the famous author hostess of soirées in London, at a time when Dickens would have been the new kid on the block, with his monthly 'Sketches by Boz' appearing in the *Monthly Magazine* from 1835. In her autobiography, Martineau alludes to the fact that they met in this period, and it is very likely that Dickens attended one of the many parties hosted by Martineau, as a young author getting connected in literary London.

In the 1840s, Martineau retreated to her sickroom while Dickens became famous as the author of widely read, monthly issued, social improvement novels such as *Oliver Twist* and *Nicholas Nickleby*. He didn't forget Martineau, however, and when in 1850 he founded and edited his own monthly journal, *Household Words* he invited her to become a regular contributor, publishing 47 articles by her between 1850 and 1854, often at his specific request. He also commissioned Elizabeth Gaskell to write for the journal, and seemed to have been keen to have the two women authors at the heart of this new venture.

Martineau had been working on *A History of the Thirty Years' Peace* in the late 1840s, in which she paid tribute to Dickens:

> Last and greatest among the novelists [of the period] comes Charles Dickens – the Boz who rose up in the midst of us like a jin with his magic glass among some eastern people, showing forth what was doing in the regions of darkness, and in off places where nobody ever thought of going to look. It is scarcely conceivable that any one should, in our age of the world, exert a stronger social influence than Mr Dickens has in his power. His sympathies are on the side of the suffering and the frail; and this makes him the idol of those who suffer, from whatever cause... while the inexhaustible humour, the unbounded power of observation, the exquisite occasional pathos, and the geniality of spirit throughout, carry all readers far away from

2. Jerome Meckier, *Innocent Abroad: Charles Dickens's American Engagements* (University Press of Kentucky, 2015), p. 28.

critical thoughts, and give to the author the whole range of influence, from the palace-library to the penny book-club.

Even at this stage, however, she was voicing reservations about Dickens which would become louder in later years:

> We may wish that he has a sounder social philosophy, and that he could suggest a loftier moral to sufferers; could lead them to see that 'man does not live by bread alone,' and that his best happiness lies in those parts of his nature which are only animated and exalted by suffering... we may shrink from the exhibition of human miseries as an artistical study; but, these great drawbacks once admitted, we shall be eager to acknowledge that we have in Charles Dickens a man of a genius which cannot but mark the time, and accelerate or retard its tendencies. In as far as its cant, he is vastly accelerating them. As to whether his delineations are true to broad daylight English life, that may be for some time to come a matter of opinion on which men will differ.

Harriet felt that Dickens's stories were not accurate pictures of life, that he had a poor theoretical knowledge of politics and economics and that he had taken over her patch of social-improvement fiction without having done the requisite research and background reading. However, for a few years *Household Words* was widely read and admired; relations between Dickens and his women contributors were amicable enough to be productive and Martineau later admitted that the financial earnings were useful at the time.

In the 1850s Dickens published an annual selection of Christmas stories. He would include in these collections tales from Martineau and Gaskell, but they appeared anonymously, while the book was titled *From Mr Dickens* – as if he had written all of the content himself. He was happy to take the credit for their contributions, and for many years these stories were not credited to their real authors.

One such story, written by Martineau and often overlooked, was 'The Deaf Child's Story', which appeared in the 1853 Christmas edition. It is the story of a young deaf boy, his struggles to make friends and how difficult this can be at Christmas. It implores readers to empathise with the deaf, but not in a patronising way:

> I began thinking of myself; but I did not suppose he did... he told me what a hopeless case he believed mine to be and what it would cut

me off from; but, he said that nothing of the sort could cut a person off from being a hero… I shall not run away from that house again, – nor from any other house. It is so much better to look things in the face!

As D. J. Taylor comments in a reproduced edition, it is a 'thoroughly modern' contribution from Martineau.[3] She did not often write about her deafness. There was an earlier *Letter to the Deaf* in which she gives advice and implores deaf people not to give up on living a full life of communication. She had a determined and defiant attitude to her own deafness that anticipates modern attitudes towards disability, exemplified in her Christmas story written for Dickens.

However, at the end of this period there was a falling out, which began with Dickens writing an article entitled 'On Strike', about the Preston Strike of 1854. It was to inform the thinking behind *Hard Times*, which appeared in *Household Words* in monthly instalments in 1855–6. Dickens was writing publicly in favour of factory and wages legislation on behalf of workers and urging better conditions in factories. Martineau retreated from her work for Dickens's journal and penned a report directly aimed at what she regarded as his inappropriate interference, in a piece entitled 'The Factory Controversy. A Warning against Meddling Legislation'. In the report she said of Dickens:

> He should not meddle with affairs in which rationality of judgement is required… If he must give the first place to his idealism and sensibilities, let him confine himself to fiction, and if he will put himself forward as a social reformer, let him do the honest thing – study both sides of the question he takes up.

These were strong words, and while Dickens did have his contemporary critics it is unlikely he had been publicly vilified in this way before. Even the *Westminster Review* refused to publish the article and it came out in a pamphlet sponsored by the National Association of Factory Occupiers. This was appropriate, as Martineau was harking back to her father's experience in the 1820s and was always adamant that industrialists and owners should be free to run their businesses as they saw fit. This argument precedes and anticipates the industrial debates of the 20th century between workers and owners. Perhaps Martineau was on the wrong side of history, but her point was that it was in the interests

3. D. J. Taylor, introduction to *The Deaf Playmate's Story* by Harriet Martineau, included in *A Round of Stories by the Christmas Fire*, Charles Dickens (Hesperus Classics, 2007), p. 98.

of owners to look after their workers, which behaviour did not require heavy-handed legislation. Unfortunately, not all factory owners were as thoughtful and benign as her father had been.

Henry Morley was the named replier to Martineau's attack but most biographers consider that it was penned and published directly by Dickens himself in *Household Words*. It was a patronising reply, calling her a 'sick lady' with a 'vomit of conceit', and saying that she had written 'hasty words', 'for a scrap or two of argument too readily adopted upon partial showing'.[4] Privately, Dickens had already written to his friend Wills that Martineau was 'grimly bent upon the enlightenment of Mankind', and he later wrote to his confidant and supporter John Forster to say she was 'wrong headed'.

Dickens was growing tired of Harriet's high-mindedness. There had been another disagreement over a Christmas story submitted by her but refused by him, because of what she interpreted as his anti-Catholicism. Martineau was no fan of the Catholic church, but she demanded a level playing field and complained bitterly about it in correspondence.

It is said that the character of Mrs Jellyby in *Bleak House* – the mother with children whom she neglects in favour of campaigning for African children – was based on Harriet. Dickens's point was that mothers should take care of their own children first before worrying about the wider world, as described here:

> Mrs Jellyby, sitting in quite a nest of waste paper, drank coffee all the evening, and dictated at intervals to her eldest daughter. She also held a discussion with Mr Quale; of which the subject seemed to be – if I understood it – the Brotherhood of Humanity; and gave utterance to some beautiful sentiments.[5]

Mrs Jellyby's visitors are in shock at the state of the house and the children: 'It must be very good of Mrs Jellyby to take such pains about a scheme for the benefit of Natives – and yet – Peepy and the housekeeping!'

In addition, the themes of *Hard Times* are a direct riposte to those critics who argued that Dickens lacked knowledge of political-economic theory. The overarching theme of *Hard Times* is that people should take notice of what is really happening and stop high-minded theorising, but also that life was for living and not to be over-analysed. He had at this time also been criticised by the historian Thomas Babington Macaulay for 'sullen socialism'. Perhaps Dickens

---

4. Charles Dickens and Henry Morley, 'Our Wicked Miss-Statements', *Household Words*, 304 (1856), pp. 13–15.
5. Charles Dickens, *Bleak House* (Penguin Classics, 1996), p. 58.

was seeking some public retribution with both Martineau and Macaulay in his writing of *Hard Times*.

By the mid-1850s Martineau was in her second health crisis and penned her autobiography, in which she reveals her state of mind as regards Dickens and the 'meddling legislation' dispute:

> Another vexation is his vigorous erroneousness about matters of science, as shown in Oliver Twist about the new poor-law (which he confounds with the abrogated old one) and in Hard Times, about the controversies of employers. Nobody wants to make Mr Dickens a political economist; but there are many who wish that he would abstain from a set of difficult subjects, on which all true sentiment must be underlain by a sort of knowledge which he has not. The more fervent and inexhaustible his kindliness (and it is fervent and inexhaustible), the more important it is that it should be well-informed and well-directed, that no errors of his may mislead his readers on the one hand, nor lessen his own genial influence on the other.

She also added late in the autobiography a complaint about Dickens and how he wrote about and treated women: '... he ignored the fact that nineteen-twentieths of the women of England earn their bread, and in which he prescribes the function of women to dress well and look pretty, as an adornment to the homes of men.'

Again, this would have had a scandalous impact had it come out soon after she wrote it, and their dispute would have been more public. However, by the time it was published, both had died – Dickens having been elevated to legendary status and buried in Westminster Abbey, and Harriet in an obscure family grave in Birmingham.

In recent years there has been much analysis of Dickens's treatment of women. Martineau was ahead of her time in suggesting that the great author was perhaps not so great in accepting intellectual women, and that his portrayals of women were not progressive in general. Patricia Ingham has written that Dickens's novels contain five female stereotypes, consistently deployed: the excessive female, the true mother, the nubile girl, the fallen girl and the passionate woman. Gaby Weiner concluded a paper on the Martineau disagreements by suggesting he had a: '... bullying characteristic – the resort to ridicule and humiliation when facing obstruction from a woman, be it unwanted wife or critical colleague – which reveals his actual rather than professed position on women and their place in Victorian society.[6]

In 1858 Dickens publicly announced his separation from his wife, and Martineau, again anticipating feminist analysis which would become prevalent 100 years later, wrote to Henry Bright:

> About the Dickens case... I am not so wholly confounded at this manifestation as many people are. I mean that I always, from the observation of a long life, distrust such an amount of sentimentality, combined with self love in the husband, as has always existed in the Dickens household. Moreover, amidst it all, he openly and thoroughly regarded his wife as 'his woman'; provided another to take care of the children & walk with him, when Mrs Dickens was unable – which she usually was – chose her to dress in black velvet, & sit at her embroidery, at leisure for him.

Martineau moves from a complaint about Dickens's vain approach to his wife to his disdain for her role as mother to their children:

> After this sort of life, – now, when she has borne him above a dozen children (9 living) & the time for collapse has come from exhaustion, indifference, indolence, is she to be turned adrift... if she does not take to the bottle, or to suicide, she will show that she has some strength.

Dickens was covering up the fact that he had fallen in love with a much younger woman, Ellen Ternan. Recent biographies of him have revealed the extent of his duplicity, showing that he actually moved in with Ternan, organised his speaking tours around the country so as to be able to see her, and ultimately burnt all their correspondence so as to not cause scandal.

Claire Tomalin, in her biography of Dickens, summarises his behaviour during this period:

> He was ready to be cruel to his defenceless wife. A raging anger broke out at any opposition to his wishes. He used lies as weapons of attack and defence. His displays of self-righteousness were shocking. He was determined to be in the right about everything. He must have known he was not, but he had lost his judgement. The specta-

6. Gaby Weiner, 'Puncturing the Image: Harriet Martineau, Charles Dickens, Gender and Power', *Martineau Society Newsletter*, 32 (2012), p. 17.

cle of a man famous for his goodness and his attachment to domestic virtues suddenly losing his moral compass is dismaying.[7]

Dickens issued a statement about the end of his marriage in *Household Words*. There was of course no mention of his affair with the younger actress. He also fell out with his publishers Bradbury and Evans over this, and they fired him. One of the partners, Frederick Evans, visited Martineau in Ambleside and one can only envisage a good session of considerable spite aimed at Dickens, between the aggrieved author and the embittered publisher. Martineau's account of this meeting to Fanny Wedgwood has been used as evidence of Dickens's poor behaviour in his marriage, as shown here in Michael Slater's biography:

> The most dramatic account of the Dickenses' marital discord at this time is to be found in a letter of Harriet Martineau's, written to her friend, Fanny Wedgwood, on 20 October 1860. Miss Martineau's source was Dickens's ex-publisher Frederick Evans of Bradbury and Evans, who had just been visiting her. He told her that he and even W. H. Wills, Dickens's 'worshipper', 'had for 2 years declined their annual visit to D's country house, because they 'could not stand his cruelty to his wife'. I asked what 'cruelty' meant; and he said 'Swearing at her in the presence of guests, children and servants;' – swearing often and fiercely. He is downright 'ferocious' now, and has quarrelled with almost every friend he had. Next to him, Forster behaved worst, – aggravating his discontent with his wife, who 'is not the sort of woman they say', Mr E declares. Dickens had terrified and depressed her into a dull condition; and she never was very clever...

One final, albeit futile, snipe back at Dickens by both Martineau and his embittered publishers came the following year, in 1861, when Bradbury & Evans published Martineau's '*Health, Husbandry and Handicraft*', a detailed look at good working practice and a fulsome tribute by the author towards the innovation and skilled small factories of Birmingham's developing Jewelry Quarter. This was a factual analysis of British industry that ran counter to what she regarded as Dickens's exaggerated stories.

Dickens and his attitude to women has been much debated by academics but has done little to slow down the global spread of affection for his books. Cer-

7. Claire Tomalin, *Charles Dickens: A Life* (Viking, 2011), p. 293.

tainly at the time when his disputes with Martineau occurred, and later at the end of his marriage, he was at the peak of his powers as a novelist. The production in the 1850s of *Bleak House, Little Dorrit, Hard Times, A Tale of Two Cities* and *Great Expectations*, all masterpieces of layered and vivid storytelling and brought to life with luminous prose and memorable characters, overshadow any reservations about his sympathy towards others in his life. Dickens is a big part of a Victorian narrative that has become very powerful, and it can be argued that it is his version of Victoriana which has become prevalent in popular mythology.

Martineau's writing highlighted, in many ways, the real experiences of 19th-century people, but she didn't have the essential, vivid characterisation and turn of phrase for her work to be treasured. Maybe her autobiography gives us as true a picture of 19th-century Britain as anything produced by Dickens.

Chapter 16: Matthew Arnold

The Arnold family were neighbours of Martineau's in Ambleside, although this simple geographic statement captures nothing of the setting. Martineau had designed her new house to look out upon a magisterial Lake District view of fell and forest, which must have sustained her every day. In the distance, halfway up a mountain could be seen Fox How, the Arnolds' house.

When Martineau arrived in the Ambleside district, in 1846, the Arnolds were still living in the shadow of the sudden death of Dr Thomas Arnold, the famous domineering schoolmaster of Rugby School, soon to be immortalised in Thomas Hughes's novel *Tom Brown's Schooldays*. Dr Arnold had rejuvenated Rugby School with moral purpose. His educational aims for the boys were to save their souls first, provide moral development second, and encourage intellectual achievement third. He emphasised religion and the classics, and while including science in the curriculum, he regarded it as secondary to spiritual guidance. National identity and a sense of national duty were also central to the teaching, and he encouraged an Eton-style prefect system in which older children had governance over younger ones. Dr Arnold's influence would be felt at many other private schools around the country, which took heed from the sense of pride at Rugby School and copied his methods. A generation of nationalistic, morally driven men was being produced, who would come to lead the expanding British Empire.

However, Thomas Arnold's influential headmastership was cut short when he collapsed and died of a heart attack, a day before his 47th birthday in 1842. His death left his wife, Mary, with nine children to nurture, all of whom were a continual source of fascination to Martineau, observing from across the valley. Throughout the rest of her life Martineau retained respect and admiration for Mary Arnold, and they regularly visited each other. She also seems to have had a more gossipy friendship with Frances Arnold, Mary's unmarried daughter, who stayed at Fox How by her mother's side and outlived both her mother and Martineau, remaining there until 1923.

An intriguing, lengthy encounter took place between the Arnolds' eldest son, Matthew, and Martineau. Matthew Arnold became well known as a poet in the 1850s, and his career has generally been portrayed as being divided between his young firebrand poetry days and his later, more staid period as an influential schools inspector. The relationship between Martineau and Arnold has often been portrayed as a tetchy one of distrust, summed up by the editor of Arnold's letters who stated that they 'never really liked or approved of each other'[1] and by Martineau's biographer Elizabeth Arbuckle, who argued that it was best described as an 'armed truce'.[2] But a different picture has emerged through the deeper investigation of Valerie Sanders and Arnold biographer Nicholas Murray, who both suggest that, while not overtly friendly, the relationship was for some time characterised by honesty and mutual respect, and that Martineau exerted her typical influence in encouraging Arnold to pursue his own views, write them down and not be overly concerned as to the consequences.

To understand the relationship it is necessary to look at Arnold's later prose writings and his influence on education and dissenting religion in the 1860s and '70s. Arnold has been best remembered for his poetry when, in fact, his later non-fiction writings were innovative, progressive and influential. This later career should definitely not be dismissed; indeed, he continued to write poetry and retained a poet's outlook on life.

Neither Arnold nor Martineau is easy to pigeonhole. Arnold had a free-thinking poet's artistic brain, with some vanity, and a foppish, almost at times dandyish, manner. He relished his time travelling alone in the continental cities of France and Italy, and idolised Wordsworth and Goethe. He was also a devoted family man who wrote to his mother every week of his life, was very committed to his wife, Frances, and became a steady civil servant in his schools' work. He was a man of contradictions.

Twenty years Martineau's junior, Arnold would later recall that one of his most vivid memories as a teenager was having his father read aloud *The Martyr Age of the United States*, published after Harriet's return from America in the late 1830s. As Arnold's father was the renowned orator Dr Arnold of Rugby School, Martineau's words would have resonated around Fox How and into the minds of the Arnold children:

> Let us not, therefore, wait, as it has been the world's custom to wait, for another century to greet the martyrs who stretch out their strong arms to bring down Heaven upon our earth; before they have stripped off care and sorrow with their mortal frame, let us make our reverent congratulations heard over the ocean which divides us from the spiritual potentates of our age.

This overt statement of human rights, which Martineau penned in 1838, would have been startling to young Victorian minds. By the time she moved in across

1. Cecil Y. Lang, Introduction to *The Letters of Matthew Arnold*, ed. Cecil Y. Lang (University of Virginia Press, 1996), p. 95.

2. Elizabeth Arbuckle, 'Introduction', *Harriet Martineau's Letters to Fanny Wedgwood*, ed. Elizabeth Arbuckle (Stanford University Press, 1983) p. XXII.

the fell, eight years later, Matthew Arnold was at Oxford University. He was in his late twenties when he first met her and was already gaining a reputation for his first poems – the poems of a young man who realised that the temptations and energy of youth were at odds with tranquillity and a calm mind:

> Calm's not life's crown, though calm is well
> 'Tis all perhaps which man acquires
> But 'tis not what our youth desires.

He portrays his early scepticism about life after death, and his belief in materialism, which Martineau would have admired, in this summary of life:

> Joy comes and goes, hope ebbs and flows, Life the wave;
> Change doth unknit the tranquil strength of men.
> Love lends life a little grace, a few sad smiles; and then
> Both are laid in one cold place, in the grave.[3]

In November 1850, he was at Fox How to receive the visiting Charlotte Brontë as Martineau marched her guest around the beautiful autumnal scenery. Each of them would later write about this day. Brontë, the newly established author, and Martineau, the established radical, seemed to relish meeting the young poet and the three of them walked to the house of Wordsworth's son-in-law Mr Quillinan and then back to The Knoll, where Martineau happily read from her about-to-be-published atheistic Atkinson letters.

Arnold wrote a letter describing the scene:

> At seven came Miss Martineau and Miss Brontë; talked to Miss Martineau (who blasphemes frightfully) about the prospects of the Church of England, and, wretched man that I am, promised to go and see her cow keeping miracles tomorrow – I, who hardly knows a cow from a sheep... I talked to Miss Brontë (past 30 and plain, with expressive great eyes though) of her curates, of French novels, and her education in a school at Brussels, and sent the lions roaring to their dens.

Meeting two such freethinking, independent-minded women was rare in 1850, and he seems to have valued the experience. However, his more conservative side reared its head three years later in his condemnation of Brontë's novel *Vil-*

---

3. Matthew Arnold, 'A Question' and 'Youth and Calm', in *Selected Poems of Matthew Arnold* (Macmillan & Co, 1910), pp. 8–10.

lette: 'The writer's mind contains nothing but hunger, rebellion and rage and therefore that is all she can, in fact, put into her book... it will be fatal to her in the long run.'

Meanwhile, Martineau performed an abrupt about-turn as regards Arnold's poetry. In private letters she had lavished praise on his early poems and recommended them to others, but as the reviewer for the *Daily News* she was suddenly scathing. One wonders whether some personal neighbourly pique was involved and it is even possible that his mother, Mary, put her up to it, but she reviews his poems as 'trite phrases and illustrations' and goes on to suggest that his character was not suited to being a poet at all, and that he should forthwith give it up as a vocation.

Two years later, in 1855, Arnold would have heard from his mother that Martineau was very ill again and predicting her own passing. By this time Charlotte Brontë had died. In response, Arnold penned the rueful poem 'Haworth Churchyard', published in *Fraser's Magazine* in May 1855, remembering their Ambleside connection five years earlier:

> Four years since, on a mark'd
> Evening, a meeting I saw.
>
> Two friends met there, two fam'd
> Gifted women. The one,
> Brilliant with recent renown,
> Young, unpractis'd, had told
> With a Master's accent her feign'd
> Story of passionate life:
> The other, maturer in fame,
> Earning, she too, her praise
> First in Fiction, had since
> Widen'd her sweep, and survey'd
> History, Politics, Mind.
>
> They met, held converse: they wrote
>
> ...
>
> Behold! The elder, to-day,
> Lies expecting from Death,
> In mortal weakness, a last
> Summons: the younger is dead.

First to the living we pay
Mournful homage: the Muse
Gains not an earth-deafen'd ear.

Hail to the steadfast soul,
Which, unflinching and keen,
Wrought to erase from its depth
Mist, and illusion, and fear!
Hail to the spirit which dar'd
Trust its own thoughts, before yet
Echoed her back by the crowd!
Hail to the courage which gave
Voice to its creed, ere the creed
Won consecration from Time![4]

His evocation in the poem of Martineau as 'a steadfast soul' who 'dared trust her own thoughts' shows that perhaps he had been tempted by her outspokenness against religion. By this time Martineau was the notorious author of *Letters on the Laws of Man's Nature and Development*, which contained her atheistic views; Arnold faced opprobrium in literary circles for this published defence of the heretic and had to defend his poetic advocacy of the ailing radical, as he did in this powerful passage in a letter to his mother:

> I do not mention her creed with the slightest applause, but only her boldness in avowing it. The wants of independence of mind, the shutting their eyes and professing to believe what they do not, the running blindly together in herds, for fear of some obscure danger and horror if they go alone is so eminently a vice of the English, that I cannot but praise a person whose one effort seems to have been to deal perfectly honestly and sincerely with herself, although for the speculations unto which this effort has led her I have not the slightest sympathy. I shall never be found to identify myself with her and her people, but neither shall I join or have the least community of feeling with, her attackers.

This powerful defence of freedom of speech is one that could be well heeded in the modern world. Arnold was moving in literary and establishment circles

---

4. Matthew Arnold, 'Haworth Churchyard', in *The Poems of Matthew Arnold*, ed. Kenneth Allnott (Longman, 1979), p. 422.

in London and the passage betrays the extent to which Martineau was now dismissed by them for her shocking secular reviews. This was 1855, four years before Darwin and Huxley would cause an anti-creationist storm. As for Arnold, his biographer summarises: 'These remarks show that the future author of Culture and Anarchy was beginning to limber up.'[5]

In fact, Martineau recovered from her illness, as we know, and although her movement was now restricted and her reputation diminished, her writing retained a radical edge. Meanwhile, Matthew Arnold became an influential inspector of schools in a growing education system. He was developing his own ideas and began to write long essays, which were widely read, and which often had Martineauesque themes. This was not surprising, as from letters it is possible to discern, in the late 1850s and early 1860s, the two developed a different discourse based on ideas. He would pop into The Knoll if he was visiting Fox How, and they corresponded at length on education, religion, culture and society. In 1862 Martineau wrote to publisher John Chapman: 'Matthew Arnold I think I told you is the most fastidious of men and scholars, met him for dinner and profoundly struck by his power and earnestness.'

In 1860 Martineau and Arnold exchanged letters on education. Arnold had visited Italy and France, and now prepared a report advocating aspects of the French education system that dated back to Napoleonic reforms. He sent the report to Martineau for comment. They agreed on the secularisation of education, but Martineau was characteristically in favour of incentives for results, while Arnold liked the prioritisation of culture and ideas in the French system.

Arnold was working towards his most explicit expression of this in his book *Culture and Anarchy,* in preparation for which he continued to write to Martineau. Tragically, Martineau's side of the correspondence in this period has been lost and the record is dependent on Arnold's letters alone. The general tenor of Arnold's view is more nationalistic: Britain needs to nurture a greater idea of its own culture, in the way that France does, through its education system. He criticises the British middle classes for not advocating 'culture' enough. He also defends Christian teaching, while keeping a level of dissent against too much superstition. In *Culture and Anarchy* he wrote:

> In modern epochs the part of high reason, of ideas, acquires constantly increasing importance in the conduct of the world's affairs. A fine culture is the complement of a high reason, and it is the conjunction of both with character, with energy, that the ideal for men and nations is to be placed.[6]

5. Nicholas Murray, *A Life of Matthew Arnold* (Hodder & Stoughton, 1996), p. 150.

Martineau seems to have replied to his letters advocating less religion and less nationalism and defending the British middle classes for their economic contribution. It prompted her to write two articles for the *Cornhill* magazine in 1864, entitled 'Middle Class Education in England', in which she argued in favour of more scientific education for everyone but pointed out that educating girls, as they were now doing more extensively in America, would have benefits for society:

> ... fitting them for the business of life or as helpers of their parents—as writing a good hand, arithmetic, and book-keeping, and such study of Natural Philosophy and Natural History as will at once make them more sensible women generally, and operate favourably on their special objects, improving their produce, yet such a school as this goes a-begging because parents are unwilling to pay for their daughters' education.

Valerie Sanders has summed up this period of correspondence between Martineau and Matthew Arnold: 'Their mutual argumentativeness was useful to both. Whatever he said on other occasions Arnold thought Martineau was worth trying to win over to his position. He is genuinely anxious to persuade her, and in the process softens his own antagonistic edge.'[7]

They both advocated more science in education, but it is interesting to note that in the 1860s Arnold was also friends with Thomas Carlyle and James Martineau (the latter by now firmly estranged from Harriet), and his own views more firmly chimed with theirs: a Christian nationalism retained within greater materialism and applied scepticism towards traditional religion. However, the work he developed in the 1860s, under the influence of Harriet, should not be easily dismissed. His advocacy of culture was to become an important part of the liberal world view, its importance in reinforcing reason and identity an accepted part of the coming left-wing movements in the 20th century. In the later 1860s, Arnold became more conservative and chose Disraeli over Gladstone. In one letter to his mother, praising the Conservatives, he muses: 'Now I have said enough to drive Miss Martineau stark mad.'

Matthew Arnold's life took a dramatic turn in 1868 with the deaths of two of his sons. His youngest son, Basil, died of fever in January, but worse was to follow when his eldest son, Thomas, died in November, aged 16, after a bad fall. The records of these untimely deaths in Arnold's letters is heartbreaking.

---

6. Matthew Arnold, *Culture and Anarchy and Other Selected Prose* (Penguin Classics, 2015), p. 217.
7. Valerie Sanders, 'Harriet Martineau and the Arnolds', *Martineau Society Newsletter*, 23 (2007), p. 4.

Martineau wrote to Fox How to say she felt the tragedy 'unspeakably'. Arnold was to lose another son in 1872 and his life was never quite the same. He greatly valued the time spent with his remaining children, and began to resent the travelling involved in inspecting schools. He became more conservative, intellectually and religiously, and his contact with Martineau did not continue. On her death, he described her to a correspondent as having 'an unpleasant nature'.

This unfortunate end to the relationship has led biographers to dismiss it as a troublesome one when, in fact, Arnold was getting older and becoming distanced from his more radical earlier self. As his own religious feeling became reinforced he no longer pursued an association with the notorious atheist. The Martineau–Arnold discourse is fascinating, being so representative as it is over Victorian tensions. Both were progressive and valued education, science, reason and culture, but both came up against the disapproval of the Christian establishment. Martineau was more defiant and radical; Arnold more in tune with 'Victorian' values and better connected.

Chapter 17: Charlotte Brontë

Harriet Martineau and Charlotte Brontë had a short but dramatic friendship between 1849 and 1853.

Brontë's novel *Jane Eyre* had been presented to the world to some literary acclaim in 1846, under her male pen name of Currer Bell, and was gaining word-of-mouth momentum. Martineau read and admired it, and sought to find out more about its author. For Brontë, *Deerbrook* had had a profound effect on her life in the previous decade, snapping her out of problems with her first novel attempts and moving her towards a different type of more revelatory, confessional writing. Martineau was the primary female author in Britain at the time. They were keen to meet each other.

The 'Currer Bell' pseudonym was a serious business: even Brontë's publishers did not know the real identity of the author of their hit *Jane Eyre*. In 1847 speculation became intense in London with the publication of Charlotte's sister Emily's *Wuthering Heights,* published under the pseudonym Ellis Bell, a book that caused consternation at the time for its emotional nature and sexual tension. Then their sister Anne added to the confusion by writing *The Tenant of Wildfell Hall* as the third Bell brother, Acton. The rumour in London was that the Bell brothers were one and the same woman. Some even suggested that it was Martineau who was penning these passionate novels. Amazingly, the Brontës were not known as authors – not even to their father living in the same house, nor to anyone else around them. It was an extraordinary period of focused, private creativity from three sisters in their remote Yorkshire parsonage in Haworth, something which has intrigued readers ever since.

The sisters resolved to reveal themselves to their publisher. Charlotte and Anne walked several miles in the rain to Keighley train station, headed to London and turned up unannounced at Smith and Elder Publications on Cornhill, much to the confusion of the young publisher, George Smith. When disclosing their true identities to Smith and Elder, they made it clear that they did not yet wish to be publicly exposed. Charlotte, in particular, made a connection with George Smith, who had been encouraging them from afar in London, and he proceeded to show the sisters around town without letting on who they were.

A few months later 'Currer Bell' was at a private gathering near Westbourne Place, when she spotted the ear trumpet that she realised signalled the presence of the distinguished author Harriet Martineau. She asked Martineau what she thought of *Jane Eyre* by Currer Bell and Harriet replied, 'I thought it a first rate book. I have ever observed that it is to the coarse minded alone that *Jane Eyre* is coarse.' Charlotte blushed and later remarked to her friend Mary Taylor that Martineau 'had no bump of secretiveness at all' but she was worried about whether she could confide in her, as how could one loudly confide 'the spirit' into an ear trumpet?[1]

In the same month, Charlotte sent a copy of her new novel *Shirley* to Martineau at The Knoll, keeping up the 'Currer Bell' cover although with a comic aspect as in her note she crossed out the word 'she' to replace it with 'he':

> Currer Bell offers a copy of 'Shirley' to Miss Martineau's acceptance, in acknowledgement of the pleasure and profit ~~she~~ he has derived from her works. When C.B. first read 'Deerbrook' he tasted a new and keen pleasure, and experienced a genuine benefit in his mind. 'Deerbrook' ranks with the writings that have really done him good, added to his stock of ideas, and rectified his views of life.[2]

An official introduction was set up in London at the home of one of Martineau's cousins. The encounter was later recorded in Elizabeth Gaskell's biography *The Life of Charlotte Brontë*, still with something of a comic element as to the gender of Currer Bell:

> Miss Martineau had invited the unknown Currer Bell to their early tea. They were ignorant whether the name was that of a man or a woman; and had had conjectures as to sex, age, and appearance. At every ring the eyes of the party turned towards the door. Some stranger (a gentleman I think) came in; for an instant they fancied, Currer Bell; he stayed sometime and went away. Another ring; Miss Brontë was announced and in came a young looking lady almost child-like in stature. She came, hesitated one moment, then went straight to Miss Martineau with intuitive recognition... a foundation was laid for her intimacy with Miss Martineau.[3]

Claire Harman, in her 2015 biography of Brontë, suggests that the meeting was eventually relaxed and mutually beneficial:

> Charlotte did reveal her real name but the Martineaus were sworn to keep it secret, and Charlotte must have been pleased with them

1. Lyndall Gordon, *Charlotte Bronte: A Passionate Life* (Hachette, 2008), p. 240.
2. Charlotte Bronte, quoted in Deborah Logan, *The Hour and the Woman* (Northern Illinois University Press, 2002), p. 193.
3. Elizabeth Gaskell, *The Life of Charlotte Bronte* (Penguin Classics, 1997), p. 337.

and with the frisson her dramatic arrival caused, for she relaxed and was able to talk to them very naturally. 'She was so pleasant and so naïve, that is to say so innocent and un-Londony that we were quite charmed with her' one of Martineau's cousins said.[4]

But 1850 was a very sensitive time for Charlotte Brontë. Her beloved sister Anne had died six months earlier, following the tragic death of Emily the previous year, both women having succumbed to bouts of consumption. Charlotte threw herself into a period of writing, in which she produced *Shirley*, and she was now emerging from this dark phase and looking for a sympathetic ear. This she found in her continued connection with George Smith, whose family she stayed with in London and with whom she toured Scotland the following year.

Soon, in appreciative and affectionate correspondence, Brontë and Martineau entered a mutual mentoring period. Martineau invited her new friend to Ambleside, and she stayed at The Knoll for four days in December 1850. Brontë relished the fortitude Martineau exuded and sought her advice on how to deal with reviews and gain confidence in her public persona. A letter by Charlotte, reprinted in the Gaskell biography, gives a vivid portrait of Harriet Martineau as she was at The Knoll at this time:

> I am at Miss Martineau's for a week. Her house is very pleasant both within and without; arranged at all points with admirable neatness and comfort. Her visitors enjoy the most perfect liberty; what she claims for herself she allows them. I rise at my own hour, breakfast alone (she is up at 5, takes a cold bath and a walk by starlight and has finished breakfast and got to her work by 7 o'clock) I pass the morning in the drawing room – she in her study. At 2 o clock we meet – work, talk, and walk together til 5, her dinner hour; spend the evening together, when she converses fluently and abundantly, and with the most complete frankness. I go to my own room soon after 10 – she sits up writing letters til 12. She appears exhaustless in strength and spirits and indefatigable in the faculty of labour. She is a great and good woman; of course not without peculiarities, but I have seen none as yet that annoys me. She is both hard and warm-hearted, abrupt and affectionate, liberal and despotic. I believe she is not at all conscious of her own absolutism. When I tell her of it she denies the charge warmly; then I laugh at her. I believe she almost

---

4. Claire Harman, *Charlotte Bronte: A Life* (Viking, 2015), p. 286.

rules Ambleside. Some of the gentry dislike her, but the lower orders have a great regard for her... I have truly enjoyed my visit here.

Brontë had been reeling from her loneliness and the mixed reception to *Shirley*, and both George Smith and Martineau gave her important succour at this time. Lyndall Gordon, in her biography of Brontë, describes the effect: 'With relief she returned to the unconventional company of Harriet Martineau; harsh she was, abrupt, despotic, but invigorating too, a model of industry... They discussed work with frankness. In this bracing atmosphere, her guest soon recovered.'

There was, though, a looming cloud hanging over the relationship. On the death of her siblings Brontë had taken refuge in her faith, and Harriet's newly professed atheism – which Charlotte must have observed first-hand when Martineau was preparing the Atkinson letters for publication – was not easy for her to stomach. On their publication she wrote to James Taylor, the managing clerk of her publishers. The letter says much about the shock which this publication caused in literary circles:

> Have you read Miss Martineau's and Mr Atkinson's new work... It is the first exposition of avowed Atheism and Materialism I have ever read; the first unequivocal declaration of disbelief in the existence of a God or a Future Life – I have ever seen... The strangest thing is that we are called on to rejoice over this hopeless blank... to welcome this unutterable desolation as a state of pleasant freedom. Who could do this if he would? Who would do it if he could? ... If this be truth – Man or Woman who beholds her can but curse the day he or she was born.[5]

When the *Letters on the Laws of Man's Nature and Development* were published later in 1851, Brontë was one of many a Martineau acquaintance who kept up a veneer of friendship with and admiration of her but who, in private correspondence, was shocked and dismayed by this secular work. However, it is interesting to note that, despite the tension in the friendship and a fundamental difference in religious opinion between these two great writers, they still had one profound thing in common.

Martineau's important point in the Atkinson letters was that the mind was within nature – part of our natural make-up – and the unconscious was an extension of the physical material world. Brontë herself would be acclaimed in

5. Juliet Barker, *The Brontës: A Life in Letters* (Little, Brown, 2016), p. 312.

the 20th century for her internalised confessional writing style and her exposition of the unconscious, which paved the way for modernist self-conscious literature and greater self-awareness. It may sound unlikely, but these two women were pioneers of the unconscious; they were both exploring the inner world that previously had been assumed to be proof of an external guiding force. Both were well ahead of their time; perhaps they were a product of their relatively isolated lives led in separate parts of northern England.

Through 1851 the friendship remained intact, but it began to come under strain with the arrival of Martineau's next work, *Oliver Weld*. Martineau had by now resolved to translate the works of Auguste Comte but delayed this work in order to write a new novel, having been encouraged to do so by Brontë and George Smith. The two younger sparks encouraged the fifty-year-old author to revive her fiction career with a follow-up to *Deerbrook*, a novel that they had both previously admired. Martineau recorded the incident in her autobiography:

> The notion of trying my hand once more at a novel seized upon me. I wrote to Charlotte Brontë, to consult her as to the possibility... She wrote joyously about it and at once engaged her publisher's (George Smith) interest... I doubted from the first whether I could ever again succeed in fiction... I let my pen go as it would when the general plan of the story, and the principal scenes, were one laid down. At Christmas I sent the first volume to Charlotte Brontë... She wrote gloriously about it but three days later came a pathetic letter from the publisher... He implored me to lay aside this scheme and send him a novel 'like Deerbrook'. That was no more in my power now than to go back to thirty years of age. (Brontë entreated me to lay aside my novel saying that some things in it were equal to, or beyond, anything I had ever written.) I did intend at first to finish it but other works pressed, the stimulus and conception has passed away, and I burned the manuscript.

The plot thickens when we see the correspondence between Brontë and Smith on this matter, and the letters from Charlotte to Harriet. Brontë was a little sceptical to Smith: 'Perhaps the nature and bent of her genius hardly warrant the expectation of first class excellence in fiction,' she wrote. And later:

> She is in fine spirits now, and they may last to the end, this enabling her to achieve a great work, but she may also be seeing things a little

too much under the rose coloured light of an excited imagination. There is something about her, very buoyant and difficult to subdue.[6]

Martineau suggested to Smith she should publish under the name 'Peter Murray' and the novel should be called *Oliver Weld*. The intrigue grows considerably when we read Smith's later description of the book. It was a futuristic, prophetic novel, portraying a scene in 1950 – imagining 100 years in the future when cities have grown considerably, so much so that the countryside has become harsh and wild. A love story ensues between a city woman and a wild man in the country, as Smith explains:

> Harriet Martineau's novel was a very surprising production. It was an experiment in what may be called prophetic fiction. The scene was laid a hundred years hence, and the story was intended to give a picture of England in those days. The England of 1950, according to Miss Martineau's forecast, will offer a spectacle of idle and desolate fields, spotted over with crowded and strongly fortified towns. The scanty inhabitants of the open country will be small droves of wild men and women, living in huts made of boughs of trees, and hunted like wild beasts by the townspeople. In the England of to-morrow, in brief, the towns will eat up and destroy the county. There was, of course, a love-plot in the story; it consisted of tender relations betwixt a town-maiden and a handsome wild man in the wilderness outside the towns. The novel, it is scarcely necessary to add, was never printed: but Harriet Martineau, in writing it, intended to describe what in her judgment, was the inevitable and near future of these islands![7]

Brontë had written to Smith:

> I feared you would be disappointed with 'Oliver Weld' when you read it, though I had not calculated on its proving so obnoxious in a business point of view as you seem to anticipate. I did not like to tell you how great was my own surprise on perusing the manuscript.

Smith had been expecting another soothing novel about the social mores of a country parson and what he got was one of the world's first science-fiction nov-

---

6. Charlotte Bronte, Letter to George Smith, November 1851, in *The Brontes, Their Lives, Friendship and Correspondence*, Vol. 3, ed. Thomas James Wise and John Alexander Symington (Shakespeare Head Press, 1932), p. 293.

7. From an unpublished, typewritten copy of George Smith's 'Recollections of a long and busy life' written circa 1895, retained in the papers of George Smith (National Library of Scotland) MS 23191.

els. Mary Shelley had written the brilliant *Frankenstein* 30 years earlier but books predicting dystopian future societies were unheard of. One can only guess how its publication would have affected Martineau's career. This was 1850 – a long time before H. G. Wells startled the world with his prophetic fiction.

In January 1852, Brontë wrote to Martineau on behalf of Smith in a brave attempt to let her down gently:

> What Mr Smith wanted and expected was another 'Deerbrook'. *Deerbrook* made you beloved wherever it was read. 'Oliver Weld' will not have this effect. It is powerful, it is vivid, it must strike but it will rarely please. Better the highest part of what is in your own self than all the political and religious controversy in the world. Rest a little while; consider the matter over, and see whether you have not another *Deerbrook* in your heart to give England.

Smith's conservative approach had stymied the adventurous spirit of the two authors. Brontë's concern about 'religious controversy' would not have concerned Martineau as she was already embroiled in those arguments. No doubt mortified by this lack of enthusiasm for her radical new writing, Martineau burnt the novel at this point. Three weeks later Brontë wrote to Smith: 'I have not heard a word from Miss Martineau and conclude her silence is of no good omen.'

And indeed, it wasn't a good omen. Martineau, presumably embarrassed and hurt, threw herself into her translation of Auguste Comte, while Brontë produced her next novel, *Villette*, published by Smith at the end of 1852. In January 1853, Martineau, by now writing for the *Daily News*, wrote her review of *Villette* for the widely circulated newspaper. It is hard to tell if this was revenge for the *Oliver Weld* episode, but it was a cutting, negative review which complained of the novel's anti-Catholicism (something that Smith had accused Martineau of in *Oliver Weld*) and its adverse effect on the reader: 'the author has no right to make readers so miserable'. In a passage that has been of interest to feminist historians ever since, Martineau criticised Brontë for her portrayal of women in general: 'There are substantial, heartfelt interests for women of all ages, quite apart from love; there is an absence of introspection, an unconsciousness, a repose in women's lives of which we find no admission in this book.'

Martineau was obviously thinking of herself and many who would come after, presaging many a modern feminist debate proposing that women should not be defined by their search for love. Brontë, who outlined this passage in red on her copy of the review, was hurt. She wrote to Martineau:

I protest against this passage and were I brought up before the bar of all the critics in England to such a charge I should respond 'Not guilty'. I know what love is as I understand it; and if man or woman should be ashamed of feeling such love, then there is nothing right, noble, faithful, truthful, unselfish in this earth, as I comprehend rectitude, nobleness, fidelity, truth and disinterestedness... To differ from you gives me great pain.

She confided to Smith that to see Martineau now would be 'perilous and inadvisable', and elsewhere she writes that she wished that they had never met. A further sorrow is that by this time Brontë's romantic friendship with George Smith was not progressing as he was in London working hard to keep the firm afloat.

Brontë and Martineau's friendship had broken down and would not recover. Charlotte married her neighbour, the highly religious Arthur Nicholl, and became pregnant, but in March 1855 she caught typhoid and died, aged 38, at her house in Haworth. This was a cause of great regret to Martineau. who wrote to Fanny Wedgwood that she was sure they could have 're-established a fuller sympathy'. In an obituary for the *Daily News* she wrote that Brontë was a 'gifted creature whose steady conviction was that the publication of a book is a solemn act of conscience... in addition to the deep intuitions of a gifted woman, she had the patience of a hero and the conscientiousness of a saint'.

On Brontë's side, while she had written of her dismay at Martineau's atheism, she also defended her in correspondence:

I find a worth and greatness in herself, and a consistency, benevolence, perseverance in her practise such as wins the sincerest esteem and affection. She is not a person to be judged by her writings alone, but rather by her own deeds and life – of which nothing can be more exemplary or nobler... Faults she has, but to me they appear very trivial weighed in the balance against her excellencies.

Had she lived, Brontë would no doubt have been open to a reconciliation, and the two women would probably have resumed their mutually supportive relationship. There was, however, to be an unfortunate postscript to Brontë's death; in talks with Mrs Gaskell about producing a biography of Charlotte, some of her private briefings against Martineau's atheism came to light, leading Harriet to write bitterly to Rev. Graves in 1857: 'I say with sorrow that I have long since ceased to consider C. Brontë truthful.' In addition, there was also a later vitriolic correspondence between Martineau and Brontë's devoutly religious father, arguing over the character and integrity of Charlotte, letters which Harriet described as 'vicious'.

Despite her protestations otherwise, Martineau was very sensitive to criticism. Her friendship with Charlotte Brontë is testament to this, both in the response to her 'prophetic novel' and also the condemnation of her atheism. Brontë, too, found disapproval hard to take, and Martineau's cutting review of *Villette* was a slight she couldn't forgive. However, here were two great pioneering intrepid writers pushing, fortifying and encouraging each other to be fearless and radical in their own important ways, even within their reproaches and criticisms. If only George Smith had summoned the courage to publish *Oliver Weld*.

Chapter 18: Elizabeth Gaskell

Harriet Martineau and Elizabeth Gaskell had much in common and shared a circle of family and acquaintances. Gaskell was a cousin of Harriet's close friend Fanny Wedgwood, and cousin-in-law to the Darwins. They shared a Unitarian upbringing, sense of duty and way of life; they were both pioneers of fiction for social improvement; they both worked tirelessly for causes such as women's education and the abolition of slavery; both idolised Wordsworth from a young age and inherited the great poet's love of travel and nature; both wrote for Charles Dickens's *Household Words*, despite their frustration with him; both consistently requested that their letters to others be destroyed; both had close connections with Charlotte Brontë and George Eliot, and disapproved of the latter's elopement with married writer and intellectual George Henry Lewes; and both were signatories to the first legislation concerning women's rights in the 1850s.

And yet there was a curious distance and coldness between Gaskell and Martineau. They only rarely corresponded and even then purely on matters of fact. They had little personal contact, meeting only on a handful of occasions. Certainly, for pioneering writers campaigning for a better society, there is very little camaraderie or support between the two. However, it is also the case that they never really fell out (although they came close to it), and they retained a mutual respect up until Gaskell's sudden death in 1865.

Mrs Gaskell, as she would popularly be known, presumably to give her an aura of respectability, kept up her Unitarianism just as Martineau turned her back on it in the 1850s. Moreover, Gaskell, while supporting initial parliamentary initiatives in the 1850s, retained a more conservative view of the role of women. Despite producing some striking storylines and characters addressing women's issues in her novels, she did not go as far as others in demanding greater freedom. Martineau was eight years older and blazed a trail which was more radical and fearless, but which would ultimately lead to an obsolete reputation, while the more respectable Gaskell would be well-remembered for her fiction.

When Martineau was recovering from her lengthy illness in 1846 and preparing to leave Tynemouth for the Lake District, Elizabeth Stevenson was now the mother of four young children in Manchester, having married a Unitarian minister, William Gaskell. She was an active reader and we know that she had recently read and admired Harriet's *Deerbrook* and *The Hour and the Man*.

She wrote to her sister-in-law Nancy Robson that she found Martineau's char-acterisation and conversation interesting, but writes of *The Hour and the Man*: 'One knows all along how it must end.'[1]

Mrs Gaskell was a doting mother, who was constantly concerned that her children should avoid infection. In a note of instruction to a nanny in 1846 she wrote: '*Please* don't let them come into contact with the Martineau children. You need not ask why but please *don't*.'[2] This must be a reference to the recent death of young Herbert Martineau, the son of James, who had died in his father's arms of typhoid that year, much to the hurt of Harriet, who felt that James should have tried her mesmeric cure on the child. Elizabeth was most worried about her daughter Marianne, and she took her and their infant son Willie to what she thought would be a typhoid infection-free retreat in Snow-donia. Unfortunately, young Marianne nevertheless fell ill with scarlet fever, but after a ten-day crisis, she pulled through, convalescing in Portmadoc. To Elizabeth's horror, however, Willie began to show alarming infection symp-toms and, too small to put up any resistance, he died on 10 August, 1846.

This tragedy threw Mrs Gaskell into a depression which lasted nearly a year, but the needs of her three remaining daughters drew her out of it, as did her husband's suggestion that she try her hand at writing some fiction. Indeed, much of her early fiction concerns young children dying, her own real expe-rience leading her to write vivid scenes that would resonate with parents both then and now. In 1848, *Mary Barton: A Tale of Manchester Life* was published. Elizabeth had experienced close contact with the changing social conditions of an increasingly industrialised Manchester through the work of her husband, who was minister at the Cross Street Unitarian Chapel, and she helped to dis-tribute soup and clothes to the poor. She wrote her observations every day and of a desire to expose the effects of growing inequality in industrialised Man-chester. The novel received good reviews in several journals including one from Thomas Carlyle.

Mrs Gaskell soon became involved with literary circles in London and, in 1849, met Dickens, John Forster and the Carlyles. Indeed, she had been born on Cheyne Walk some 40 years earlier, near the Carlyle residence, only to be sent as an infant to live with her aunt when her mother suddenly died. She recon-nected with her Wedgwood cousins and soon after visited the Lake District where she stayed at Fox How and met Wordsworth, almost certainly recon-necting with Martineau too. Jenny Uglow, in her biography of Gaskell, pre-

---

1. Elizabeth Gaskell, as quoted in Arthur Pollard, *Mrs. Gaskell* (University of Manchester Press, 1965), p. 25.

2. Elizabeth Gaskell, as quoted in J.A.V. Chapple, *Elizabeth Gaskell: A Portrait in Letters* (Manchester University Press, 1980), p. 34.

sents this period as one of great spiritual speculation and discussion, of which these two women were now a part:

> The intensity of contemporary arguments about belief, all taking place within the same small circles and communities, is hard to convey today. In July 1849 Harriet Martineau looked in amazement, for instance, at the residents and tourists gathered around Ambleside, marveling at: 'the diversities of faith within our valley! Let us see, We have High Church, Low Church and Middle Church families; Catholics, both in and out of communion; Independents, Unitarians, Quakers, Swedenborgians, Wesleyans, Plymouth Brethren, and some who belong to no Christian sect at all.'

Elizabeth's slightly standoffish stance with Martineau can begin to be explained by a comment Uglow reports from this time. Intrigued by mesmerism, but wary, Gaskell wrote to a friend: 'I have rather a dread of it altogether, I think because I have a feeling that it twisted Miss Martineau's mind.'

Martineau already had a reputation for taking the materialist view emanating from science further than others, and suggesting that religion should be forsworn. Even her description of the different faiths in the neighbourhood suggests she already saw religion as a man-made construct that simply varied from place to place. To many in their circle it seemed that she was indeed 'twisted'.

Gaskell didn't shy away from controversy in her writing, however. *Mary Barton* was very critical of factory owners and the rich; subsequently she came in for some disapproval locally in Manchester. Uglow suggests Gaskell may have had Martineau in mind when she wrote in the preface, 'I know nothing of political economy'. She was a recorder of the effects of economic policy on towns and cities but didn't have an interest in the economic theory. Martineau may have provided her with a great example of a woman writer but Gaskell was distancing herself from the analytical and secular views emanating from Ambleside.

When Dickens founded *Household Words* he wanted women writers. He commissioned Martineau, who must have been somewhat like the old soldier, and recruited Gaskell as the new kid on the block – very much *his* block. One of the first pieces she wrote for Dickens may have had the Martineaus in mind as it was entitled, 'Traits and Stories of the Huguenots'. Soon she was producing the episodic *Cranford* for *Household Words* about the effects of a small bank on a

3. Jenny Uglow, *Elizabeth Gaskell* (Faber & Faber, 1993), p. 231.

small town, as seen through the eyes of a group of productive women. *Cranford* quickly gained a reputation and was avidly followed by readers. These stories also centred on the arrival of a doctor into a small town, a storyline surely taken directly from Martineau's *Deerbrook*, and yet in Gaskell's hands told with much greater wit and warmth.

Both Martineau and Gaskell became friendly with the newly famous Charlotte Brontë in 1850, though the latter soon became wary of Martineau's atheistic opinions, and found Gaskell's views chimed more closely with her own. They became firm friends, visiting each other several times in the early 1850s, although it seems that Brontë's marriage to the strict Anglican Nicholls curtailed the visits.

Gaskell was by now writing her next novel *Ruth*. Mrs Gaskell's modern reputation is not one associated with controversy but *Ruth* caused a minor scandal when it was published anonymously. It tells the story of a 15-year-old seamstress who is seduced by an employer and has his illegitimate child. She is rescued by a Unitarian minister (Mr Benson) who takes her in, but she is soon exposed, causing a scandal. She finds redemption as a nurse in a fever epidemic and dies a martyr. Reviews were openly hostile and copies were publicly burnt. Martineau wrote to Fanny Wedgwood, unaware that *Ruth* had been written by Fanny's cousin Gaskell:

> I hope some woman will arise who, with power like, or equal to Charlotte Brontë's, will bring us up to high art again – 'Ruth' won't help us. All strewn with beauties as it is, it is sadly feeble and wrong, I think. Amidst much wrong, I think making Mr Benson such a nincompoop is fatal... What a beautiful 'Cranford' Mrs Gaskell has given us again!

Gaskell's work had Unitarianism running right through it, and this is both a strength and a weakness. As Uglow summarises she doesn't avoid controversy but 'she elevates sympathy and communication above radical change.'[4] Both Gaskell and Martineau were infused with the Unitarian duty to do something in the face of those struggling through life, but they chose to express it in different ways. Martineau's approach was to change the system or to free the individual up for human nature, initiative and drive to have effect. Gaskell, in tune with Elizabeth Fry, Charles Dickens and many others, was to hold out a hand of sympathy to the poor. Arthur Pollard in his 1965 biography of Gaskell observed

---

4. Jenny Uglow, 'Gaskell, Elizabeth Cleghorn (1810–1865)', *Oxford Dictionary of National Biography*, ed. Professor Sir David Cannadine (Oxford University Press, 2004), p. 604.

the distinction in relation to the writing of *Mary Barton*: 'Mrs Gaskell saw the whole matter not as a question of economics but of morality and even religion. It is thus that Mary Barton differs so obviously from work such as Harriet Martineau's... The book's imaginative energy is nourished on close experience, deep sincerity and immense compassion.'

This distinction can also be observed in the growing ideological differences between James and Harriet Martineau in the late 1840s and early '50s, Gaskell being close to this divide. James was advocating a Unitarian theology which emphasised emotion, and maintained that internal conscience was a good guide to life and wasn't in conflict with reason. Harriet was more interested in evidence and around this time responded to a query about the best approach: 'Use evidence with benevolence,' was her reply. This presages 20th-century debates within the philosophy of science about the relevance of experience and intuition versus cold, hard evidence-based facts. In her writing Gaskell fell on the side of James Martineau, for emotion and compassion, as indeed did Dickens who grew wary of over-analysis.

In March 1855 Charlotte Brontë died. By now Harriet had been through the scandal of the Atkinson letters and had fallen out with Brontë over the review of *Villette*. Many people in the wider Unitarian circles they shared had turned away from Harriet, and certainly Elizabeth may have felt that James Martineau's review, castigating the 'mesmeric atheism', represented well the views of Unitarians, a community within which she and her husband were well known.

The three-way authorial relationship between Elizabeth Gaskell, Charlotte Brontë and Harriet Martineau had become quite intense and would continue to play out as Gaskell was charged with writing a biography of Brontë. Charlotte's widower, Nicholls, and her domineering father, Patrick Brontë, were on one side, and Martineau on the other, with Gaskell in between: it very quickly descended into a war of words. Martineau wrote to their mutual friend Monckton Milnes, in July 1855:

> Mr Brontë and Mr Nicholls beg her to write a life of 'Currer' & the old gent sends her 'facts' which appear to her & me as irreconcilable with what 'Currer' told us. Mrs G comes here (stays at Fox How) to learn all I can tell her & compare letters & consult.

Martineau handed over letters and reported the visit from Gaskell, which ended with hugs and tears. However, when Martineau wrote of it later, to Fanny Wedgwood's daughter Julia (known as Snow), she added a caustic follow-up:

Mrs G is bound by her professed principles [Unitarianism] to consider the publication of that book [the Atkinson letters] and every other of deliberate and express speculation, a laudable act, – I repeat, it is only for her own sake that this matters; ... I admire the book [the Brontë biography] – the doing of it, – so much! I shall make myself easy – well knowing the lady, and having been consulted and concerned in it – she came over on purpose, you know, to consult with me, and see and hear what I could give her. She covered us all with kisses and wept when she went away, and asked, as the greatest favour, that she might write occasionally, to tell me how she went on. She never wrote a line, nor even sent me a copy!

Snow had worked with Mrs Gaskell's daughter, Meta, to annotate Brontë's letters for the biography and Harriet would have known that this comment would reach Elizabeth. By then the first edition had come out and had been threatened with several lawsuits, mainly from William Carus Wilson from Cowan Bridge School, whom Gaskell had portrayed as partly responsible for the deaths of Anne and Emily Brontë. Copies were withdrawn and apologies issued in *The Times*. For her part, Martineau didn't sue but she wasn't happy. In the Brontë biography, Gaskell had written:

I suspect that the disappointment arose from the great susceptibility to an opinion she valued much – that of Miss Martineau, who both in an article on 'Villette' in the Daily News and in a private letter to Miss Brontë, wounded her to the quick by expressions of censure which she believed to be unjust and unfounded, but which, if correct and true, went deeper than any merely artistic fault.

Then, explaining that an author is very sensitive to the views of another author, she concluded: 'Thus, in proportion to her true, firm regard for Miss Martineau, did Miss Brontë suffer under what she considered her misjudgement not merely of writing, but of character.'

Gaskell then suggests it wasn't all Martineau's fault and that the two women had made an agreement to be honest with each other: 'The promise then given of faithful truth-speaking. Miss Martineau fulfilled when 'Villette' appeared. Miss Brontë writhed under what she felt to be injustice... the misunderstanding was the cause of bitter regret to Miss Brontë.' She goes on to transcribe a letter that Charlotte wrote after the falling out, in defence of Martineau to her critics, which ends:

I believe if you were in my place, and knew Miss Martineau as I do, – if you had shared with me the proofs of her genuine kindliness, and had seen how she secretly suffers from abandonment, – you would be the last to give her up; you would separate the sinner from the sin, and feel as if the right lay rather in quietly adhering to herein the strait, while that adherence is unfashionable and unpopular, than in turning on her your back when the world sets the example.

Gaskell concludes the passage in the biography: 'In spite of their short, sorrowful misunderstanding, they were a pair of noble women and faithful friends.'

There is a surfeit of underlying tension portrayed in this exchange of words, and Martineau would have been very sensitive to the published result. Even in the quoted letter at the end, when Charlotte is defending Harriet's right to say what she wants, the words 'sinner' and 'sin' would have leapt off the page as would Gaskell's earlier comment that Brontë had been 'wounded... to the quick' by the review. In reading the book and seeing other Brontë letters, Martineau became convinced that Charlotte had been duplicitous and this led to the war of words with her father and husband. As for Gaskell, Martineau wrote to their mutual acquaintance Susannah Winkworth in June 1857: 'I do mourn that Mrs G ever came in the way of that awful family.'

Then, in November that year, when the dispute with the Brontë men had just about been settled, she wrote to R. P. Graves: 'I fancy these gentlemen (who are not gentlemen however) have never before been opposed or called to account. In their own parish they reign by fear; I hope it may be good for them to find they can be wrong... If only they will now let Mrs Gaskell alone.'

The interaction between Bronte, Gaskell and Martineau in the first half of the 1850s can now be seen to arrive at an evocative time in the history of women in the Western world. These pioneering writers were challenging the entrenched male establishment and the growing industrial money makers. They were utilising an unprecedented opportunity for women to express themselves honestly and earnestly particularly through fiction. However, they had disagreements about how far religion should be challenged and also as regards what was appropriate for women. The two novelists have rightly been widely read and well remembered but both owed a debt to Martineau for setting a clear example of the possibilities.

There would be more correspondence and collaboration between Elizabeth Gaskell and Martineau showing that, despite some differences over the Bronte biography, they didn't fall out. By the late 1850s, Gaskell had sent her daughters to study in Liverpool at the girls' school set up by James and Harriet's older sister Rachel Martineau, where James was a guest teacher, thus confirming their shared Unitarian beliefs, although at this time there was not much choice of education for girls.

In 1859, Gaskell became convinced that George Eliot could not be a woman and believed a rumour that the author of *Adam Bede* was one Joseph Liggins, pretty much based on Liggins standing up in a London restaurant, perhaps having had one too many, and proclaiming himself the author of the novel sweeping the nation. Gaskell wrote to Martineau: 'You heard truly that I have stuck out that I believed a man wrote them. I am shaken now, and should like much to receive your evidence. I would rather they had not been written by Miss Evans.'

Both Martineau and the publisher George Smith had to write to Gaskell before she would believe that Mary Ann Evans was indeed George Eliot. Although her original horror at the prospect may have been driven by jealousy, once convinced, she was magnanimous and wrote to Evans in November 1859: 'I must tell you how earnestly fully and humbly I admire them. I never read anything so complete, and beautiful in fiction, in my whole life before.'

Martineau and Gaskell also collaborated in helping to alleviate the effects of the cotton supply collapse in Manchester caused by the American Civil War. Gaskell did much work with her daughter to arrange for the retraining of cotton factory workers, particularly women, in Manchester, while Martineau wrote about the work in the *Daily News*. They understood the effects of the end of slavery on the cotton industry, and how the Manchester economy still depended on it, and shared a sense of duty to try and do something to alleviate the effect on the poor.

In studying Martineau and Gaskell together we get a good sense of how much their Unitarian creed influenced the whole Victorian progressive movement. One suspects that Harriet was aloof towards Elizabeth because she threatened to move in on her political economy territory, while Elizabeth continued to regard the overt religious scepticism of Harriet as 'twisted'. However, even though Martineau had turned her back on religion, she still felt a duty to make a better society. They shared a belief in the teachings of Hartley and Priestley that society was built by the people in it and the actions you took. This infused not only their writing but also that of Darwin and Dickens, and collectively they influenced the Brontës and George Eliot.

The late 1840s and early '50s are often presented as an oncoming scientific age, when Darwin, Huxley, Hooker, Lyell, Owen and other scientifically minded men established themselves with the arrival of greater technology and industry. The 1870s are seen as representing the 'first wave' of feminism. But between these two periods, the voices of Martineau, Gaskell and the Brontës made a powerful impression on the intellectual scene, supported by determined Unitarian and Quaker women demanding a better world. In the 1850s Martineau and Gaskell did much to encourage women's education, backed by others such as the writer Anna Jameson and campaigner Elisabeth Reid, with Fanny Wedgwood assisting. The power of independent-minded women was beginning.

This work was continued by the daughters of Gaskell and Fanny Wedgwood, and by Mary Carpenter, Rachel Martineau and Frances Lupton (Harriet's niece), along with a new generation who took inspiration from the pioneers. This mid-19th-century change was mirrored in America, and these British pioneering female writers to some extent lit the flame that would spread around the world, and continues to spread now.

Chapter 19: George Eliot

Unlike Currer Bell, the male pseudonym of George Eliot has survived so that the real Mary Ann Evans remains somewhat mysterious. Indeed, it has been said that the great novelist George Eliot was a construct of the partnership between Evans and the writer and intellectual George Henry Lewes, which began when they eloped together in 1854. No doubt Mary Ann had the talent and wrote the words, but 'George Eliot' became a powerful brand for those words and was fiercely protected by Lewes.

Harriet Martineau's period of closeness to Evans came in the years before the elopement, and had some similarities with her brief friendship with Charlotte Brontë around the same time. Like Brontë, Evans came to stay at The Knoll. She admired the older, pioneering author, and all three shared a progressive outlook towards the art of writing. As with Brontë, the friendship ran into trouble over moralities of love and passion. But unlike Brontë, Evans, particularly under the influence of Lewes, was sympathetic towards the materialist secular philosophy Martineau developed. Indeed, Lewes himself had written in support of Comte's Positivism.

Martineau and Evans may have first had contact when Evans was involved with the *Westminster Review* in the late 1840s. Their shared publishing circle included John Chapman and the John Murrays (who had enraged Martineau when they pulled out of publishing her theological travelogue *Eastern Life*). Around this time Chapman decided to buy the *Westminster Review*. He had recently broken off a brief affair with Evans, but hadn't forgotten her literary talent and brought her into the editorial team at the *Review*.

Both Harriet and James Martineau had previously had articles published in the *Westminster Review*; indeed, Harriet's 1839 *The Martyr Age of the United States* was one of the *Review*'s most famous pieces. Mary Ann Evans was an impressionable 20-year-old when it had been published and, like Brontë, had also read and admired *Deerbrook* in the previous year.

Evans was a progressive thinker and a great writer, but she had a romantic weakness for intellectual men. After a failed affair with emerging writer Herbert Spencer, she travelled to Edinburgh in a vulnerable state to stay with the phrenologist George Combe. On the way back she visited Martineau in Ambleside for several days in October 1852.

Within only a few years of being at Ambleside, Martineau had instituted a building society to help provide local people with affordable housing. The two ladies toured the recently built cottages, in which Harriet was proud to have played her part. It was typical of Martineau that she was trying to do something about the already established issue of tourist visitors driving property prices too high for locals.

Evans's stay at The Knoll seemed to do the trick. She was fortified by both the veteran writer's resilience and experience and their bracing walks in the Lake District fells. She wrote to her friends the Brays:

> The coach brought me to Miss Martineau's gate at half past six yesterday evening, and she was there with a beaming face to welcome me. Mr Atkinson joined us this morning, and is a very agreeable addition. There has been an intelligent gentlemen visitor to-day, who is interested in Miss Martineau's building society; and we have been trudging about looking at cottages, and enjoying the sight of the mountains, spite of the rain and mist. The weather is not promising, that is the worst of it. Miss M. is charming in her own home – quite handsome from her animation and intelligence. She came behind me, put her hands round me, and kissed me in the prettiest way this evening, telling me she was so glad she had got me here. I send her note that you may have an idea of 'The Knoll'.[1]

Martineau also wrote in a letter to publisher John Chapman: 'Miss Evans' visit was a vast pleasure... The only drawbacks were wet roads and that she could not stay longer.'

Evans also met Henry Atkinson during her visit and must have passed on the latest thoughts of the phrenologist Combe, as well as having lively, religiously sceptical, discussions. Subsequently she called the *Letters on the Laws of Man's Nature and Development* 'the boldest I have seen in the English language', but she also saw that it would affect Martineau's reputation, saying it was 'studiously offensive'.

The developing friendship between the two pioneering writers was based more on respect than affection, but that respect came under great pressure with the arrival of George Henry Lewes in Evans's life. Introduced to each other by Chapman, the intellectually inquisitive but socially awkward Lewes wasn't initially to Evans's taste, but he gradually won her round. His marriage was foundering and he had moved from the family home into temporary lodgings. Evans began to extricate herself from the *Westminster Review*.

In an unfortunate accident of timing, Martineau and Lewes both produced

---

1. George Eliot, 'To the Brays', in *The Letters of George Eliot*, ed. R. Brimley Johnson (Bodley Head, 1926), p. 76.

books promoting Auguste Comte and ended up in competition during 1853. T. H. Huxley reviewed Martineau's contribution for the *Westminster Review* very favourably but criticised the Lewes book. Evans inevitably took the side of her new beau and tried to get Chapman not to run the review, but he insisted on editorial impartiality and published the review anyway.

This was a few years before the arrival on the public stage of 'George Eliot', in the late 1850s, with *Adam Bede* and *The Mill on the Floss*. However, the elopement to Germany of Evans and Lewes caused a scandal in literary circles, and certainly Martineau wasn't impressed. To this group, Lewes was a married man with children, and he was deserting them for a flirtation with a younger woman. Evans's own brother didn't speak to her again, and there was much condemnatory gossip. The Victorian age was progressive in many ways, but the importance of morality within marriage became, if anything, stronger.

Eliot's biographers Kathryn Hughes and Gordon Haight have been very harsh on Martineau for her role in the malicious gossip of this time, based on a letter from her to Thomas Carlyle, of which there is only circumstantial evidence. Haight describes it as 'irrational antipathy' and Hughes goes further, portraying Martineau as having 'paranoid fantasies'. Some of this is based on speculation and rumour with, perhaps, some stirring by Carlyle, Evans and Lewes.

However, Martineau's biographer Deborah Logan has said there is very little evidence for these accusations. It wouldn't be surprising if Martineau distanced herself from the scandalous couple but, in fact, as time went on, the gossip blew over. Martineau read and admired the novels of George Eliot, and Evans herself wrote to her friend Sara Hannell of Martineau:

> I respect her so much as an authoress, and have so pleasant a recollection of her as a hostess for three days, that I wish that distant impression from herself and her writings to be disturbed as little as possible by mere personal details. Anything she may do, or say, or feel concerning me personally, is a matter of entire indifference.

For her part Martineau wrote to Henry Reeve in 1859, as Eliot's star was rising, that she had 'admired her abilities, beyond expression', but that 'I did not like her', confirming the impression of respect between the two as opposed to affection.

Both Valerie Sanders and Deborah Logan have drawn out similarities in the work of Eliot and Martineau and have even argued that Harriet was possibly the model for Eliot's most famous creation, Dorothea Brooke, in *Middlemarch*. As Logan outlines:

> Eliot's *Middlemarch* heroine, Dorothea Brooke, with her innovative plans to provide affordable housing for the poor, finds a prototype in Martineau and her Ambleside cottage scheme. There are parallel themes shared by *Deerbrook* (1839) and *Middlemarch* (1871): the village doctor whose promising career is compromised by local political intrigues and the ill-fated romance resulting in marriage motivated by duty rather than love. Further, scholars have noted striking parallels between Martineau's account of the Reform movement in her 'History of England' (1844–51) and Eliot's fictional rendering in 'Felix Holt – the Radical' (1866) as well as between Eliot's title character in Silas Marner (1861) and Martineau's 'The Hill and the Valley'. All of this suggests that, in Eliot's case, Martineau played the role of mentor and literary grandmother without formally being asked to do so.

The parallels between *Deerbrook* and *Middlemarch* go even further. Martineau made a radical point in the denouement of *Deerbrook* that to endure life it was much better not to dwell on the big subjects – that humans were not built with this in mind, but it was much better to focus on the small, local things, should you be looking for personal happiness. In *Middlemarch* we find the grand thinkers in the shape of Edward Casaubon and the village doctor, Tertius Lydgate, both running into trouble with their philosophical ways. Casaubon drives himself to distraction and a premature death, while the doctor, with his scientific visions of a better world, gets into financial difficulties and loses standing with his wife and the local community. The message from George Eliot is the same: better to keep grounded with local matters, do work that is of practical benefit, than to indulge in progressive philosophising or grand theorising.

In his book *Building Jerusalem*, an account of the social-improvement movements of the 19th century, Tristram Hunt also spots Martineau's influence on Eliot:

> In her *History of the Thirty Years' Peace* the liberal intellectual Harriet Martineau sang the praises of 'the great middle class of which history told so little', who 'busy about their private affairs, their manufactures, and their commerce – busy about their local affairs, their magistracy', had founded England's urban civilisation while the 'idle and

indifferent' carried out the plunderous wars 'of which history tells so much'. In doing so she provided a template for the wondrously understated ending of George Eliot's *Middlemarch*.[2]

Certainly, it is hard not to think that Eliot is channelling Martineau in the famous final sentences of *Middlemarch,* in which she summarises the life of her heroine Dorothea:

> Her finely touched spirit had still its fine issues, though they were not widely visible. Her full nature, like that river, of which Cyrus broke the strength, spent itself in channels which had no great name on the earth. But the effect of her being on those around her was incalculably diffusive; for the growing good of the world is partly dependent on unhistoric acts.[3]

It may be that, George Eliot also had Martineau partly in mind when creating the protagonist of *The Mill on the Floss*, Maggie Tulliver. The character's life is comparable to Martineau's as an aspiring author in the late 1820s. The novel is set around an industrial mill, and is famous for the intense relationship between Maggie and her brother Tom. By the time Evans was writing she would have been well aware of the psychological tension between Harriet and her brother James, which had become notorious in literary circles. Maggie Tulliver is an independently-minded woman with pretensions of being a writer that are put down by the men around her. She has a series of failed romances and a doomed intimacy with her brother, which revolves around the failing mill and a dying father. This is surely very much like Martineau's experience with her own father and brother and her struggles to establish herself.

What these likenesses bear out is that these two authors had a similar view of the world. They believed women had every right to be heard and to have a degree of independence; that science was progressive where religion was not; that small communities should be built from the bottom up and need good honest leadership, which demands application of a moral sense of right and wrong. They were forging a model of the future through writing – one that was radical at the time but had great resonance throughout the 20th century and is still relevant today.

It may seem that too much is being made here of the similarities, but they support what many modern feminists have said about Martineau: that

---

2. Tristram Hunt, *Building Jerusalem* (Weidenfeld and Nicolson, 2005), p. 133.

3. George Eliot, *Middlemarch* (Penguin Classics, 2003), p. 688.

as a public intellectual writer, struggling to overcome societal barriers in the 1830s, she had an unprecedented career and was an unprecedented woman. Which other women would George Eliot have been inspired by in the 1830s and '40s? Gaskell and Nightingale came later. Other women, such as Elizabeth Fry, were known for their charitable work and Jane Austen was a famed author and great storyteller, but not as progressive in a political or feminist way. The restless urging and insistence on progress in Martineau's life and writing, and her inquisitiveness about human nature, would provide great source material for George Eliot to apply in her brilliantly dramatic novels.

Kathryn Hughes's biography of Eliot concludes with a passage that could have been written by, or about, Martineau: 'She would have hated the defeatedness of Postmodernism. For Eliot believed it was possible for society to move forward from the centre. The pace would be slow, the mood both sceptical and humble. But there would also be value, purpose, a sense that this was right.'

Martineau's autobiography was published in 1877, a year after her death. Soon after Harriet's passing George Eliot wrote to Sara Hannell, confirming that she retained a close connection: 'We are waiting with some expectation for Miss Martineau's Autobiography, which, I fancy, will be charming so far as her younger and less renowned life extends.'

George Henry Lewes died in 1878. Evans read Martineau's autobiography aloud to him during his final illness, which makes for an interesting scene, given the book's brazen opinions about their mutual acquaintances. Evans was shocked at its openness and vowed that she couldn't leave the same thing as a legacy to her friends. But she wouldn't have been reading it to Lewes at all without the assistance Martineau had given, to make their careers possible.

Chapter 20: Auguste Comte

In 1852–3 Martineau translated the philosophical writings of the French philosopher and teacher Auguste Comte. Comte himself lived and taught in Paris and by this time was nearing the end of his life. His five-volume *Cours de Philosophie Positive* had been completed ten years before. It was a comprehensive study attempting to unify all branches of science and made a strong case for science over religion. It gave structure to scientific philosophy in proclaiming that mankind went through three distinct phases of progressive development in all fields of knowledge: the 'theological' stage, the 'metaphysical' or 'abstract' phase and the final 'positive' stage, as represented by science.

Comte had developed his ideas in the 1830s and '40s, having come under the influence of Henri de Saint Simon in early 1820s Paris, while working as his assistant. Throughout his life Comte seems to have walked a thin line between sanity and insanity. In 1825 he was sectioned and then released, after his symptoms were brought under control, though this didn't stop a failed suicide attempt in 1827 when he jumped into the Seine from the Pont des Arts.

In the 1830s he published his Positivist ideas, which gained a following in France and beyond. His small but select band of notable English supporters included the philosopher John Stuart Mill, Frederick Knight Hunt (editor of the *Daily News*) and George Henry Lewes (soon to be the partner of George Eliot). Martineau had some connection with all of them, and had read about Comte in a short tribute by Lewes in Knight Hunt's weekly volume and in writings by Emile Littré, who went on to found a journal, *The Positivist Review*.

By the time she decided to embark on her translation in 1852, the Martineau–Atkinson correspondence had just been published and was about to receive a vitriolic response, and Martineau's own progressive histories, *Eastern Life* and *A History of the Thirty Years' Peace,* had recently come out. It is easy to see how Comte's progressive scientific philosophy would have chimed with Harriet at this time.

Knight Hunt was a key figure in her life at this time, inviting her to write regular leaders in his newspaper about world events and sharing with her a high regard for the work of Comte. Martineau wrote to Knight Hunt in January 1853, as she was about to embark on her main period of translating work:

> What a thing it is to old people like me to see the next generation
> about to have to vindicate the rights of opinion again & not over

well fitted to do it. This comes as Comte said 20 years ago, of free enquiry having been erected into a dogma, whereas so used, it is but a negation. Protestantism, in its proper sense, will go down, and our fight must be for Positivity.

Martineau and Knight Hunt had made a connection based on a shared desire to challenge the religious establishment and to advocate the scientific approach. He made a timely entrance into Martineau's life that would ensure many of her remaining years were taken up with restless journalism. Tragically, however, Frederick Knight Hunt died suddenly in November 1854 of typhus, aged 40, leaving a wife and children. Martineau, however, was always grateful for his encouragement and she wrote regular letters to his widow offering condolence and assistance.

The idea of Martineau producing a translation of Comte arose in the middle months of 1851. At this early stage a Mr Edward Lombe, a former High Sheriff of Norfolk, now resident in Florence, Italy, and a follower of Comte, offered Martineau £500 for the translation. In 2005, sociologist Michael Hill unearthed a letter written by Martineau in April 1851 to publisher John Chapman, saying that her surgeon uncle, Philip Meadows Martineau, had played a role in amputating Lombe's leg when she was a child, and his apparent fortitude in this matter showed he was a man to be trusted. She then expanded her thoughts about producing a publication on Comte:

> My notion about Comte would be that if any quarterly could be found brave enough, a careful and finished sketch of his philosophy should be given there, & be followed up by an abridged English version. But pray don't say that I am meditating any such thing. I must study & think much before I could make up my mind to do it & I want a holiday in the first place. I have worked excessively hard for 3 ½ years; and I now must rest a while. Mr Atkinson will look back through the Edinburgh for the article on Comte but I have no idea that an Edinburgh reviewer would dare to present him as he is.

This letter betrays both the radicalism of this project and that it was a continuation of her partnership with Atkinson. Michael Hill reflects:

> It was a brave project... The end result was no small matter in the history of sociology: Martineau's translation, underwritten by Edward Lombe, published by Chapman, effectively introduced Comte's founding sociological treatise to large numbers of English-

speaking readers, for the first time in a comprehensive and detailed manner.

The process of producing the book is recorded in Martineau's autobiography. She describes how the work was initially delayed by her suddenly deciding, on the encouragement of Charlotte Brontë, to write a new novel. This was the *Oliver Weld* episode, which Martineau was soon pleased to put behind her and, instead, focus on the translation. John Chapman had agreed to publish Martineau's condensed version of Comte's work, perhaps emboldened by Lombe's donation and Martineau's suggestion that some of the money should go towards the production of the book and some should go to Comte himself. John Stuart Mill was dismissive, claiming that any interested intelligent people could read the original text in French. Meanwhile, George Henry Lewes prepared his own volume on Comte.

Martineau had a strong inclination to produce a work that would reach out to a wider public. This was not going to be a straight translation; it was to be a popular interpretation of Comte's work. She was explicit about this in the preface: 'My strongest inducement to this enterprise was my deep conviction of our need of this book in my own country, in a form which renders it accessible to the largest number of intelligent readers'. Under Martineau's supervision the five volumes would be condensed into a single, still detailed, book.

She began in the second half of 1852, in between articles about Ireland and America and completing her annual series of public lectures in Ambleside. As she describes in her autobiography: '[It was] Christmas Day when I finished the first of the six volumes...' The first months of 1853 were freed up for her to work on the translation:

> I finished Astronomy in the middle of January, and biology on the twenty third of April; so that I had five months for the three last volumes, which were by far the easiest to do, though half as long again as the first three. I had a perpetual succession of guests, from April till the end of September; but I did not stop work for them; nor did I choose to leave home till I had fulfilled my engagement.

The autobiography was penned just 18 months later, with the onset of her illness in 1855, and the experience of working on Comte was still clear and resonant in her mind:

---

1. Michael R. Hill, introduction to 'On Edward Lombe, Translating Auguste Comte and the Liberal English Press: A Previously Unpublished Letter', *Sociological Origins*, 3 (2005), p. 100.

I often said to myself and others, in the course of it, that I should never enjoy anything so much again. And I believe that if I were now to live and work for twenty years, I could never enjoy anything more. The vast range of knowledge, through which one is carried so easily, is a prodigious treat; and yet more, the clear enunciation, and incessant application of principles. The weak part of the book, – the sacrifices made to system and order, – just happens to fall in with my weak tendency in that direction.

She seemed to revel in the task of translating a work that was so in tune with her philosophy, and she was clear that she was producing her own interpretation of Comte:

My work was not mere translation: it involved quite a different kind of intellectual exercise; and much as I enjoy translation – pleasant as is the finding of equivalent terms, and arranging them harmoniously – it is pleasanter still to combine with this the work of condensation. To me, in truth, nothing was ever pleasanter. It was like going to school again while doing the useful work of mature age and I should relish nothing better than to go on with it as long as I lived...

This was more than enjoyment as a translation task; it was a spiritual connection. She added: 'Many a passage of my version did I write with tears falling into my lap.'

The finished article was published with a Martineau-penned preface, containing the clearest depiction yet of her own scientific, materialistic views in relation to the human race, and of the importance of people viewing it as a whole objectively to gain a clearer understanding:

The theological world can not but hate a book which treats of theological belief as a transient state of the human mind. And again, the preachers and teachers, of all sets and schools, who keep to the ancient practice, once inevitable, of contemplating and judging of the universe from the point of view of their own minds, instead of having learned to take their stand out of themselves, investigating from the universe inward, and not from within outward, must necessarily think ill of a work which exposes the futility of their method, and the worthlessness of the results to which it leads. As M. Comte treats of theology and metaphysics as destined to pass away, theolo-

CHAPTER 20: AUGUSTE COMTE

gians and metaphysicians must necessarily abhor, dread, and despise his work.

This was spiritual writing about science – a conscious decision to portray religion as man-made and replace it with evidence-based enquiry in all fields of knowledge. Her preface is an explicit continuation of Martineau's great internal revelation that nature, as described by science, supersedes religion:

We find ourselves suddenly living and moving in the midst of the universe, – as a part of it, and not as its aim and object. We find ourselves living, not under our capricious and arbitrary conditions, unconnected with the constitution and movements of the whole, but under great, general, invariable laws, which operate on us as part of the whole. Certainly, I can conceive of no instruction so favourable to aspiration as that which shows us how great are our faculties, how small our knowledge, how sublime the heights which we may hope to attain, and how boundless an infinity may be assumed to spread out beyond.

She castigates those who take pride in forging 'belief without evidence' and acclaims the 'scrupulous and humble' who are prepared to wait and gain the evidence. Martineau concludes with a direct challenge to the religiously minded to accept the inevitable and give in to science, evidence and progress, as represented by Positivism:

My hope is that this book may achieve, besides the purposes entertained by its author, the one more that he did not intend, of conveying a sufficient rebuke to those who, in theological selfishness or metaphysical pride, speak evil of a philosophy which is too lofty and too simple, too humble and too generous, for the habit of their minds. The case is clear. The law of progress is conspicuously at work throughout human history. The only field of progress is now that of Positive Philosophy.

John Chapman published the book at the beginning of 1854. T. H. Huxley, a few years short of his own notoriety, wrote a positive piece on it for the *Westminster Review*, while being less than warm about Lewes's book on Comte. He quoted Martineau's combative, idealistic preface at length, no doubt assimilating it ready to fulfil his destiny as 'Darwin's Bulldog', concluding: 'That some interpreter should stand between Comte and the public, is no more than what is necessary. By Miss Martineau all that is needed has been done; boldly, with rare fidelity, and as a labour of love.'[2]

Sales were acceptable but other reviews were hard to come by. Martineau took the liberty of writing to Comte himself:

> It is not this order of men that understand or will ever receive your work. It is the men who do not write that are your true disciples. The book is read and it must be by such. Down in that lowly valley where human life goes on under the feet of the proud, the seed is sown and will flourish. You and I shall never see the gathering of the harvest, except in the eye of faith; but I am sure that is all that we desire.

Comte himself liked the English edition and would recommend it to his students rather than his own earlier volumes.

In her autobiography, Martineau deals with criticisms of Comte's works that had been put to her personally. To counter them she refers to a letter by Atkinson arguing that a true science of human nature, objective measurable observation of human action, was what the future held. She had previously outlined this herself in a letter to her friend Mrs Ogden, as the Comte book was coming out:

> You will see at once that interest in theology must exist till we have a Positive Science of Human Nature – a thing which is only just beginning to be dreamed of. Positive science has exorcised the outward frame of nature, – got rid of Apollo and Neptune, and Isis and the Naiads and the relation of the Supernatural and Metaphysical systems is now SO the human mind and they will be the supreme interest till a science of human nature exists and is completely established... My anticipation is what it has been for many years – that we shall have strifes and disorders and no peace for a course of years and that the result will be the over throw of dogmatic theology altogether... You and I shall not see this; but I feel very confident that there will be no stopping short of it.

Martineau invokes the struggles that a science of human nature will have, and anticipates the problems and antipathy that will develop between sociology and socio-biology in the second half of the 20th century. Comte's work, and Mar-

---

2. T. H. Huxley, 'Comte's Positive Philosophy', *Westminster Review* (July 1854), p. 194.

tineau's advocacy of it, are seen as greatly influential in the development of the coming social sciences. Yet Martineau, Comte, Atkinson and, indeed, Darwin saw no divide between social, natural or life sciences. Humans were very much within the natural purview. These were revolutionary views not readily accepted in a 20th century marked by increasing division and niche study in science, and a stubbornness in philosophy to keep man on his pedestal, above nature.

American sociologist Susan Hoecker-Drysdale makes the important point that Martineau's influence on sociology should not be restricted to the Comte translation. Comte resonated with Martineau, because she had also written her own analytical scientific approached to human life, particularly in *Society in America* and in *How to Observe Morals and Manners* in the 1830s.

Cultural historian Lesa Scholl compares Martineau's translation with Comte's original work, and puts forward the view that aspects of the original that would have been harmful are played down – particularly Comte's dismissal of women as workers and an anti-English slant. She goes so far as to suggest that Martineau becomes 'his saviour from intellectual obscurity', and concludes: 'Within her ostensible appearance as a passive, evangelising disciple, Martineau is active, she is not a mere instrument of the original author, but a messenger in her own right.'[3]

As for Comte himself, in her autobiography Martineau reports somebody saying that 'he has gone mad', which she refuses to believe and refutes. In fact, by 1855, towards the end of his life, Comte *was* losing touch with reality. His life had changed when he fell deeply in love with Clotilde De Vaux in 1844. Despite being an unconsummated passion and Clotilde's untimely death from tuberculosis two years later, this experience of love inspired Comte to push on with his new 'Religion of Humanity', which proposed a new calendar of 13 months, each of which would be named after great writers and thinkers, including Homer, Caesar, Dante and Shakespeare. The all-male months did not preclude him remembering his love, however, with the institution of Saint Clotilde's Day on 6 April.

Comte's new religion had a lasting impact in France and in Brazil (several individuals who were instrumental in the establishment of a Brazilian Republic in 1889 were followers of Comte). Both countries still have Positivist chapels, and the Brazilian flag bears the Comtean motto 'Order and Progress'. Its wider influence comes in another phrase adopted for the religion, '*vivre pour altrui*' ('live for others'), from which comes the word 'altruism'. For outside observers,

---

3. Lesa Scholl, 'Provocative Agenda's: Martineau's Translation of Comte', in *Harriet Martineau: Authorship, Society and Empire*, ed. Ella Dzelzainis and Cora Kaplan (Manchester University Press, 2010), p. 97.

Comte's leadership of the religion increasingly took on a hierarchical dimension, inevitably placing himself at the top of a priesthood as the new God.

This was an unfortunate turn of events for his British followers, and subsequently Mill, Lewes and Martineau all distanced themselves from, and generally rejected, his need to establish a new religion to replace the old ones. Huxley memorably described Comte's 'Religion of Humanity' as 'Catholicism without the Christianity'.

Hoecker-Drysdale reflects on the subsequent differences between Martineau and Comte:

> While she concurred with Comte's secularism, in the shedding of old theologies and metaphysical systems, Martineau was repulsed by his desire to establish a new quasi-religious morality and hierarchical social system. As she saw it. Martineau's original interest in Positivism was ultimately to make empirical findings and their interpretation available to the decision-makers and the public. This was far different from the authoritarian management approach of Comte. Martineau wanted to learn about social reality; Comte wanted, following his own philosophy, to reorganise it.[4]

Martineau had a determined belief in education and knowledge, and her work on Comte – like all her work – had reason and purpose for social betterment behind it. She distanced herself from Comte when he seemed to be replacing one religion with another, or producing more despotism, against which Martineau had an immediate internal reaction. She refused Comte's requests to translate his other books and distanced herself from his work in later years.

The other weakness in Comte's philosophy was, as Martineau predicted in the autobiography, one that they shared. Both sought structure and certainty where they don't exist. Their three-pronged progressive stages were too simplistic. They were committed to science but in a way that was ironically quasi-religious, and science brought new determinist laws that could not be avoided. Today, science has become powerful but exists alongside theology and metaphysical views of the world. It has brought method and measurement, but it describes a complex pluralistic universe rather than one with simple progressive laws.

Reading the translated work now, the first striking thing is that it is an achievement in itself. Martineau's year-long dedication to the translation was

---

4. Susan Hoecker-Drysdale, 'Harriet Martineau and the Positivism of Auguste Comte' in *Harriet Martineau: Theoretical and Methodological Perspectives*, ed. Michael R. Hill and Susan Hoecker-Drysdale (Routledge, 2003), p. 186.

the culmination of several strands in her life: her family's French origins and her fluency in the French language; the breadth of her reading and her growing scepticism towards religion. Its publication both reflected and stimulated the growth of scientific attitudes in mid-19th-century Britain.

The book's theme of unifying science was not realised, as science became ever more divided in the 20th century, and its overarching philosophy is flawed. However, its advocacy of science and secularism in 1850s Britain helped to lay the foundations for much modern thought as well as thousands of university departments around the world. Comte's Positive philosophy has become a founding text of sociology and Martineau's translation had a considerable influence on this, particularly in Britain and America where sociology would flourish.

In his essay 'The Original Modernizers', the writer and philosopher John Gray charts the influence of Positivism on the development of economic theory: 'Without realizing it, the majority of economists have inherited their way of thinking from the Positivists... Comtean ideas have become the standard methodology of economics.'[5] What Gray is referring to here is the marriage of free market views to a progressive faith in science and technology, and though he fails to recognise her contribution, this is a world view Martineau would have been seeking to pursue in her translation of Comte's work. Gray is drawing attention to the hidden influence of ideas: 'Technology – the practical application of scientific knowledge – produces a convergence in values. This is the central modern myth, which the Positivists propagated and everyone today accepts as fact.'

An intriguing subplot of the Martineau–Comte partnership was the resulting cooling of relations between George Eliot and Martineau. Kathryn Hughes, in her biography of Eliot, suggests that Harriet deliberately sought to outdo the work on Comte by Eliot's new love partner George Lewes. Deborah Logan argues that the effect of Martineau's positive reviews, set against the more negative response to the latter's, did cause some bad feeling. From the correspondence and Harriet's autobiography it seems unlikely that she was very preoccupied with Lewes's work, and we can clearly see how the translation fits into her own philosophical trajectory. As we have seen, however, this did help lead to a cooling of relations between Martineau and Eliot.

In the first half of the 1850s Martineau was responding to a higher calling, using a spiritual language about science that is the antithesis of the better-remembered

5. John Gray, 'The Original Modernizers', *Gray's Anatomy: Selected Writings* (Allen Lane, 2009), pp. 271–273.

writing of George Eliot and Charlotte Brontë from the same period. Human intrigue and the details and difficulties of life perhaps have a more eager readership than the elevation of mankind through science into a golden future. Ironically, this is surely reflective of the human nature that Martineau was so keen to pin down and elucidate.

Part V: The 1860s

The 1860s see the advent of a more self-conscious Victorian culture and fashion, which becomes popular around the world. It is an era of continued industrial development and the growth of trade unions, fighting for better working conditions in large factories. This decade also sees the beginning of the Gladstone and Disraeli age of politics. However, the major world event is the American Civil War between 1861 and 1865, which heralds the end of the slave system in the Southern American states.

Martineau's journalism in the late 1850s and '60s had a global view, drawing upon her experiences and contacts in Ireland, the Middle East and particularly America. She received regular updates from her American abolitionist friends, and presciently anticipated the arrival of Abraham Lincoln as President, correctly predicting that war was the only possible resolution to the crisis. Supporting the North in the war was still controversial in Britain, where powerful vested interests – including *The Times* newspaper – backed the status quo. Several commentators have suggested Martineau's was a lone British voice of clarity on this world-changing issue which, along with her campaigns in support of Florence Nightingale and feminist and social reformer Josephine Butler, made the late 1850s and '60s a productive era for Martineau, in terms of her influence on world events, despite her journalism appearing anonymously.

Chapter 21: Florence Nightingale

In 1858 Martineau was over the worst of her illness, but she would never again be as active as she had once been.

The newly famous Florence Nightingale was exhausted too, from her time in the Crimea, having only just survived an infection that left her permanently weak. She wrote to Martineau, enclosing her war report, and requesting help to publicise and write up her findings from the Crimea. Martineau wrote back saying that she would help where she could but that 'every stroke of my work is more likely than not to be my last', to which Nightingale replied in equally fatalistic mode: 'I too have no future and must do what I can without delay.'[1] In reality, over the next ten years they would form a partnership that would not only change the world, but would directly save a multitude of lives; their own lives carried on actively, if not healthily, for a good while longer.

The issue over which the two women collaborated was the evident need for better, more hygienic, hospitals, and the need for them to be attended by well-trained nurses. Of course, Nightingale is well remembered as the mother of nursing, and it would be stretching a point to give Martineau equal billing here. However, at a crucial time, Martineau brought her experience, her contacts and her pen to bear to help publicise Nightingale's causes and to start a trend that would continue to resonate around the world throughout the 20th century. Neither woman is particularly remembered for advocating better hospitals. Such is the power of mythology – in this case, a romantically reassuring feminised image of Nightingale as created by 19th-century newspaper spin – that Nightingale is famous as the 'Lady of the Lamp' and the founder of an order of nursing 'angels', when she was also hard-headed and determined, with a clear vision of what was needed.

Martineau and Nightingale had previous links. Nightingale had read and admired *Society in America* as an 18-year-old, and it fuelled her determination to become someone who would change things. She came from a wealthy, privileged background but grew to despise the upper classes and the evident inequalities in society. In the late 1840s, she travelled up the Nile and read the recently published *Eastern Life*. Although she might have been repelled by its sceptical approach to religion, she would have revelled in its radicalism and the traveller's tales.

The two women also shared a significant mutual acquaintance in Richard

---

1. Florence Nightingale, as quoted in Mark Bostridge, *Florence Nightingale: The Woman and her Legend* (Viking, 2008), p. 326.

Monckton Milnes, who had been a poet in 1830s' London and a part of Martineau's radical dissenting circle. Harriet wrote to him from Egypt in January 1847:

> What new knowledge comes to one in the presence of the past which one has read and thought about all one's life? It is a knowledge, not only of those old and wonderful people, but through them, of the whole race. I had of late years got some glimpse of what is now as plain to me as anything. I have discovered for myself, that the true history is the history of great ideas of which human usages and men themselves (though they have a history of their own) are but illustrations.

Monckton Milnes and Nightingale were in the middle of a nine-year courtship, which she finally broke off in 1850, much to his disappointment. Nightingale had a higher calling than domestic life and chose to remain independent and celibate throughout her life, so as to make room for her duty. Their shared Unitarian background, their higher calling, and their need to try and make society better would soon bring Martineau and Nightingale together.

Contained in the report that Florence sent Harriet was incontrovertible evidence that armies at war were much more likely to lose men from disease than from battle. Nightingale showed that in the Crimean War, from which she had just returned, 1,760 men had died in battle or from wounds, while 16,300 had died from disease – nearly 20 per cent of the whole army. Nightingale had been sent to introduce better hygiene to the Crimean hospitals and had shown great leadership in reorganising provision for the wounded and emphasising good nursing. However, the basic hospital set-up, the food provisions and the government back-up were still inadequate. Moreover, hospitals at home were scarcely better. They were locally organised and dependent on volunteers, neither nursing as a profession nor nurse training being well established.

Nightingale had assembled her evidence, but she was not a writer, lobbyist or publicist. Martineau was all three, and she immediately wrote a series of articles for the *Daily News* on sanitation in hospitals, the need for an Army medical department and professional nursing. She explained to Nightingale that she intended to keep to the facts, and encouraged her not to be distracted by superficial fame: 'My object was to have you entirely let alone…keep the crowd off you and leave you air and space and liberty.'

Martineau's articles formed the basis of a book, *England and Her Soldiers*, published in 1859. It wasn't a big success in Britain but it was also published in America, where its central message spread. It was the first book in which the famed pie chart of Nightingale's evidence was printed, clearly showing the numbers of lives that would be saved by more hygienic hospitals. Martineau went further:

> In every way there must be General Hospitals. They cannot be established and worked without immediate and constant command of experience, knowledge and habit. We cannot have good hospitals abroad unless we have been accustomed to them at home. We cannot have good hospitals in war unless we have had them in peace. We must have one at home, at once.

In *England and Her Soldiers* Martineau presents Nightingale as a serious professional, collecting data. As Mark Bostridge has observed in his biography of Nightingale: 'It is light years removed from the sentimental individual of popular myth.' There seems to have been a clear understanding between the two women that any personal credit or adulation was irrelevant – it was the concerns at the heart of the campaign that mattered.

They formed a remarkable partnership during this period of health reform. Both were by now often stricken with illness and often bed-bound. Yet they offered each other support via regular correspondence and both had routes into power and influence. Nightingale had the constant ear of Sidney Herbert at the War Office who did so much to implement her suggested reforms, which would transform health provision for the British army. In 1861 he died of kidney failure and Nightingale was stricken with grief, both for her friend but also with the fear that this would be the end of her life's work. After one of her last meetings with Herbert she wrote to Martineau: 'I see death written in the man's face. And, when I think of the possibility of my surviving him, I am glad to feel myself declining so fast.'[2]

Two years after Herbert's death, Nightingale had been lobbying the government for a sympathetic successor. Her preference was for Lord De Grey and at the beginning of April 1863 she wrote a telegram in her own hand to Martineau: 'Agitate, agitate for Lord De Grey to succeed'. The very next day a Martineau penned leader column appeared in the *Daily News* in praise of De Grey and by the end of the month Prime Minister Lord Palmerston announced him as the new Minister at the War Office. Nightingale's ongoing reforms would continue.

Following publication of *England and her Soldiers* in America, Maria

2. Florence Nightingale, as quoted in Cecil Woodham Smith, *Florence Nightingale* (Book Club Associates, 1972), p. 358.

Weston Chapman in Boston passed on a request from the American Secretary of War, Simon Cameron, that he be sent the report and statistics. Martineau and Nightingale duly obliged, dispatching a package from London, though Martineau was adamant that the evidence should be available to both sides in the American Civil War, despite her deep bias for the pro-abolition North. Cameron wrote to thank both women. Martineau informed Maria Chapman of what she had told the American Secretary of War:

> I took occasion to say that we should be thankful to furnish the results of our experience and our reforms to all armies, everywhere, if we had the power. It is F.N.'s and my doing and nobody's else and we should have done the same by any other army if we could. If duly attended to, I really hope and believe these documents may save some of your good soldier's lives.

The reports sent to America were backed up by further articles by Martineau in the *American Monthly* in 1861, entitled 'Health in the Camps and Health in the Hospitals'.

Martineau encouraged Nightingale to publish her own book *Notes on Nursing* and then wrote a glowing review of it in the *Quarterly Review*. She recommended it to P. P. Carpenter:

> We have been saving for you, on your return, a copy of Miss Nightingale's 'notes' which I now send. If you have seen the book I need not say a word about it, for it is literally beyond all praise, but I will ask you to send it wherever you think it may do good. To us nurses it is like a new life... Surely to have done such a work must be a consoling thought to Miss Nightingale in the midst of her suffering. She seems to be sinking faster now – our last account was that she cannot live very much longer.

In fact, Nightingale was to live for another 50 years, and her partnership with Martineau was far from over. In 1865 they pushed on with the recruitment and training of nurses and midwives, particularly in Manchester with the help of Elizabeth Gaskell – in response to women being laid off by cotton mills due to the American Civil War. Martineau wrote in the *Daily News*:

> There is a mission for women, a vocation for them, honoured, undisputed and well rewarded, which is left so nearly unnoticed that one would suppose the champions of the sex had never heard of it.

While we have an unmanageable crowd of hungry and disappointed women, poor and idle, on the one hand, we have on the other an absolute destitution of nurses of all classes, sick nurses for the household, hospital nurses, midwifery nurses and nurses for our civil and military stations in India and elsewhere.

She reminds her readers that the need for nursing goes hand in hand with the need for better hospitals: 'Hospital reform is proceeding, both at home and wherever we have settlements abroad and the want most difficult to supply is that of trustworthy and capable nurses.'

Of course, the 'settlements abroad' in 1865 consisted of large portions of the world, including India, Canada, several African nations, Australia and New Zealand, amongst many others. The *Daily News* was read around the world, as were Martineau's books, and the action she requested would subsequently be carried out by governments all around the world in the 20th century, with nursing becoming a vocation and an occupation for women in hospitals of all types in all countries.

It is easy to see why much feminist analysis and sociological thought has been expended on the work of Martineau and Nightingale. They both held nuanced positions on the rights of women, particularly Nightingale, who didn't support women going into medicine as doctors. In one sense they were creating a characterisation of women as natural carers, and potentially marginalising them as regards other professions. However, it is important to remember the context. It was unusual for women to be employed in any profession in the 1850s and '60s: university was barred to them, and the vast majority of men still expected women to stay at home, bringing up the children. Championing the idea that women could do a trained, paid, professional job was a pioneering, radical breakthrough.

The partnership between Harriet Martineau and Florence Nightingale continued in the form of their support of Josephine Butler's opposition to the Contagious Diseases Act. Having been two lone dissenting voices against the original passing of the Acts in 1863 and '64, with Nightingale supplying Martineau with statistical evidence providing the basis for her series of *Daily News* articles arguing against the Contagious Diseases Act, which was so biased against prostitutes, Nightingale showed a rare humour in suggesting that prostitutes she had seen around soldiers 'deserve good service pensions' from the government for the sheer level of activity. However, the Act passed at the time and both

women gladly welcomed the new impetus of opposition led by Josephine Butler a decade later.

Nightingale always had an ambivalent attitude towards greater women's
rights and several times wrote that her work was to save the lives of everyone,
regardless of race, creed or gender, yet her name appears alongside Martineau's
as signatories to John Stuart Mill's three separate parliamentarian petitions in
the 1860s for greater women's suffrage. However, their greatest achievement
together remained the widely disseminated, evidence-based writing of
1859–61, proving incontrovertibly that more hygienic hospitals would save
lives both at home and, during wartime, in the field. Behind the historical
mythology were two determined women using scientific evidence, and the
written word, to change the world in a way that we now take for granted.

Each woman was able to pay tribute to the other on dying: Martineau had
penned an obituary of Nightingale in the 1860s, which the *Daily News* used in
1910 when Nightingale finally passed away. It read:

> She was no declaimer, but a housewifely woman; she talked little,
> and did great things. When other women see that there are things for
> them to do, and train themselves to the work, they will get it done
> easily enough. There can never be a more unthought-of and marvel-
> lous career before any working woman than Florence Nightingale
> has achieved; and her success has opened a way to all others easier
> than anyone had prepared for her.

Florence Nightingale, for her part, paid homage to Martineau in a letter that
formed part of the Memorials that would appear with Harriet's autobiography
in 1877:

> She was born to be a destroyer of slavery, in whatever form, in what-
> ever place, all over the world, wherever she saw or thought she saw
> it… To the last her religious feeling, – in the sense of good work-
> ing out of evil, into a supreme wisdom penetrating and moulding
> the whole universe; – into the natural subordination of intellect and
> intellectual purposes and of intellectual self to purposes of good, even
> were these merely the small purposes of social or domestic life.

Chapter 22: Josephine Butler

In the history of feminism, the 1860s and '70s are usually described as the 'first wave', paving the way for the Suffragettes and other subsequent organised women's movements; the last flourish of Harriet Martineau's campaigning pen came in 1868–70 in support of a concerted, women-led effort to oppose the Contagious Diseases Acts. These three Acts, passed in 1864, 1866 and 1869 by an all-male Parliament, were aimed at curbing sexually transmitted diseases by men from prostitutes, particularly in garrison towns. The Acts blamed the spread of disease solely on the women, and sought to control it by allowing the police to arrest any woman suspected of prostitution, who could be forcibly checked and treated. The Acts also instituted a system of registration and health checks for brothels and prostitutes.

The campaign against the Acts was led by Josephine Butler who was one of the first of a new breed, overtly working to organise women to campaign for women's rights. By all accounts, she was a charismatic individual who could be very persuasive in person. She was an evangelical Christian, and a mother of four children with a supportive husband, who became a champion of radical causes, particularly those concerning women's rights.

On the establishment of the Ladies National Association for Repeal of the Contagious Diseases Acts in 1869, one of Butler's first letters was to request the help of the now elderly and immobile Martineau. Harriet seized the opportunity, probably remembering that she had predicted 20 years earlier to friends that she would one day become involved in a campaign concerning prostitution. She immediately suggested to Butler that she would galvanise her old employer, the *Daily News*, and that she would write to parliamentarians.

However, the *Daily News* would not accept Martineau writing the articles as leaders, one of the paper's proprietors raising strong objections. She was therefore forced to pen four lengthy letters on the subject, which she sent to the paper's acting editor, Thomas Walker. He was ill in bed and his wife read the letters to him. At first shocked, she then insisted that her husband publish them fully.

In fact, Martineau had written leaders in the *Daily News* in 1863–4 when the first Act was passed, and they were now collected and reprinted in pamphlet form. The new letters were signed 'An Englishwoman' and printed in the *Daily News* in December 1869. The first letter showed how the legislation could be extended to any woman and called on readers to remember Lady Godiva, who took direct action on behalf of the poor, to support the action of Josephine Butler and her association:

> ... These honourable women who are now putting away the most sensitive of personal feeling, to help us out of the peril we have incurred to destroy the risk for all future time. Their deed is of a quality kindred to Godiva's while its scope is wider and its import infinitely deeper. She pitied starvation in poor men's homes. These are striving to save home itself, and to preserve the most sacred of institutions, and one hitherto pre-eminently our own – the Family.

This crusade was the culmination of much of Martineau's own personal campaigning, and her mention here of 'the Family' is an overt reference to something she had always believed in: the importance of responsible family life. She supported women until the point they left their husbands; she didn't support Factory Acts because she felt parents needed strength not to send their children to work in factories. She advocated responsible parenting and education at home – surprising, perhaps, because she had a difficult relationship with her own domineering mother and in later life had a major schism with her brother. Plus, she had remained resolutely single. Martineau had an idealistic vision of the importance of family life, which had very rarely been part of her own life.

The second letter of hers to appear in the *Daily News* in 1869 contained an outline of how the system was failing women:

> The legal position of women has been deprived of its most essential security. The incredible part of the case will be that this has been effected in the dark and in silence. The press has not fulfilled its function and its trust in regard to the most recent act. In Parliament no warning voice was raised. The most sacred liberties of half the people of England are gone, without being missed; and now it is the women, for the most part, who have to insist on their restoration.

She went on to suggest that the Acts only served to legitimise prostitution and all the actions around it:

> Prostitutes, observing the provisions of the Act, are pursuing their trade under the sanction of Parliament. Young men, entering the world, find this kind of vice recognised as necessary by Parliament, the police, the magistracy and the law; and with this discovery, a host of scruples and shames and difficulties vanish... the law and the gov-

ernment are enlisted on the side of animal passion and against the institutions of Marriage and the House.

These passages highlighted her belief in a good moral life and the importance of loyalty and responsibility within marriage and the family. She wasn't a puritan or a prude, she had a clear idea of what men were like in their 'animal passion' and wrote elsewhere at this time of how men needed to channel their 'war instinct'. Martineau also penned the official call to Parliament on behalf of Butler's National Association, which went forward with 128 signatures, including, at the top, Martineau's, Butler's and Florence Nightingale's. In the final paragraph of this document Martineau wrote:

> The conditions of the disease, in the first instance, are moral, not physical. The moral evil through which the disease makes its way separates the case entirely from that of the plague or other scourges, which have been placed under police control or sanitary care. We hold that we are bound, before rushing into the experiment of legalizing a revolting vice, to try to deal with the causes of the evil, and we dared to believe that, with wiser teaching and more capable legislation, those causes would not be beyond control.

In her original leaders she had made a plea to 'treat men as moral agents and not as animals'.

In this campaign, Martineau was a link between the past and the future; she was providing an ideological framework for a new movement. Her earlier writings on women's rights, particularly in *Society in America*, came 30 years before this first wave of feminism. But here she was providing the basis for many a future ideological battle. In the 1960s, modern feminism was born on the back of sexual freedom, itself made possible by birth-control technology, part of a movement championing individual freedom over censure and regulation.

The 'moral' approach to legislation has rarely worked. Most modern attempts to institute 'family values' through government and legislation have fallen on the stony ground of hypocrisy, partly because the 'animal passions' of both men and women have been allowed to thrive thanks to the greater goal of individual freedom. Martineau's whole career was spent navigating this tension. Her advocacy of 'human nature' was in effect an acceptance that individuals want greater freedom. She fought injustices on behalf of women and the family, rejected religion as the arbiter of a moral life, but was the living embodiment of individual freedom which, perhaps, she knew would win out in the end.

She spent her life within a strongly patriarchal system and has been mistrusted by male-dominated history. However, her own philosophy was brilliant and original and superior to that of most of the male philosophers preceding her. Yet her challenge to religion, her championing of science, her support of a mind within human nature, is wrapped up in letters to Atkinson, in journalism, translations of Comte and travelogues to America and the Middle East. She did not have the confidence, nor was she encouraged, to explicitly lay down her own philosophy in a straightforward text, reflecting her place as a woman writer. A woman philosopher was unthinkable in the 1850s.

Martineau had at times been judgmental of Mary Wollstonecraft, who had written *A Vindication of the Rights of Woman* in 1792, berating her for living a morally loose life. However, Martineau's recognition of their shared situation, and of the coming wave of liberty, led her to change her mind, as revealed in a letter to her American abolitionist comrade Maria Weston Chapman, in 1850:

> You will live to see a great enlargement of our scope, I trust; but, what with the vices of some women and the fears of others, it is hard work for us to assert our liberty. I will, however, till I die, and so will you; and so make it easier for some few to follow us than it was for poor Mary Wollstonecraft to begin.

Josephine Butler provided the prototype for what would become the Suffragette movement. She went from town to town with a small but loyal following and spoke at public meetings. She would often invoke Martineau as the elder stateswoman when she spoke in front of the Royal Commission in London. Butler's presence was not always welcome, though, and meetings were often disrupted by hired thugs or groups of unhappy prostitutes who felt she should not interfere with their livelihood. When this happened in Colchester, Martineau quickly penned a direct appeal in the *Daily News* entitled, 'To the Women of Colchester'. In the Memorials, Butler paid tribute to Martineau and suggested that prostitutes were akin to black slaves: 'Faithful to the end to the cause of liberty, justice and purity, faithful to the end to the cause of the white slaves of Europe as she had been faithful to the black slaves of America.'

Martineau had provided great impetus to the first wave of feminism in aiding the Contagious Diseases Campaign and was true to her word in working for women's liberty for the rest of her life. Unfortunately, she didn't live to see the resolution of the crisis, dying ten years too soon in 1876. The system of brothel regulation was suspended in 1883 and the Acts were repealed in 1886, a victory for women's rights and one that would change for ever the landscape of political discourse in Britain.

Chapter 23: The Two Marias

In the final phase of her life, Harriet Martineau had two profound relationships with two very different women, both called Maria. Maria Weston Chapman was the American abolitionist Martineau had met in America, in 1835, and with whom she became increasingly intimate in correspondence – so much so that in the 1850s Martineau took the surprising decision to bequeath her papers and journals to Chapman, for her to disseminate to the public, and to place Chapman in charge of the production of her autobiography.

The second Maria to have a deep and lasting impact on Martineau was her niece, Maria Martineau. The daughter of her brother Robert, Maria went to The Knoll, in her late twenties, to help nurse her aunt through her latest illness in 1855, and ended up staying there until her own tragically premature death in 1864.

The two Marias provided Harriet Martineau with her two closest relationships in the second half of her life, to the extent that they have led to speculation regarding Harriet's sexuality. In *Harriet Martineau: A Radical Victorian*, R. K. Webb is explicit in stating his view that Martineau was gay, but that her orientation almost certainly did not manifest itself in a sexual way. This has been the source of some consternation to Martineau scholars and followers: it is seen by some as idle and unnecessary conjecture and by others as simply not true.

There may be evidence that Martineau loved the two Marias and they loved her, but it had no means of expression, except in companionship in Maria's case and appreciation from afar in Chapman's. Martineau had no such deep feelings for any men, and the two Marias filled an emotional void in her life, which remained empty during the last ten years of her life, following her niece Maria's death.

Maria Weston Chapman was a strong charismatic character who was much more than Garrison's deputy in the abolitionist movement. She galvanised many, wrote her own polemics and was a successful fundraiser for the movement. In 1835, a meeting of minds and stout hearts led Chapman to ask Martineau to speak out in public against slavery – something that would change Harriet's life. Chapman then became a continual first-hand source of American events, feeding the English journalist with much material. This intensified in the 1850s as the Civil War loomed, and their own relationship deepened when they both lived to see Lincoln's emancipation of slaves and the end of the war in the North's favour.

Chapman visited The Knoll, as did her daughters. Her husband had died in 1842, leaving her, her sister and four daughters, who all chose to live unmarried. This caused Harriet Martineau to remark:

> There you see a kind of American women who really are moulded by the spirit of their country. I never knew of such practical admiration as they have excited. – I mean of so many opportunities of marrying, in all manner of tempting ways: but they seem not to be disposed, – under the circumstances of the times. Though such cases are not rare in England one seldom or never sees a whole family so passing through life by choice – only one of the many sisters marrying.

Martineau's decision to bequeath her writings to Chapman in 1855 and place her in charge of the autobiography was a snub to her brother, James, but drew the two women closer together. Martineau wrote in the 1850s that she would be afraid to live with Mrs Chapman as, being with such a powerful character, she would lose her own self-reliance.

The autobiography would eventually be issued with a large addendum of Memorials, assembled by Chapman as a mixture of their own letters, other correspondence, and tributes from those Martineau had worked with, including Garrison and Nightingale. However, Chapman's input was almost embarrassingly sycophantic and R. K. Webb claimed that the 'ineptitude' of the Memorials did not help Martineau's reputation. Overly effusive and randomly ordered, they are a bit of an oddity, although they are also interspersed with some of Martineau's most explicit secular writings.

The deep connection with Maria Weston Chapman, and Martineau's lifelong connection with America in general, presages how she has been better remembered in the United States than in her home country. Chapman commissioned a large statue of Martineau by Anne Whitney, which stood at the all-female elite ladies' Wellesley College until it was destroyed by fire in 1914. A bust of Martineau remains in the gallery there.

Harriet had been close to her brother Robert's family in Birmingham, staying with them if she was passing through to London and on occasional Christmases. When she became seriously ill in 1855 her niece Maria was either sent or summoned to help nurse her through the crisis. The deep connection between them was immediate and did much to bring the author through her latest health crisis. In March 1857, Harriet wrote to her follower and secular sympathiser Sara

Hannell of Maria: 'I wish you knew her. She is something that one hardly meets twice in a lifetime, for power convertible to any purpose while STURDY in its virtue as the stars in their courses. She is the member of the clan.'

Maria threw herself into life at The Knoll, playing an active part in the sustainable farming project as well as indulging Harriet by administering her mesmeric cures. Maria was cook, housekeeper and companion. She must have also provided family support in defending her aunt in her feud with Uncle James. Her hard work and organisation freed Harriet to concentrate on her writing so that the Nightingale campaign and much other journalism were possible. As time went on, it seems she also took on the role of proofreader and editor of Martineau's output – evidence, were it needed, that Harriet had absolute trust in her niece. She wrote to her friend Henry Grote:

> My greatest pleasure is in witnessing the capital health and cheerfulness of my beloved Maria, under such a responsibility as the care of me. She does everything well, – as well as can be, – from cooking sick messes to revising my articles; and such a sense of power as she must have is a great sustainer… of our mutual attachment.

Such was Maria's efficiency that she was lent to Florence Nightingale in times of need and she, too, developed a deep appreciation of the younger woman. It was therefore an immense sadness to both old campaigners when their nurse became fatally ill with typhoid in 1864. Harriet wrote to her old friend Erasmus Darwin in London:

> I shall be glad to give you (who understand) particulars. But I cannot… I am very ill myself and can hardly get through anyhow. Till you hear again, I think you must suppose that, while she may live, the chances are infinitely against it. – Tell Fanny what I say.

Maria died the following day and all Martineau's biographers mark this loss as a significant point in Harriet's life. She went into deep grief for months and, while she lived for another twelve years, she never had the same energy and spirit. Other nieces and nurses came and went but none made the same connection as Maria Martineau. In 1866 Harriet wrote to Fanny Wedgwood: 'The truth is, the mainspring of my life snapped when I lost Maria, as I doubt not you understand; and I need not say more.'

From her new home near Regent's Park in London, George Eliot confirmed her connection with Martineau by having an instinctive shudder at the news of Maria's death, as she wrote to Sara Hannell:

I was more sorry than it is usually possible to be about the death of a person unknown to me, when I read of Maria Martineau's death. She was a person whose office in life seemed so thoroughly defined and so valuable. For an invalid like Harriet Martineau to be deprived of a beloved nurse and companion, is a sorrow that makes one ashamed of one's small grumblings.

In 1867, Harriet wrote to Henry Grote's wife that her relationship with Maria had run much deeper than that with a nurse or housekeeper: 'For nine years my niece Maria lived in a companionship so close that few married people are so much and so exclusively together; and I verily believe that, in those years, there never was one passing moment of discontent of either with the other.'

Maria Weston Chapman cast Maria Martineau as the daughter Harriet never had, while Deborah Logan sees her more as a mother figure. Whatever the characterisation, Maria was the life partner that Harriet wanted and needed. She felt deep love for her, so much so that towards her own death many years later Maria was still uppermost in her mind: '... and now I desire nothing except in the languid way which is all I ever feel since I lost Maria... I care as much for the great and the distant as ever.'

Perhaps in a more modern and liberated era Harriet Martineau would have lived as an openly gay woman. She had a deep mental connection with Maria Weston Chapman and Maria Martineau, and both acted as confidant, support and emotional crutch at difficult times. It is incorrect to see Harriet as a cold, emotionless spinster who became bitter, as portrayed. With Maria Martineau particularly, she shared an emotional relationship of great mutual support and love. The sadness caused by Maria's death, and the gap she left behind, was a heavy weight on Harriet's final years.

Chapter 24: James Martineau

Harriet's brother James Martineau was famous in his own right in the 19th century. To this day, it is only his name that appears on the plaque outside the house in which the Martineaus grew up in Magdalen Street, Norwich. There is also a memorial to him at Harris Manchester College in Oxford, recognising his long work as a theologian and teacher for the College at its different homes in York, Manchester, London and Oxford.

The tale of Harriet and James is a lifelong sibling drama played out in public. It begins with them as close as two children can be, yet is strained by fame and ideological differences, burst asunder by a betrayal and ends in a lengthy feud. To followers and scholars of Harriet Martineau, James is generally regarded as the 'bad guy' who deserved what he got, but there are historians who claim Harriet was oversensitive regarding her brother.

Their similarity in character is often overlooked. Both became defined by a scepticism towards dogmatic, doctrinal, miracle-based religion, which they developed together in a dissenting Norwich environment, spurred on by reading Priestley, Hartley and Wordsworth. They shared a restless inquisitiveness allied to a stubbornness that would turn both of them into religious controversialists.

In recent years, the picture of their early life growing up together has become clearer with the publication of James's third-person summary of Harriet's letters to him. Unfortunately, she insisted that he destroy the originals, and he obliged. From these letters we get confirmation that the two young siblings were very close, as seen here when Harriet was writing to him as a 19-year-old: 'Harriet is longing for my return and the long walks and talks we shall have together', and, 'Before I leave she must tell me how deep is her love and that in parting from me she feels the loss of her better half', and, later in the same year, '... after death we might meet where no painful separation will disturb the enjoyment of our interchange of affection'.

Generally, the early letters from Harriet to James appear to be gushing in their affection for him. She shares her reading and experiences from Bristol, urging James also to study under Lant Carpenter. He follows her advice and soon comes under the influence of the freethinking preacher, eventually becoming his assistant in the 1820s.

The letters between the two of them record the death of their eldest brother Thomas, who had been a mentor to them, after which they embark on a very Wordsworth-like walking tour of Scotland, covering some 500 miles together. I imagine them reciting the words of the great poet, for whom they shared such a deep appreciation, as they went.

In 1825, James was away when their father was taken ill, and his precis of Harriet's letters are foreboding: 'My father has been ill from some obscure internal complaint. Harriet attributes it to great anxieties and precariousness of business affairs.'

In the spring of 1826, James records Harriet's letter as reporting: '... a sudden and terrible relapse in my father's state and the appearance of fatal symptoms.' Their father died in June 1826 with both Harriet and James in the house.

There then follows an episode in which James tried to matchmake his sister with a college friend, John Worthington. She writes to him in August 1826, saying she is ready to commit but at the same time has obvious reservations: 'Harriet's letter is an unreserved opening out of her feeling to me, with an obvious longing to accept J.H.W.'s proposal, yet a misgiving about her ability to realise his hopes, and some sympathy with the fears of his friends respecting his health.' Indeed, Worthington had been depressed for some months and the engagement was doomed.

In 1830 Harriet wrote several long letters to James, who by now had taken a post as Minister at Eustace Street Presbyterian Church in Dublin, in which she discussed her dilemmas in dealing with her publisher W. J. Fox:

> The first letter from the scene of her new and stimulating existence under the influence of W.J. Fox, at whose house and in whose study she spends day after day. Aunt Lee's present of her hearing trumpet enables her to enjoy in fullest measure his extraordinary conversation, as well as that of Dr Southwood Smith who would be tremendously interesting to her if she only heard him and never saw his face with its utterly 'vile expression' which it was impossible to trust.

She also presented here a picture of unrest back home in Norwich, which is not the peaceful easy country city it is easy to envisage. 'Norwich is in a very fractious and disturbed condition; murder and vitriol throwing being not infrequent, in the conflict of passions no one is safe.'

In 1831 Harriet went to Dublin to stay with James and his new wife Helen. James was getting a reputation as a deep thinker and a good pulpit orator, though this letter to W. J. Fox already hints at a developing divide between the siblings as regards religion:

> I believe ja's influence here is great over some ½ a dozen thinking

people, & there are very many who wonder at him, which is almost as good; and then Mr Armstrong intimates pretty extensively that he is a heretic... But his gentleness & forbearance with these people – I won't begin on this! I see in the eyes of a few that they would follow him on their knees through the world... I hear nothing of his sermons being too metaphysical, as I feared I should.

The letters reflected Harriet's growing reputation and career as a writer. She regularly wrote to James with updates and to ask his advice, as in 1832:

Harriet then reported the struggle she had to go through in facing and honestly treating the population problem in her political economy tales. She had taken courage to deal with it as Malthus himself did, like a moral and social question of fundamental importance and not to be shirked.

With Harriet's new-found fame and busy life in London, the letters became less frequent. James had married Helen Higginson, in 1828, and was planning a family as well as establishing himself as a cleric with his own ideas. Harriet repeatedly asked him to come on a 'continental' trip with her and he persisted in saying that it was not practical. It is possible to see that, by now, they were leading very different lives – she a freewheeling, famous writer and he a family man and cleric. It is also possible to sense his disapproval of this turn of events.

In 1832, James moved to Liverpool to take up a post at Paradise Street Chapel, though not before he and his wife had to bury their firstborn daughter who had died of fever in Dublin. They travelled with their two remaining children and would set up home in Liverpool for the next 25 years. James began expressing his own philosophy; having grown up in the Martineau family home, he was trying to reconcile religion and reason, and in 1836, when Harriet was preparing her own radical volume after returning from America, James wrote *The Rationale of Religious Enquiry*, advocating that religious truth must not be contrary to reason, expressed in the phrase: 'A divine right to dictate a perfectly unreasonable faith cannot exist.'[1] He was taking a critical approach to scripture and tradition, and advocating a religion based on feeling, sympathy and duty. This book was widely read, including in America, and would be republished several times under the title *What is Christianity?*

The growing divide between the siblings was exacerbated in the late 1830s by Harriet's outspoken advocacy of slavery abolition and her criticism of the

---

1. James Martineau, *The Rationale of Religious Inquiry* (Chapman, 1853), p. 27.

American system. James was not a great abolitionist and was developing establishment friends with vested interests, who would have had sympathy for the Southern slave-holders. Nevertheless, when Harriet was taken ill in Venice in 1840, it was James who led the party to bring her home and who made the arrangements with their older sister in Tynemouth.

The 1840s, however, saw them continue to pull apart from each other. James was developing and writing his own philosophy and becoming well known in Unitarian circles. He rejected the need for dogma and superstition but did not, like his sister, lose his faith in a direct higher power. His philosophy was influential in the developing Unitarian sense of duty to contribute to the community in order to make it better and it was not without influence. One of his direct disciples was George Dawson, who became instrumental in the establishment of Birmingham City Council. Together, the two men put forward the idea of local politics and government, through democracy and accountability, and argued that local people of standing had a duty to contribute and get involved.

James was no fan of Harriet's mesmerism and in 1843 the siblings had their first dispute. When James's young son Herbert became very ill, Harriet persisted in suggesting a mesmeric cure. James ignored the pleas and, tragically, his son died. Harriet quietly resented that her ideas had not at least been tried.

In the later 1840s, Harriet wrote several times to request visits from her brother but none were forthcoming. James may have felt he had been replaced in her life by the younger Henry Atkinson and, meanwhile, he was very busy with his own family life and in his burgeoning career. In 1848 he would have read *Eastern Life* and realised that their spiritual ideas were now incompatible, although Harriet wanted to set ideological matters aside and continue with family life, particularly as she valued seeing Helen and the children.

The seismic event that would cast the once inseparable siblings asunder for ever arrived in 1852, with James's review of the Martineau–Atkinson *Letters* in the *Prospective Review*. He portrayed Atkinson as an amateurish charlatan who had led his sister down a garden path of foolishness:

> The authors appear to live exclusively among people who see through brick walls, taste and hear across half the land; who have electric telegraphs laid into the future and the past, and can report histories they have never learned, and coming events that have made no sign of their approach.

Harriet, at home in The Knoll, must have felt a terrible betrayal, and her letters around this time lambast James, particularly for his treatment of Atkinson. She wrote to James's wife Helen:

> He has lost my esteem by public conduct, – not only not requiring 'explanation' but so bad as to disentitle him to it. On the face of it, – his taking advantage of his safe position as my brother to slander and insult Mr. Atkinson… leaves me no alternative but to disown him. This is obvious to all the world… It is not personal offence, but moral reprobation that I feel… I am sorry not to see the young people; but my course of conduct is clear. Fidelity to the truth, both general and personal, leaves me no choice in the test James has thought fit to impose.

There are two more similar letters in the following months, and one declining a visit from Helen and the children – even without James. The two siblings would not meet, speak or write to each other directly again. Harriet quietly seethed and seems to have felt it more than James, the feud perhaps encouraging her to undertake the Comte translations as she knew this was pushing the science-based philosophy which irritated him. Indeed, in 1858 James wrote a negative assessment of Comte in the *Westminster Review*, while Harriet lobbied to prevent him becoming Minister at Harris Manchester College, saying he had not enough faith to take the post. She failed in her attempt as he was elected, but later she successfully lobbied to stop him becoming Professor of Philosophy at University College London; she was part of a coalition that blocked his appointment because they saw him either as too religious or not religious enough. It was controversial at the time and led to resignations in the UCL governing body.

When the *Westminster Review* ran into financial trouble under the stewardship of John Chapman and George Eliot, Harriet heard that James was going to try and assume control and so she offered Chapman a loan of £500 to stop this happening. The siblings' hostility became widely known and talked about in literary circles, probably not reflecting very well on either party. In her autobiography Harriet mentions her disappointment at her brother's review but doesn't dwell on it and prefers to remember their friendly childhood. When he came to write his own memorial, James reflected: 'I think it open to reasonable doubt whether it was well for me to become the critic of the "letters"', and said that it had caused an 'epoch' in his life.[2]

Their estrangement did lead to a family schism: the Birmingham party,

---

2. James Martineau, *Biographical Memoranda* (Harris Manchester College Oxford, 1902), p. 54.

including Robert and his daughter Maria, generally took Harriet's side; the Liverpool contingent, including their sister Rachel who established a school in the city, stayed closer to James. There is an apocryphal story that, early in the 1860s, James went to Ambleside to attempt a reconciliation and knocked on the door of The Knoll, but it was closed wordlessly in his face.

James attended Harriet's funeral in Birmingham, alongside Robert's sons, and was one of the six people who bore her coffin into the Key Hill Cemetery family grave. This was the final meeting in what Maria Weston Chapman in her *Memorials* would call 'The Life Sorrow' of two siblings who had torn apart their own deep bond.

Part VI: The 1870s Onwards

Harriet Martineau's last years were clouded by her loneliness, isolation and a sense that she was physically hanging on to life. She occasionally wrote letters, but her mind was not the restless word machine it had once been. Meanwhile, the world was moving on apace, with strident ideas of racial and Christian superiority taking hold, justifying the empire as the Scramble for Africa unfolded. She would also have been aware that across the Atlantic the legacy of the American Civil War was one of bitterness and recrimination. These worldwide developments are well explored through her largely distant relationship with Queen Victoria.

Martineau's ongoing legacy and reputation have taken some strange twists and turns. Included here is a posthumous encounter with Arthur Rackham as representative of her publishing legacy, which has mainly amounted to reprints of her children's tales. And her links with America have borne fruit as she was in effect rediscovered by a new generation of American sociologists in the 1960s and '70s. In recent years, interest in Martineau has been sparked by a recognition that many women have been written out of history, but it may have been helped by the fact that there is a direct line of descent from the Martineau family in Norwich to Kate Middleton, who, all being well, should become Queen of England at some point in the future.

Chapter 25: Queen Victoria

Harriet Martineau was renowned around the world when the 18-year-old Alexandrina Victoria ascended to the throne in June 1837. Martineau's fame was at its peak, with her economic tales and American books widely read in Britain and its colonies, as well as in continental Europe and Russia. The young Victoria had read Martineau's early work in the 1830s and admired the *Illustrations of Political Economy*, particularly the tales of Ella of Garveloch, with her independence and sense of purpose.

Martineau was no fan of royalty per se, but she was generally defensive of Victoria in her journalism. The two women were never formally introduced, although Harriet did attend the coronation in Westminster Abbey. Her later description of it finds Harriet revelling in her own somewhat eccentric behaviour on the day. She was up at 4am and arrived at the Abbey early, where she sat down on a pew and ate her packed lunch. As it got more and more crowded, she took up a precarious perch so that she could see the ceremony: 'In order to see the enthroning, I stood on the rail behind our seats, holding by another rail. I was in nobody's way though every moment expecting that the rail would break.' Her reflection on the ceremony, written 18 years later in her autobiography, also finds her rather sceptical about the religion and pomp involved:

> It was a wonderful day; and one which I am glad to have witnessed but it strengthened instead of relaxing my sense of the unreal character of monarchy in England... There was such a mixing up of the Queen and the God, such homage to both, an adulation so like in kind and degree that, when one came to think of it, it made one's blood run cold to consider that this was commended to all that assemblage as religion... There is I believe, no public religious service which is not offensive to thoughtful and reverent persons, from its ascription of human faculties, affections, qualities and actions to the assumed First Cause of the universe.

At the time she had great regard for the young queen and soon after the coronation wrote to an American Unitarian friend the Revd William Ware: 'We are all somewhat romantic about our young Queen, poor thing! What chance has she got of growing up simple and good? But she really is an exceedingly good girl at present.'

After Victoria had been on the throne for a year, Martineau wrote a piece for the newspapers which was optimistic: 'Everyone who has seen her intelligent face knows that the comparisons by which utter incapacity is insinuated against the Queen are alike unfeeling and false.'

There is a sense in Martineau's correspondence that, having seen the Queen when she was young and watched her develop, she regarded her as a real person trying to do her duty. In these early years the Queen and Prince Albert, her husband and cousin, were both in tune with the restless improvement demanded by the writers and reformers of the era. This was before the historical myth of Victoria – symbol of the progressive 'Victorian' era, spreading British influence around the world – grew in the later years of the 19th century. After the death of her husband in 1861, Victoria went into a long retreat and only emerged to revel in her symbolic role as the head of a growing empire, publicly characterised when she was crowned Empress of India in 1877.

On occasion Martineau tried to connect with the Queen, requesting her endorsement of campaigns she was engaged with: for example, the issue of children working in factories, which became such a big debate in the 1850s and '60s. We can trace Martineau's own journey on this issue. In 1843, while she was in her Tynemouth sickroom, she wrote to Monckton Milnes about her attempt to make contact with the Queen and the result:

> When the Queen was a girl, she was fond of my political economy tales... You probably know how grave and sorrowful she has been of late about the factory children... I wrote to her accordingly, pleaded my years, my being the daughter of a manufacturer, – and my having studied these matters a good deal. In order to secure perfect freedom of speech, I pledged myself that she should not be committed in any way, that her name should not be used at all.

This foreshadows Martineau's disagreement with Dickens over the Factory Acts, ten years later. At this stage she was on the wrong side of history: she was convinced that the natural responsibilities of parents and employers would be enough to protect children from being abused through overwork. She certainly wasn't in favour of children working, but she was instinctively against the need for legislation to interfere in a free market of labour.

By August 1863, some years after her falling out with Dickens, and now fully engaged with producing regular leaders for the *Daily News,* Martineau wrote of a newly released report recommending the introduction of factory inspectors appointed by the government, particularly in response to the deaths of children working in the potteries. She seemed to be apologising for her earlier position and having a conversation with her former self:

> Thirty years ago the whole question of the rights and wrongs of children and young persons in their industrial capacity was one of our most embarrassing social jungles, which it seemed scarcely possible either to penetrate or leave untouched... Thus it is admitted to be for the benefit of all parties but bad employers and bad parents that the interests of the children should be secured in a way already proved to be safe and beneficial; and the only debate is about the method.

In concluding this piece, she referred to the serious 1860s problems of typhoid and cholera, scientific battles that she had written about before. She suggested that new child labour legislation was only the start of further improvements that would inevitably come from democratic pressure – something which would prove to be true:

> The further we look into each case the more important it is seen to be in relation to the future interest of the country; when the ravage of disease and death is stopped there is something else of not less vital interest to be looked to... we have only opened up the first aspect of a very expensive disclosure.

In 1870, elderly and battling her health, Martineau resurrected her pen. Exasperated and chastened by the lack of action on the part of employers, she sought redemption by actively supporting the 1870 Factory Act, convinced by then that legislation was necessary, allied to Forster's Education Act to make education for children compulsory. As R. K. Webb summarises:

> Her activity on behalf of the Factory Bill was enormous. She wrote herself 'sick and weary'. She wrote directly to the Queen to put the case, since she had heard that Queen Victoria was concerned about the plight of factory children. She hammered at all her friends in any position of political power. ... education was a case where delay was impossible, where the voluntary principle would not work because the very people most in need of education were those least capable of demanding or wanting it, or even of conceiving of it.

By this time Martineau was calling for Queen Victoria to come out of her self-imposed exile. Several times in the *Daily News* she politely suggested that the mourning had gone on long enough and that the country needed its monarch to play a part in public life. However, not only was Victoria uninvolved in public life, but she also became more conservative in her older years. She was not an advocate for women having the vote or greater political rights and was no longer particularly helpful to any reforming causes, much preferring the Conservative Disraeli to the reformer Gladstone. Victoria embraced her role as head of the British Empire, whereas Martineau several times in the *Daily News* expressed sympathy with the idea of Indian people having self-rule and warned against too much British power on the subcontinent.

Modern Sociologist Gayle Graham Yates summarises the Victorian situation as regards the rights of women, suggesting that Victoria herself became a negative influence on progress towards accepting women, choosing to live their own lives: '... in the 1830s women and women's rights made great advances only to fall back under the influence of Queen Victoria and the Victorians... Faith in individual women's accomplishments was a central point of Martineau's feminism from the beginning.'

The Victorian era, and the role of the Queen herself, is full of contradictions. It was a time of progress for women, a golden era of new women writers, particularly in the 1850s and '60s, with the appearance of the Brontës, Elizabeth Gaskell and George Eliot. The first organised campaigns for women also came about in that era, as did the developing notion that education for women and girls might be a good idea. However, it was also a time when family values became entrenched and the sanctity of marriage more powerful than ever. Moreover, the taking of colonies for practical economic reasons transformed into a macho philosophy of global dominance, espoused by prominent late-Victorian Christian men. The idea that the Victorian era was a great one for Britain is largely based on this power-grabbing philosophy, rather than the notion of progress towards greater equality of human rights.

Martineau was active as a journalist and a journal contributor in her latter years, an historical era that has been characterised as the 'Civilising Mission': a mission to make the wider world more like the Western industrialised 'civilised' nations. Martineau wrote leaders for the *Daily News* constantly between 1856 and 1863, and this journalism, in these fascinating historic years, perhaps caps her entire oeuvre. She wrote 1,600 leading reports on world affairs for the newspaper, of great variety and scope, all published anonymously, using her contacts around the world to give readers a global insight.

In her book *Harriet Martineau, Victorian Imperialism, and the Civilizing Mission*, Deborah Logan portrays an ambivalent body of work during this period. Harriet was a campaigner for science and education, which she saw as progress for the world, but she was also a champion of human rights and hated wars, particularly unnecessary ones, such as the Crimean War. As the years went on and British forces became more aggressive and indigenous people objected to their subjugation, the empire entered its most controversial phase. Logan takes a sociological approach, which leads her to question whether Martineau was culpable in encouraging British imperial ambitions.

> Martineau's commitment to the Civilizing Mission as a justification for imperialism was particularly challenged during 1857–63, when she was preoccupied with Ireland's education reforms, India's Sepoy Mutiny, Africa's slave trade, China's Arrow War, the Sarawak uprising, chronic unrest in the West Indies, the Trent affair that nearly resulted in war with the United States, and the American Civil War. Martineau's intense engagement with all these issues and events – her anger, despair, and optimism – resulted in some of the most impassioned and effective writing of her career. Seen in the broader context of intellectual history, her thinking reflects Enlightenment optimism, she was a positivist committed to the perfectibility of the human race and to the viability of democratic principles, free-trade capitalism and empirical science as the means to accomplish that aim.[1]

Martineau was unusually empathetic to indigenous peoples and several times wrote in favour of home rule for colonies. If she assumed a British superiority in this era it was because it was difficult to avoid. The *Daily News* gave her a platform for her campaigns such as anti-slavery, better hospitals and opposition to the Contagious Diseases Act. It would have been difficult to write anti-patriotic leaders in a national newspaper. It is easy to take a retrospective approach and suggest she could have done more to stop the excesses of the empire, but the facts of atrocities were not always obvious. Logan concludes that Martineau, on balance, is not guilty:

> Martineau was not without contradictions, and this study of her writing reveals her struggle to reconcile humanism with scientific objectivity and imperialism with democratic principles. Although she never doubted the superiority of Western civilization she viewed it as complementary to, not a substitute for, the heritage and traditions of indigenous cultures.

1. Deborah Logan, *Harriet Martineau, Victorian Imperialism and the Civilizing Mission* (Ashgate Publishing, 2010), p. 243.

Going further, one could say that Martineau deserves credit for taking an empathetic view of indigenous peoples; that her overriding principles of economic fairness, freedom and racial equality were very unusual at the time. Britain, as the first industrial nation, with huge global trading wealth, experienced a juggernaut momentum towards empire in the 1860s, '70s and '80s, the ideology of which was difficult to counter. But Martineau was a consistent alternative voice, with a global, universalist view, anticipating the modern liberal attitude to world issues that developed a century later in the 1960s.

These two women, Queen Victoria and Harriet Martineau, make for an interesting comparison. Victoria has become symbolic of a great era of reform and progress – a period when Britain ruled the waves. Victoria herself is intensively studied, in particular her life story, with its emotional upheavals. By contrast, Harriet Martineau has virtually disappeared from view, despite her life-long campaigns for women's rights, racial equality, better hospitals and trained nurses; her economic analysis favouring fairness and free markets; her challenging of religion and advocacy of science; and her pioneering journalism – ideas which have gone on to have enormous influence throughout the world. Yet history makes the myth, and it is myth that takes hold.

Chapter 26: Arthur Rackham

Arthur Rackham was nine years old in 1876 when Harriet Martineau died. This event was insignificant to him, living in a poor London suburb, the fourth of 12 children. But his career would collide with Martineau's writing at a later date.

Harriet's last years had been painful, both emotionally and physically and she finally died at her house in Ambleside in June 1876, aged 74. She never recovered emotionally from the death of her niece, maid and companion Maria, and physically she found it increasingly difficult to move around. She was still a restless spirit and would write regular letters in favour of greater education, better hospitals and in support of Josephine Butler's campaign, as well as keeping up her American correspondence, particularly with Garrison and Chapman.

She had resigned from the *Daily News* in the late 1860s after writing regular leaders for nearly 20 years. She was surprised and touched to receive several letters in tribute to her journalism from fellow scribes and from the Editor, who paid her fulsome tribute in the paper. Her *Daily News* work was wide-ranging, and agitated for improvements to be made around the world. It set a precedent for campaigning journalism which would be much copied in the 20th century.

The letters from her later years are also marked by an increasing depression about world affairs. Her work had always been marked by optimism about human progress and she had embraced Positivism and its philosophy that humankind's journey towards rationality and science was the route to peace and a better world. However, the technology created by science also brought more brutal wars. The conflicts in India, the violence of the American Civil War and the new large guns utilised in the Franco–Prussian War of 1870 would have dismayed her, as did the continued growth of poverty in the industrial cities. Around this time, she wrote to her niece Sarah Martineau:

> ... the increase of pauperism is beyond all former experience for the deadly character of it, – rotting away the working classes who have hitherto been our hope and pride. At such a time, we have no statesmen except Gladstone and there is no knowing what turn he will take next... Then it is a black outlook as regards the Royal Family, no help and only hindrance to be looked for there... My concern is purely & solely for the country & those in it who have to witness the coming times. It is an immense relief to me that I am leaving it, as I can do no good.

Harriet was buried in the family grave at Key Hill Cemetery in Birmingham, alongside her beloved niece Maria, her brother Robert and her mother. The record of the funeral in the *Birmingham Post* was brief, but significantly mentioned that her estranged brother James was in attendance:

> The funeral was a private one, and the arrangements were of a simple character. The hearse containing the body, followed by two coaches in which the mourners arrived at the cemetery about half past ten. The mourners were the Rev. Doctor Martineau (brother of the deceased), Councillor T. Martineau, Councillor R.F. Martineau, ... on reaching the cemetery the coffin, borne by six persons, and covered with a black velvet pall, was taken into the chapel. The Rev. Charles Clarke read the lessons and prayers contained in the service book which is commonly used by English Presbyterians, addressed the mourners and friends of the diseased who were present: 'during twenty years and more it has been known to most of us that there was a servant of God and of righteousness whom we knew dwelling in the neighbourhood of the Cumberland lakes, whose health was much impaired, and who might at any moment be called from the things seen, which are temporal, to the things not seen, which are eternal.[1]

An autopsy found a large ovarian cyst, which would have been the cause of her previous health crises that had ailed her over the years. She offered to leave her ears and her brain to medical science but they were declined. Many newspapers lazily chose to run the obituary she had written for herself, when she thought she was dying 21 years earlier. This was a typically modest account, alluding to neither her later work, such as her partnerships with Florence Nightingale and Josephine Butler, nor much of her journalism. Martineau was dismissive of much of her own writing in her obituary, as seen here, regarding her fiction:

> None of her novels or tales have ever had, in the eyes of good judges or in her own, any character of permanence. The artistic aim and qualifications were absent; she had no power of dramatic construction; nor the poetic inspiration on the one hand; nor critical cultivation on the other, without which no work of the imagination can be worthy to live.

---

1. 'Funeral of Miss Martineau in Birmingham', *Birmingham Post*, 5th July 1876, p. 48.

Advocates of Martineau have been partly fighting the lady herself, so keen was she to rubbish her own writing. The effect and influence of her fiction are both, here, missing. *Deerbrook* was greatly admired by a new generation of female novelists; *The Hour and the Man* was a radical tale of racial equality; the economic tales had a worldwide readership and an impact on connecting people with policy; and even the children's stories, with their cultivated communities and scepticism, have been widely read.

Her lifelong battle with *The Times* didn't stop the newspaper coming up with its own obituary, which included the following:

> Her 'illustrations' extended to twenty numbers; they were translated into French and German, and have helped perhaps more than any other work of modern times to spread abroad, in other countries as in our own, a knowledge of that science which til our own day had been so little known and studied... to mere pleasure seekers and idlers and triflers she had an unconquerable aversion; but if anyone sought to benefit these fellow creatures, high or low, rich or poor, and to lead a useful life as a social being, and a member of humanity at large, to him or to her the doors of Miss Martineau's house and of her heart were at once open. To the last in spite of a painful chronic illness she took the greatest interest in every movement which had for its object social, physical or moral improvement of the world, in which her lot was cast, and she corresponded largely with various leaders of such movements, who seldom sought in vain for her counsel and advice. If any lady in the nineteenth century in England or abroad, may be allowed to put in a claim for not having lived in vain, that woman, we honestly believe was Harriet Martineau.[2]

When her autobiography was published, with its appendix of other tributes assembled by Maria Weston Chapman, it received very mixed reviews and the atheism contained in it was still unpalatable to many. Scottish writer and critic Margaret Oliphant dismissed the book and castigated Harriet for a lack of feminine qualities saying, 'She never was much of a woman'.[3]

Martineau's career and profile had been on the wane since the early 1850s, when she alienated many of her friends and members of the literary circle with her radical secularism. Her ongoing journalism was largely produced without her name attached, as was the practice of the time, her longer journal articles

2. Harriet Martineau, 'Times Obituary', in *The Times Great Victorian Lives*, ed. Ian Brunskill (Times Books, 2007), p. 152.
3. Margaret Oliphant, review of Harriet Martineau's *Autobiography*, *Blackwood's Magazine*, 121 (1877), p. 54.

often being signed, 'From the Mountain', or something similar. By the time of her death the world was no longer interested in Harriet Martineau and some expressed surprise that she was only recently dead.

In the Memorials appendix to the autobiography there is a section, not very subtly entitled 'Waiting for Death', in which Chapman printed some of Harriet's final letters to loyal correspondents, as well as stating that one of the last people to visit her was the statesman and education reformer W. E. Forster. Final letters to Chapman, Nightingale and Garrison were part of the compilation; of course, many of her close friends had already died. To the end, she was swapping letters to Henry Atkinson. Both were still defiantly materialistic in the face of death, as here in her last letter to him:

> I see no reason for supposing it is not an actual and entire death. I have no objection to such an extinction... we are fully aware how mere a glimpse we have of the universe and the life it contains. Above all I wish to escape from the narrowness of taking a mere human view of things, from the absurdity of making God after man's own image.

The publication of this in 1877, along with the other autobiographical content, would have confirmed in the minds of the reading public that she was an avowed atheist, and this was no more palatable 25 years since the first publication of correspondence letters between Martineau and Atkinson than it had been at the time. The Memorials appendix, compiled by Chapman, was confusingly arranged as well as morbid, sad, atheistic, overly sentimental, and not a good overview of Martineau's career.

Martineau's principal legacy in the late 19th and early 20th centuries were her children's stories, particularly those commissioned as *The Playfellow* series in the 1840s, written from her Tynemouth sickroom. So it was that her collision with Arthur Rackham occurred in 1899.

Feats on the Fjord, as illustrated by Rackham and published by Dent & Co., was to become a popular children's book in the first part of the coming century, and is one of the most collectible and valuable of Martineau's books, largely because of his illustrations.

It was one of the first books Rackham was commissioned to illustrate, only a few years after he became a full-time artist and illustrator. He would go on to produce fantasy drawings of incredible detail and imagination; such that his work in the modern era is highly regarded artistically and loved by numerous followers, his original drawings and artwork being much sought after by the art houses of the world. Rackham became known for retaining a level of realism and materiality in his art while still suggesting fantasy worlds. His work in *Feats on the Fjord* is underdeveloped, but it is possible to see his natural talent. In fact, he took the job very seriously and it was a breakthrough for him. He even visited Norway to get an accurate depiction of the Fjords and villages that the story revolves around.

Feats on the Fjord is an interesting read and it is safe to assume that, even in her children's books, Martineau was making the same arguments she did in her other writing. This is the story of several members of a village on the edge of the Norwegian fjords. On three separate occasions there is a marked reaction to a superstitious event in the village, which turns out to have been concocted by humans, and the superstitious are shown to be foolish. There is a female role model of independence and strong mind, and there is a powerful sense of what the village needs for their traditional way of life to be sustainable, with everybody playing a useful, productive role. There is danger and derring-do on the fjords and a somewhat sympathetic portrayal of pirates. Unexpectedly for Martineau, the narrative also includes a love triangle, which resolves itself in a happy ending.

Within the story she presents vivid descriptions of the geology and geography of the Norwegian fjords and draws attention to the effect of long northern days:

> The golden light which blesses the high and low places of the earth, did not disdain to cheer and adorn this humble chamber, which at the bidding of nature, the waters had patiently scooped out of the hard rock. Some hours after darkness had settled down on the lands of the tropics, and long after the stars had come out in the skies over English heads. This cave was at its brightest. As the sun drew to its setting, near the middle of the Nordland summer night, it levelled its golden rays through the cleft, and made the place far more brilliant than at noon.

It is a thoroughly modern, dramatic and vivid tale, which could still be popular. The book ran to many editions, and still crops up in private libraries; the extent of its reach is indicated by the fact that two other illustrators were commissioned for further editions: P. Ebbutt, who took a fairly literal view of the tale with his elegant drawings, and the Scottish social realist artist Enoch Ward, who would go on to greater things. It is perhaps very appropriate that Arthur Rackham should have been given a Martineau book to work on, and his illustrations are the more complex of the three, bringing to Martineau's oeuvre a mixture of reality and mystery.

Harriet advocated science and materialism and the need for evidence throughout her life, but also retained a view that the answers to some questions were unknowable to humans. Moreover, her view was that mysterious things did exist and could be explained in materiality. However, she wasn't a supporter of science to the detriment of every other view. A more scientific world was preferable, but human life also had complexity and imagination attached to it. In her lifelong appreciation of poetry and fiction, she embraced human products of the imagination and, in proposing *Oliver Weld* to George Smith, she even saw a future world where progress and technology had divorced people from nature.

She would have been pleased that her book was the subject of Rackham's illustrations and that it was an important step in his development as an artist. He came from a large, poor family and had a difficult childhood. He was sent away on a trip to help him come out of himself as a teenager, and his flowering as an artist was not entirely different from hers as a writer, 70 years earlier; nothing pleased her more than helping people to fulfill their talent.

That *Feats on the Fjord* is the book of Martineau's that has been most widely read and circulated since her death, perhaps suggests the world can accept a woman as a children's fiction author but not as a radical philosopher. In her sniping review of the autobiography a year after Martineau's death, Margaret Oliphant set the scene for this by writing: '*Feats on the Fjord* is the only one of her productions that specially deserves to live.' She was pursuing a true science of human nature and we can see a great irony here that human nature means that people prefer a good story of childhood derring-do to hearing that material life is all there is and that perhaps there is no God. The world was not ready for Martineau's radical philosophising in the 19th century, though she had given her all in the name of pursuing truth and progress. When she died in 1876, in her 75th year, she must have felt the satisfaction of having been an influential writer and of leading an unprecedented life through an unprecedented age.

Chapter 27: Kate Middleton

One hundred and eighty years after the ascent of Queen Victoria, two family lines have come full circle and collided. Prince William, sixth-generation descendant of Victoria and second in line to the throne, has married Catherine (Kate) Middleton, sixth-generation descendant of Harriet Martineau. It does feel noteworthy that Kate Middleton, a modern symbol of independence and female capability, yet within such a highly managed institutional context, has come from a long line of non-aristocratic women, several of whom helped to establish education for girls. One can only guess at Martineau's reaction to the news that her descendant would marry into the royal family, with a strong possibility of becoming Queen of England, for she was no fan of royalty or privilege. She may also have been nonplussed by the fuss around modern fashion and celebrity culture which seems to relentlessly follow the Duchess of Cambridge. It is safe, I think, to assume that Harriet would have been urging Kate to make her own independent mark and to use her position for progressive change.

The line of descent is via Frances Lupton, Harriet's niece, who was much influenced by her aunt in becoming a powerful supporter of schools for girls in the Leeds area, in particular, and in the North in general. The Martineau and Lupton families shared a Unitarian background and both families went on to build political dynasties, the Martineaus with five generations of mayors in Birmingham and the Luptons with two mayors in Leeds. Both families were instrumental in building local government and social reform at a city level, and shared a sense of public duty. However, they were outsiders to the church and London establishment. Unitarians were barred from attending university until the mid-19th century.

Kate Middleton has obviously benefited from living in a world in which people from all backgrounds can receive an education and advance up the social ladder. Her lineage links her to the great Unitarian families of the Midlands and the North, including the Martineaus, Wedgwoods, Darwins, Chamberlains and Kitsons, all of whom drove reform with a social conscience. These families had a great influence on the industrialising world at a crucial time. The fact that the future Queen of England comes from this background and lineage is symbolic recognition of a great breakthrough, even if some of the same social problems and inequalities battled by her ancestors persist.

At the time that Kate Middleton became engaged to the future king, the *Daily Mail* ran an article that said she would do well to heed one of the stories written by her ancestor, Great Great Great Aunt Harriet Martineau, namely *The Peasant and the Prince*. One of *The Playfellow* series produced by Martineau in the 1840s, this story is aimed at young adults and focuses on the last days of royalty before the French Revolution. Portraying Martineau's real feelings about royalty, aside from her affection for the young Queen Victoria, this short book contains some radical passages – so much so that American sociologist Jackie C. Horne has suggested that it was in effect deliberately suppressed by the Victorian establishment, who intimidated its publishers.

The Peasant and the Prince is two stories in one, the first half being a description of the terrible conditions that French peasants were left to live in under the aristocracy, and the second half showing young Prince Louis's struggle to cope with the Revolution. This half begins with the passage the *Daily Mail* recommended for the Duchess of Cambridge, suggesting as it does that royals should not get carried away:

> It is a common belief, among those who have not learned to be wiser, that to be a king, or one of the king's family, is the same thing as to be perfectly happy… The truth is that royalty does not exempt from sickness and death, and from the troubles of the heart and mind.

The book ends with one of Martineau's clearest evocations of what greater equality could be. It sounds like socialism, confirming that, though she was a fan of free markets, she saw them as the best route to democracy and equality:

> God gave to the French nation one of the richest and most beautiful countries in the world. This country, with its sunny hills, its fertile plains, its great forests, and brimming rivers, can easily produce more of all the good things of life than are wanted for the use of all its inhabitants. No man, woman, or child within its boundaries ought ever to be in want of the comforts of life.

For Jackie C. Horne, this children's book fits her theory that the socio-economic context of industrialisation brought a new type of children's literature. Her *History and the Construction of the Child in Early British Children's Literature* contains another constructivist sociological take on Martineau from America. She reveals that *The Peasant and the Prince* was regarded as subversive at the time:

> If twentieth century critics fail to see the radical nature of *The Peasant and the Prince*, Martineau's contemporaries were far more aware; an

anonymous article on the state of books for children in the *Quarterly Review* 'purposely omitted' *The Peasant and the Prince* because of its 'reprehensible purpose and tendencies'.[1]

Horne explains that 1840s England saw the beginnings of Chartist rumblings, with fears of mob demands for greater democracy. She concludes:

> To preach understanding of the people who made up these faceless mobs as Martineau does in *The Peasant and the Prince* is for the *Quarterly Review* to extend an invitation to the mob violence characteristic of late eighteenth century France onto unsullied British ground.

Many subsequent purveyors of subversive literature will recognise that the establishment can bury unwanted ideas in subtle ways, although this is perhaps not so prevalent in children's literature.

Another unheralded Martineau influence comes with the publication of Mark Twain's *The Prince and the Pauper* in the 1880s, 40 years after Martineau had penned her version. Twain would have been aware of *The Playfellow* series, which was popular in the United States. Although based on the British monarchy and a tale of mistaken identity, Twain's basic aim is very similar – to demystify royalty, to show that they are people just like you and me and that the inequality they symbolise should be challenged. Twain was channelling the anti-establishment spirit of Harriet Martineau.

Martineau's story reveals the modern dilemma for royals in that, over the last 200 years, deference towards royalty and upper-class superiority has been eroded. Kate Middleton, a real life example of a commoner becoming a royal personage, has benefited from the modern breakdown in class barriers. However, the media hype surrounding her has never been greater, particularly as a duchess who has come from ordinary stock. The public and media interest in Kate mean that she is becoming an important public role model, famous around the world, with a carefully presented royal image.

It may be seen as ironic that Kate will never have the freedom that Harriet Martineau had 180 years before her. Her role will always be conflicted: however much she may dote on her children, enjoy her charitable work, love her husband, it must all be presented in accordance with maintaining – or, indeed, creating – a positive and, perhaps most importantly, appropriate image of the royal family.

This betrays the ongoing pressures that still exist for women. There are

---

1. Jackie C. Horne, *History and the Construction of the Child in Early British Children's Literature* (Routledge, 2011), pp. 166–7.

great restrictions on freedom of choice, particularly if we take a worldwide view. Headway has been made in the Western world but in large parts of the rest of the world women are still restricted to societal norms that say they must stay at home to rear children. Freedom of choice for women still has a long way to go. Kate Middleton is symbolic of class fluidity and a new type of royalty, but she still faces great pressure to be presented in a traditional role. This helps us recognise the radicalism of the handful of public women who were prepared to present a different front.

In 1850 in America, the first congress was held for women's rights. Martineau had been an inspiration for many of the women who established this event, but although she was invited she could not make the trip. She could not attend the second congress in 1851 either, but was invited to pen an address to be read out. It may have surprised her female comrades that she chose to say that freedom and rights for all people, not just women, were still some way off but could be attained. The following quotation from her address to this congress is included because it represents a profound philosophy – one that has rarely been so clearly elucidated and could still form the basis of much change. She saw no great collision between accepting laws of nature and retaining individual free will. The division of sciences since the 19th century has created a false divide. Martineau is one of very few people to write that humans exist within natural laws but are left with freedom, diversity, great capabilities and potential in every individual, which should not be shackled but should be encouraged and set free.

Harriet Martineau's 'Address Read Aloud to the 2nd American Women's Rights Convention, 3 August 3 1851':

> My thoughts and best wishes will be with you when you meet. I cannot accept your hearty invitation to attend your Convention, but you may be assured of my warm and unrestricted sympathy. Ever since I became capable of thinking for myself, I have clearly seen – and I have said it till my listeners and readers are probably tired of hearing it – that there can be but one true method in the treatment of each human being of either sex, of any color, and under any outward circumstances – to ascertain what are the powers of that being, to cultivate them to the utmost, and then to see what action they will find for themselves. This has probably never been done for men, unless in some rare individual cases. It has certainly never been done for women.
>
> It will appear to be no less absurd to have argued, as men and women are arguing now, about what women ought to do, before it

was ascertained what woman can do. Let us see a hundred women educated up to the highest point that education at present reaches – let them be supplied with such knowledge as their faculties are found to crave, and let them be free to use, apply and increase their knowledge as their faculties shall instigate, and it will presently appear what is the sphere of each of the hundred. One may be discovering comets, like Miss Herschel; one may be laying upon the mathematical structure of the universe, like Mrs. Somerville; another may be analysing the chemical relations of nature in the laboratory; another may be penetrating the mysteries of physiology; others may be applying science in the healing of diseases; others may be investigating the laws of social relations, learning the great natural laws under which society, like everything else, proceeds; others, again, may be actively carrying out the social arrangements which have been formed under these laws; and others may be chiefly occupied in family business, in the duties of the wife and mother, and the ruler of a household. If among the hundred women, a great diversity of powers should appear, (which I have no doubt would be the case), there will always be plenty of scope and material for the greatest amount and variety of power that can be brought out.

Chapter 28: Harriet Martineau and Me - A Personal View

In the 1990s I went back to university to do a part-time Masters degree in history, realising that I hadn't made the best of my previous attempts at studying. In my own scientific spiritual awakening, I had been reading Darwin and the great modern writers on evolution, Richard Dawkins and Stephen Jay Gould. I was very lucky in gaining a tutor, Stephen Inwood, who was open-minded and encouraging, a few years before his own great success with *A History of London*.

There seemed to be a big difference between Darwin's description of natural selection and how it was popularly conceived, even how it was often described within science. I became mildly obsessed with this conflict and with tracing how it had come about. It seemed to my untrained mind that a good understanding of evolution was a prerequisite for intellectual activity. In particular, the open-ended, non-purposeful character, and ecological aspects of natural selection were ignored or wilfully misunderstood, and yet to me this aspect of natural selection revealed much about the complex, haphazard, under-designed, imperfect world as it exists. The popular understanding of evolution as a concept had been heavily influenced by the Victorian context of its birth.

In pursuing this for several years, I became involved in a London scene and it is no exaggeration to say that I was present at the birth of modern-day evolutionary psychology. Helena Cronin at the LSE invited me to help run the LSE Darwin Seminars, my prior professional experience as an events manager being of some use. In the mid 1990s I was able to help spread the word about the seminars, which featured influential talks by the Darwinian luminaries of the day including Steven Pinker, Daniel Dennett, Steve Jones, John Maynard Smith, Peter Singer, Matt Ridley, Mark Ridley, James Watson and Lewis Wolpert, amongst others, and were attended by many of the UK's top scientific thinkers. It now seems to me that Helena Cronin was the Harriet Martineau figure in this 1990's all-male club, and she deserves much credit for stimulating public debate about evolution during that decade.

Throughout this time, I became more and more convinced that there was a neglected aspect of evolution, and that the imposition of purpose onto natural selection – that there was an active selector, which Darwin hadn't described – was quite common even in this informed complex thinking circle. Darwinian natural selection is the twin factors of reproduction and survival leading to organisms becoming shaped by their ecological niche over millions of years.

As a species, we are much more the result of specific environmental challenges than the winners in any active competition with other groups or species. Social Darwinism had been powerful in America, and dictated a view dominated by a dog-eat-dog, survival of the fittest notion that is still very common today.

In the 1990s, evolutionary psychology developed a reputation for just so explanations, for easy answers to complex questions, and encouraging a determinist view, denying free will. It is right to be wary of these and other factors in overstating the control of evolution on our lives. However, the basic premise that the human brain and its resulting 'mind' have evolved alongside other organs – and, indeed, other minds within nature – is surely right. Engaging with this should not be controversial.

I then spent 15 years trying to write up my own emphasis on the purposeless, open-ended aspect of natural selection, and trying to get it published in various guises. Other than a few articles, a couple of which generated a vitriolic response from creationists, my audacious book proposal failed to become more than just that: a proposal. I had also chosen to keep working and eschew academia, partly because I wanted to be involved in culture, not on its sidelines. This is not something I regret: I learnt as much about society, politics and human nature by working as a manager at the Millennium Dome as I would have done at any university. However, it also took its toll on my nervous system and I retreated back to my home town, Norwich, to eventually become Director of the Norwich Arts Centre.

Through my study of the 19th-century context of evolution I had been made aware of Harriet Martineau. In particular, James Moore and Adrian Desmond mentioned her time and again in their magisterial 1991 biography *Darwin*, as a radical influence on him at a crucial time. I then found out that she was from Norwich and I knew that there was very little recognition of her in our shared home town. Harriet Martineau became part of my escape from the capital.

I began to read more about Martineau and discovered her sociological side and that she was revered in American academia. I invited myself to a one-day conference about her at University College London, mainly attended by formidable American women academics. As I'd found when studying Darwin, they went into great theoretical detail and debate about Martineau, with limited understanding or recognition of her place in the wider world.

At this point the Martineau Society came into my life – a wonderful mix of academics, Unitarians, enthusiasts and eccentrics, their meetings always friendly, humorous and stimulating. I received some encouragement for my pursuit of the links between Martineau and Darwin, as well as discovering a myriad of other 19th-century connections between her and other luminaries. Studying a neglected historical figure can be something of a joy in that you end up delving into unexpected nooks and crannies of history. My research has included clandestine meetings, discovery of forgotten writings and meeting modern Martineau family members. Finding an original copy of *Letters on the Laws of Man's Nature and Development* became a difficult quest, as they are rare, and it was with some excitement that I finally held one in Cambridge University Library.

For the 200th anniversary of Darwin's birth in 2009, Moore and Desmond published their follow-up to the original biography, *Darwin's Sacred Cause*, giving Martineau even more credit in the evolution story, and I disseminated their work into papers and talks. All the while, Harriet Martineau was beginning to reveal to me previously hidden depths in her writing and thought, while her fascinating life was an example in itself of so many historical forces. The Martineau Society meeting in Boston Massachusetts in 2010 was life-changing for me, partly as it brought Harriet's American journey alive, but also because the historians and librarians I encountered there were incredibly enthusiastic about her in a way I hadn't experienced in the UK. I realised I was onto something and had accidentally carved myself a niche.

The personal connection grew. The pursuit of truth rather than accepting the predominant culture, the power of reading and writing, and the mixture of high theory and real improvement to lives, were all aspects of her career that had motivated me in my own life. I've never been overly concerned about disproving religion and, like Martineau, I realised that the consoling power of religion in life is stimulated by human nature.

Understanding the wider natural context, that humans are a part of nature as are other animals, shouldn't be hugely controversial in the light of evolution, but it is still problematic to many people going about their lives and to many scholars trying to make sense of it all. This was just one of Martineau's insights, which I began to think should be recognised.

It is not easy to trace where the modern liberal approach to life, the assumed right of freedom, democracy and respect for every individual, comes from, but I began to understand that Martineau was way ahead of others in promoting individual human rights, racial equality, women's rights, economic fairness, freedom from religious persecution, opposition to slavery, greater democracy, better health provision. These ideas have become powerful, and provide the bedrock of the United Nations' Universal Declaration of Human Rights of 1948. Of course, I am not claiming Martineau was their single greatest advocate, nor the originator, but she was the only woman in, and was at the head of, a generation which made enlightenment ideas real and she was at the forefront in a crucial era in terms of determination and steadfastness in the face of opposition. She was central to the so-called 'radical 1830s', the consequences of which would reverberate around the world, partly through the historical accident of British industrialisation and empire. Those liberal ideas have come from somewhere and have needed supporters.

Moreover, her championing of science and progress were part of a massive historical force towards more detailed knowledge, better technology and longer lives. If only one thing chimes from the encounters I've recorded here, it is surely how far we have come from having to accept the deaths of our children. So many people, just 150 years ago, had to accept this, and it scarred the lives of Charles Darwin, Elizabeth Gaskell, James Martineau, Matthew Arnold and William Wordsworth amongst others in this story.

The religion that runs through this account is surely linked to this ever-present spectre of mortality, particularly for people whose children died before them. But a battle between faith-based religion and evidence-based science becomes ever more present in the 19th century and Harriet Martineau has a prominent role in this at the time. In adolescence, Harriet and James Martineau were obsessed with religion and both were a part of an era in which blind adherence to the gospels dissipated and which had to be reconciled with reason. Nineteenth-century Britain was a period when most public figures were working out the implications of 18th-century scepticism and, in the case of Tom Paine, outright rebellion against religion, as well as an increasing presence of science and technology.

In modern times, religion is explained broadly in two ways. On the one hand, according to, for instance, Richard Dawkins and Daniel Dennett, it is a 'delusion' – a foolishness that should be dropped forthwith. On the other, evolutionary psychologists such as Steven Pinker, Robert Wright or anthropologist Scott Atran, argue that religion is a part of human nature – it exists for good reasons, and has therefore manifested itself in different faiths in various cultures throughout the world and throughout history. Martineau was well ahead of her time in advocating the latter, and I would generally agree with her.

Of course, religiously minded people are not concerned with this. They are busy accepting a future life, a more optimistic view and more palatable to human nature. I myself don't feel the need for this consolation but do not get upset with people who do (other than those who set out to kill others to prove the superiority of their particular God) though the pernicious influence of religion as a human institution has to be guarded against. Martineau's position was a sophisticated one: that ultimate explanations are beyond the scope of the human mind. Having stuck to her guns in the early 1850s, she wrote to Maria Weston Chapman in 1856 to explain her Positivist position and in doing so was at her combative best:

> While the disciples of dogma are living in a magic cavern, painted with wonderful shows, and the metaphysical philosophers are wandering in an enchanted wood, all tangle and bewilderment, the positive philosophers have emerged upon the broad, airy, sunny common of nature, with firm ground underfoot and light overhead... Infant man – the race and the individual – instinctively transfers his own consciousness or experience to everything his senses encounter... I need not say how puerile and barbaric appear to us the views of Christian Fetishism... It is not 'another life' that people desire and expect, but the same life.

However, we now live in an era where the progress those liberal, science advocates once took for granted, and which gained momentum after the disaster of the Second World War, is now being challenged. The internationalist, global view of the liberals is coming up against nationalism and opposition to the free movement of peoples. Human rights and respect for people are under pressure from increasingly vocal prejudice and vitriol. Global technological growth is challenged because of the impact it is having on the planet's natural resources. Science, despite its robust methods, can be contradictory and does not always have the trust of the public. The era of assumed progress is coming to an end.

So these things are not straightforward, but I felt increasingly strongly that Harriet Martineau was an underestimated figure in the history of progressive human rights, internationalism and scientific advancement and I began to push harder to get her recognition. It had become a mission.

I was invited to write about her in when Norwich became the first English city to receive UNESCO City of Literature status – a bid with non-conformist writing at its heart. On the back of that, with the help of Chris Gribble at Writer's Centre Norwich, I founded an annual Harriet Martineau Lecture as part of the Norfolk and Norwich Festival, the first one in 2012 being brilliantly delivered by author Ali Smith. This was appropriate given that the festival had been founded by Harriet's surgeon uncle Philip Meadows Martineau, as a concert fundraiser for the new Norwich hospital in the 1770s. I made a plan for the book and left my job, partly to write it, and partly to revisit my Darwin studies.

Even the acceptance by Unbound to publish this book has seemed right. Martineau's original publication of *Life in the Wilds* came about through subscriptions, and so the crowd-funding I embarked upon – backed up as hers was, by supporters, friends and progressives of Norwich – felt appropriate. One of the staff at Unbound had attended the 2015 Harriet Martineau Lecture, delivered fittingly and tellingly by the Russian journalist and thorn in Putin's side, Masha Gessen: Martineau's books had been ordered to be rounded up and burnt in Russia by Tsar Nicholas I, 180 years before.

As I've approached my fifth decade I've felt another connection with Martineau – we both went through a demystification of people in London. Martineau knew intimately some of the top politicians, writers and artists of the day and became a focal point of attention amongst them. In her autobiography she presented them as rounded humans both vulnerable and with character flaws, as well as purveyors of influential work. In my London years I met some of the great evolutionary thinkers, such as James Watson, Bill Hamilton and Richard Dawkins (it is still a very male-dominated field), but I also met many cultural luminaries. Politicians, royalty and stars of film, music and TV can soon lose their mythical status when you've had to spend a day or two with them (for me this included amongst others Tony Blair, Charlton Heston, Gerard Depardieu, Luciano Pavarotti, Greta Scaachi, George Best and Princess Diana) and, if nothing else, you quickly realise they are just people. Some are more talented than others, some more hardworking and some plain lucky, but all are the same – people like you and me.

I believe that Martineau would have been both mystified and dismayed by modern academia, designed as it is to create hierarchies of knowledge. Indeed, it is worth noting that very few of the great thinkers in this book went to university or, if they did, they wasted their time in revelry, like Darwin. The increasingly pointless niche study, the veneration of hierarchical progress, the bureaucracy of modern universities is something Martineau would have abhorred, so focused was she on knowledge to make people's lives better.

Martineau's career is strikingly symbolic of a major schism in intellectual history. The birth of social science and of sociology, which she influenced in the middle of the 19th century but which came to fruition towards the end of the epoch, led to a growing divide between the natural and the social sciences. In particular, a split occurred between those accepting the influence of nature and human nature, and those denying it as an influence. Sociology increasingly rejected what came to be seen as the opposite of freedom; biology equated with determinism became a dogma; and Social Darwinism was rightly dismissed as a pariah. Human life was instead seen as one of social construction, shaped by society, so that if society could be changed then human life would improve.

The sexism to which Martineau fell victim was a result of a patriarchal system developed as a power structure.

So a considerable irony here is that Martineau herself was an advocate of nature, and of the notion that humans are greatly influenced by that nature. She herself was the living embodiment of independent-minded free will within the wider boundaries of nature. She did not see individual freedom, the existence of free-will, as being in opposition to humans existing within influential natural systems. Her work in the 1850s anticipated the idea of an evolved mind. She foresaw evolutionary psychology, which many in the social sciences still oppose as anti-freedom and deterministic, despite the protestations of those within it.

This also chimed with my own experience of meeting those people who shaped the new evolutionary psychology in the 1990s. It was very rare to find deniers of individual freedom. As Steve Jones said during a Darwin Seminar I helped produce in 1998: 'There are no genetic determinists in genetics'. There is a huge difference between saying genetics *influence* humans, which is obviously true, and saying genetics *determine* the future in an unavoidable way. The dogma created by social sciences, to resist the influence of nature and demonise biology, has been a major wall in a true understanding of ourselves. It takes an intellectual leap, one that Harriet Martineau made, to realise there is freedom in nature. Accepting that free will is produced by nature, is an intellectual revolution still waiting to happen.

In my own work I've written several times about 'The Spirit of Harriet Martineau', which I've characterised as embracing freedom of speech, encouraging the potential of people, using evidence where possible, having steadfast determination and taking up the cause – sometimes against the odds – against history and against prevailing opinion, and not being afraid to investigate an issue yourself. Martineau was by no means perfect, but in the battle of ideas and the historical forces of conservatism versus improvement, she was a heroine. I do believe that, generally, we should always be ready to listen to radical outsiders.

Several people have expressed puzzlement at my pursuit of the Martineau story and some see no value in looking backwards at all. But what does it say about history and the collective memory? Surely we need to learn from the past, and observing previous battles and celebrating ideological pioneers, particularly progressive ones, says something about our current society. History is the same battleground as life: it is a battle for a better future. Studying the history of the development of ideas such as evolution is one way in which this study is very much alive and relevant. The establishment will by definition try to reinforce the status quo. If there is one lesson from Martineau's life and philosophy it is that human life is made by humans. We can influence our future but the past, and the battle for it, is relevant.

In another time Harriet Martineau could have been lauded as a great philosopher and encouraged to write up her ideas of freedom, family, women's rights, human nature and how they manifest in human systems of economic life, rather than them appearing piecemeal in 'tales' or letters and journalism. Or indeed, she could have been a great politician and leader, so convinced was she of the importance of good leadership backed up by clear ideas of how the system should relate to people. But these options were unthinkable to her as a woman in 19th-century Britain and help us appreciate the progress that has been made for women in a relatively short period of time, in both the intellectual and the political worlds.

For what it's worth, my own determination lies in pointing out that the open-ended quality of natural selection is still poorly understood. As the accepted driver of life on Earth within science, it is surrounded by myth and wilful misunderstanding in wider culture. The uncertainty of outcome, the concurrence and simultaneity of factors in life, the complex mix of nature and nurture, are inherent in evolution. Freedom exists because it has evolved. We all live in a complex web of tensions arising from evolution but to reach this we have to have a more subtle understanding of natural selection.

Martineau egged Darwin on towards a fearless challenge of religion. She instinctively understood his idea because she was open-minded about nature as an influence. The future of intellectual, academic study must include a break-down of the barrier between biology and sociology, between the natural and social sciences. The science she advocated is increasingly showing that genetics and complex biological development of every being is real and influential, but it is not counter to individuality – it is the *cause* of individuality.

So Harriet Martineau has become my inspiration, my cause and my model. Her life demonstrates that embracing nature is not denying freedom, for the application of her own free will was formidable and her determination to speak out through the written word considerable. She was attuned to the bigger picture of history and events of the world, while still being able to recognise that the individual lives of ordinary people needed to be better. Idealism and practicality can run alongside each other. She spoke her own mind and accepted that others should, also. Ongoing inquisitiveness and ongoing debate, fought through words, written and spoken, were the substance of life.

The history of ideas runs through these encounters, alongside the fallibility and character of humans. In so many ways – and it doesn't always seem so –

we live in a better world than the Victorians, with greater freedom, longer and richer lives, easier access to learning, food, culture, sport, entertainments and communications. But this world was built by people with independent, creative minds from previous generations. In Martineau's eyes the world was not made better by cold, detached, statistical analysis, nor by macho political posturing. There were real problems for ordinary people, which needed real, working solutions in which everyone could play a part.

From these 19th-century stories, we can see how far we have come thanks to the work of outspoken individuals, that human life is not pre-destined – it is the result of conversation, collaboration, research and individual visions, of human action, advocated by leading lights talking and working with others. It is what we make it. And I'd like it to be recognised that through her steadfast indomitable determination, not many lights have shone as brightly and consistently for improvement for people in this world as Harriet Martineau.

Selected Bibliography

Harriet Martineau Letters

Arbuckle, Elisabeth Sanders (ed.), *Harriet Martineau's Letters to Fanny Wedgwood* (Stanford University Press, 1983)

Hooper, Glenn (ed.), *Letters from Ireland: Harriet Martineau* (Irish Academic Press, 2001)

Logan, Deborah Anna (ed.), *The Collected Letters of Harriet Martineau* (Pickering and Chatto, 2007)

Logan, Deborah Anna (ed.), *Harriet Martineau: Further Letters* (Lehigh University Press, 2011)

Sanders, Valerie (ed.), *Harriet Martineau: Selected Letters* (Oxford University Press, 1990)

Harriet Martineau Selected Works

Arbuckle, Elisabeth Sanders (ed.), *Harriet Martineau in the London Daily News* (Garland, 1994)

Atkinson, Henry George and Harriet Martineau, *Letters on the Laws of Man's Nature and Development* (John Chapman, 1851)

Comte, Auguste, *The Positive Philosophy of Auguste Comte*, trans. and condensed by Harriet Martineau (John Chapman, 1853)

Logan, Deborah Anna (ed.), *Harriet Martineau's Writings on Slavery and the American Civil War* (Northern Illinois University Press, 2002)

Logan, Deborah Anna (ed.) *Harriet Martineau and the Irish Question* (Lehigh University Press, 2012)

Martineau, Harriet, *Illustrations of Political Economy: Selected Tales*, ed. by Deborah Anna Logan (Broadview Editions, 2004)

—*The History of England during the Thirty Years' Peace 1815–1846* (Charles Knight, 1850)

—*Autobiography, Volumes 1 and 2* (Elibron Classics, 2005)

—*Biographical Sketches* (Forgotten Books, 2012)

—*Deerbrook* (Penguin Classics, 2004)

—*Eastern Life, Present and Past, Volumes 1–3* (Edward Moxon, 1848)

—*England and Her Soldiers* (Cambridge University Press, 2010)

—*Feats on the Fiord* (Ward, Lock & Co, 1890)

—*Forest and Game Law Tales* (Edward Moxon, 1845)

—*Health, Husbandry and Handicraft* (Bradbury and Evans, 1861)

—*Household Education* (Edward Moxon, 1849)

—*How to Observe Morals and Manners* (Transaction Publishers, 1989)

—*Life in the Sickroom* (Edward Moxon, 1844)

—*Middle Class Education in England* (Cornhill Magazine, November 1864)
—*Miscellanies, Volume 1 of 2* (Forgotten Books, 2015)
—*Retrospect of Western Travel* (Saunders and Otley, 1838)
—*Society in America, Volumes 1–3* (Transaction Publishers, 2000)
—*The Factory Controversy: A Warning Against Meddling Legislation* (The National Association of Factory Occupiers, 1855)
—*The Hour and the Man, an Historical Romance* (Edward Moxon, 1841)
—*The Peasant and the Prince* (Tutis Publishing, 2008)
—*The Settlers at Home* (George Routledge and Sons, 1885)

Other Selected Bibliography

Ackroyd, Peter, *Dickens* (HarperCollins, 1991)
Arnold, Matthew, *Culture and Anarchy and Other Selected Prose* (Penguin Classics, 2015)
Arnold, Matthew, *Selected Poems* (Macmillan, 1910)
Ashton, Rosemary, *Thomas and Jane Carlyle: Portrait of a Marriage* (Chatto & Windus, 2002)
Aubyn, Giles St., *Queen Victoria: A Portrait* (Hodder & Stoughton, 1992)
Barker, Juliet, *The Brontës: A Life in Letters* (Little, Brown, 2016)
Barrett Browning, Elizabeth, *The Collected Poems of Elizabeth Barrett Browning* (Wordsworth Editions, 2015)
Bostridge, Mark, *Florence Nightingale: The Woman and her Legend* (Viking, 2008)
Bronte, Charlotte: *The Brontes: Their Lives, Friendship and Correspondence*, ed. Thomas James Wise, John Alexander Symington (Shakespeare Head Press, 1932)
Browne E., Janet, *Charles Darwin: Voyaging* (Jonathan Cape, 1995)
Cazamian, Louis, *The Social Novel in England, 1830–1850* (Routledge, 1973)
Chapple, J.A.V., *Elizabeth Gaskell: A Portrait in Letters* (Manchester University Press, 1980)
Clubbe, John (ed), *Carlyle and his Contemporaries* (Duke University Press, 1976)
David, Deirdre, *Intellectual Women and Victorian Patriarchy: Harriet Martineau, Elizabeth Barrett-Browning, George Eliot* (Cornell University Press, 1987)
Desmond, Adrian, and James Moore, *Darwin* (Michael Joseph, 1991)
— *Darwin's Sacred Cause* (Allen Lane, 2009)
Desmond, Adrian, *Huxley: The Devil's Disciple* (Michael Joseph, 1994)
Dickens, Charles, *A Round of Stories by the Christmas Fire* (Hesperus Classics, 2007)
— *Bleak House* (Penguin Classics, 1996)
Dzelzainis, Ella, and Cora Kaplin (eds.), *Harriet Martineau: Authorship, Society and Empire* (Manchester University Press, 2010)
Eliot, George, *Middlemarch* (Penguin Classics, 2003)
— *The Letters of George Eliot* (Bodley Head, 1926)
Froude J.A. *Thomas Carlyle: A History of His Life in London* (Longmans, 1885)

Gaskell, Elizabeth, *The Life of Charlotte Bronte* (Penguin Classics, 1997)

Gordon, Lyndall, *Charlotte Bronte: A Passionate Life* (Virago, 2008)

Gray, John, *Gray's Anatomy: Selected Writings* (Allen Lane, 2009)

Harman, Claire, *Charlotte Bronte: A Life* (Viking, 2015)

Hawthorne, Nathaniel, *English Notebooks* (Randall Stewart, 1941)

Heffer, Simon, *High Minds: The Victorians and the Birth of Modern Britain* (Random House Books, 2013)

— *Moral Desperado: A Life of Thomas Carlyle* (Weidenfeld and Nicolson, 1995)

Hill, Michael R., and Susan Hoecker-Drysdale (eds.), *Harriet Martineau: Theoretical & Methodological Perspectives* (Routledge, 2003)

Hoecker–Drysdale, Susan, *Harriet Martineau – First Woman Sociologist* (Berg, 1992)

Holme, Thea, *The Carlyles at Home* (Persephone Books, 2002)

Horne, Jackie C., *History and the Construction of the Child in Early British Children's Literature* (Routledge, 2011)

Hubbard, Elbert, *Harriet Martineau* (Kessinger Legacy Reprint, 2010)

Hughes, Kathryn, *George Eliot: The Last Victorian* (Fourth Estate, 1998)

Hunt, Tristram, *Building Jerusalem: The Rise and Fall of the Victorian City* (Weidenfeld and Nicolson, 2005)

Hunter, Shelagh, *Harriet Martineau: The Poetics of Moralism* (Scholar Press, 1995)

Hutcheon, Pat Duffy, *Leaving the Cave: Evolutionary Naturalism in Social Scientific Thought* (Wilfrid Laurier University Press, 1996)

Kaplan, Fred, *Thomas Carlyle: A Biography* (Cambridge University Press, 1983)

Lang, Cecil Y. (ed.), *The Letters of Matthew Arnold* (University of Virginia Press, 1996)

Logan, Deborah A., *Harriet Martineau, Victorian Imperialism and the Civilizing Mission* (Ashgate Publishing, 2010)

— *The Hour and the Woman* (Northern Illinois University Press, 2002)

Martineau Society, *A Harriet Martineau Miscellany* (Martineau Society, 2002)

— *A James Martineau Miscellany* (Martineau Society, 2005)

Mayhew, Robert, *Malthus: The Life and Legacies of an Untimely Prophet* (Belknap Press, 2014)

McCarthy, Barbara, *Elizabeth Barrett to Mr Boyd* (Yale University Press, 1955)

Meckier, Jerome, *Innocent Abroad: Charles Dickens's American Engagements* (University Press of Kentucky, 1990)

Mermin, Dorothy, *Elizabeth Barrett Browning: The Origins of a New Poetry* (University of Chicago Press, 1989)

Miller, Florence Fenwick, *Harriet Martineau* (W.H. Allen & Co, 1884)

Morrow, John, *Thomas Carlyle* (Hambledon Continuum, 2006)

Murray, Nicholas, *A Life of Matthew Arnold* (Hodder & Stoughton, 1996)

Nevill, John Cranstoun, *Harriet Martineau* (F. Muller, 1943)

Paston, George, *At John Murray's: Records of a Literary Circle 1843–92* (John Murray, 1932)

Pichanick, Valerie *Harriet Martineau, the woman and her work, 1802-76* (University of Michigan Press, 1980)

Pickering, Mary, *Auguste Comte: An Intellectual Biography* (Cambridge University Press, 1993)

Pollard, Arthur, *Mrs Gaskell* (University of Manchester Press, 1965)

Roberts, Caroline, *The Woman and the Hour: Harriet Martineau and Victorian Ideologues* (University of Toronto Press, 2002)

Sanders, Valerie, *Reason over Passion: Harriet Martineau and the Victorian Novel* (Harvester Press, 1986)

Slater, Michael, *Charles Dickens* (Yale University Press, 2009)

Taplin, Gardner B., *The Life of Elizabeth Barrett Browning* (Yale University Press, 1957)

Thompson, Kenneth, *Auguste Comte: The Foundation of Sociology* (Thomas Nelson, 1976)

Todd, Barbara, *Harriet Martineau at Ambleside* (Bookcase, 2002)

Tomalin, Claire, *Charles Dickens: A Life* (Viking, 2011)

Uglow, Jenny, *Elizabeth Gaskell* (Faber & Faber, 1993)

—*The Lunar Men* (Faber & Faber, 2002)

—*George Eliot* (Virago 2008)

Vint, John, *Harriet Martineau: 'The Wealth of Nations' and 'Life in the Wilds'* (Manchester Metropolitan University, Martineau Society Conference Paper, 2014)

Webb, R. K., *Harriet Martineau: A Radical Victorian* (Heinemann, 1960)

Wheeler, Sara, *O My America!* (Vintage, 2014)

Whitney, Janet, *Elizabeth Fry: Quaker Heroine* (George Harrap & Co., 1937)

Wilson, A.N., *The Victorians* (Arrow Books, 2003)

Wilson, D.A., *Carlyle on Cromwell and Others* (Kegan Paul, Trench, Trubner, 1925)

Wood, Anthony *Nineteenth Century Britain, 1815–1914* (Longman, 1960)

Woodham-Smith, Cecil, *Florence Nightingale* (Book Club Associates, 1972)

Yates, Gayle Graham (ed.), *Harriet Martineau on Women* (Rutgers University Press, 1985)

Selected Online Resources

The Darwin Correspondence Project: https://www.darwinproject.ac.uk/
The Carlyle Letters Online: http://carlyleletters.dukeupress.edu/

Acknowledgements

Thanks to the staff at Unbound and Whitefox who have helped so much with producing this book particularly Phil Connor, Xander Cansell, Molly Powell, Mathew Clayton and Annabel Wright. Invaluable research help was provided by Megan Bradbury and Margaret Hobday, with much needed copy help from Jan Robertson, Jane Haynes and Ffion Jones. Members of the Martineau Family and the Martineau Society have provided nothing but encouragement, with particular thanks to Gaby Weiner, Sharon Connor, John Vint, Beth Torgerson, Jeremy Martineau, Iain Crawford, Deborah Logan, Susan Hoecker-Drysdale and Valerie Sanders.

Great thanks to all those who contributed to the funding of this book, to Chris Gribble and the staff at Writer's Centre Norwich and the staff at the Millennium Library in Norwich. This book has been a long time in the making with much needed support from friends too numerous to mention, but particular thanks to Grace Jackson, Rosie Arnold, Jenny Allison, Ian Brownlie, Asa Hardy-Brownlie, Mark Howe, Steve Forster, Steph Potts, Katie Utting, Stephen Allen, Robin Worden, Penny Edwards, Ben Smart, Mike Talbot, Guy Martin, Ian Nettleton, Kathy Gill, Anjali Joseph, Deborah Arnander, Anna Sims, Julie Cleminson, Cathy Eden, Richard Fair, Lucy Hogg, Jean Hogg, Sarah Power, Mark Cocker and Clare Haynes. Finally to my sister Marion, my brother Keith and their families, and especially to Mum and Dad – thanks for your unstinting support.

Patrons

Rosie Arnold
Jessica Asato
Daisy Bourne
Sarah Bower
Kate Bowgett
Niki Braithwaite
Dave Cantin
Ian Carrell
Kaavous Clayton
Joanne Connolly
Paul Dolman
Lauren Dove
Cathy Eden
Mark Edwards
Mary Epworth
Ann Farrant
Charlotte Featherstone
Dee Fowles
Keiko Funaki
William Galinsky
Dudley Garner
Estelle Gee
Celia Rose Halifax
Hilary Hammond
Victoria Harris
Clare Haynes
Keith Hobday
Sophie Hunter
Matt Hutchings
Cerian Hutchings
The Itinerant Poetry Library (Norwich-born, too)
Anjali Joseph
Philip Langeskov
Adrian Lever
Tamasin Little

Janet Robertson and Louisa Lloyd
Geraldine Locise
Lissy Lovett
Katherine Mager
Guy Martin
The Martineau Society
Judith McGlincey
Adam McKeown
Helen Mitchell
Steve Morphew
Deborah Muir
Nicola Naismith
Lawrence Napper
Claire Nelmes
Vikki Nelson
Ian Nettleton
John Osborne
Sarah Power
David Pullin
Jenni Rant
Kelly Robb
Sam Ruddock
Jane Ryan
Alex Sanders
Sharon Sanderson
Dee Scholey
Claire Sharland
William Thomas
Bill Vine
Maggie Wheeler
Luke Wright
Brent Hopwood
Judith McGlincey